From Goethe to Gide

Feminism, Aesthetics and the French and German Literary Canon 1770–1936

This collection of essays provides a major reassessment of those literary figures from the later Enlightenment to the beginnings of Modernism who are most studied on French and German courses in Britain and around the world today.

By investigating the works of these canonical male French and German writers through the optic of feminist criticism, the contributors lay bare some of the fundamental aesthetic questions raised by these works: the function of art and of the artist; the limits of Realism; the relation of gender and genre. Readers new to French and German can study one author in depth or engage in comparative analysis, while specialists will find much to stimulate their critical thinking.

Editors: Mary Orr is Professor of French at the University of Southampton. **Lesley Sharpe** is Professor of German at the University of Exeter. Both have published major monographs on canonical writers of French and German literature as well as working on women writers and feminist criticism. Mary Orr is one of the General Editors of *Forum for Modern Language Studies* and Lesley Sharpe was for six years Germanic Editor of the *Modern Language Review*.

From Goethe to Gide

Feminism, Aesthetics and the French and German Literary Canon 1770–1936

edited by
Mary Orr and Lesley Sharpe

UNIVERSITY
of
EXETER
PRESS

First published in 2005 by
University of Exeter Press
Reed Hall, Streatham Drive
Exeter EX4 4QR
UK
www.exeterpress.co.uk

British Library Cataloguing in Publication Data
A catalogue record for this book is available from the British Library.

Hardback ISBN 0 85989 721 4
Paperback ISBN 0 85989 722 2

Typeset in 10½/13pt Plantin Light
by Kestrel Data, Exeter, Devon

Printed in Great Britain by
Athenæum Press Ltd, Gateshead

Contents

Preface

The twelve essays in this volume are designed to stimulate debate on what we the editors consider a vital issue in contemporary criticism: the extent and value of the contribution of feminist criticism to scholarly analysis of canonical male writers and the potential of such criticism to enrich and diversify scholarly debates in the future. The project was born of our sense of the need to take stock of the impact of an enormously varied and sometimes incompatible set of feminist critical approaches that had often been only sporadically applied to major canonical writers in the French and German traditions. These approaches and their interpretative possibilities had, moreover, often been marginalized in mainstream critical debate. In harnessing the rich critical tools of feminist criticism and by foregrounding its usefulness, our aim was also to demonstrate the increasing sophistication of those approaches and hence their potential to probe not only received interpretations of canonical texts but also the aesthetic assumptions underpinning them and their reception. Our hope is that the essays in this volume will encourage further dialogue within feminist criticism and, by demonstrating that criticism's flexibility and productiveness, help in questioning assumptions about the formation of literary values and traditions.

All the contributors to the volume are experts in their fields. They present original work and an immense background of accumulated scholarly expertise in a manner accessible to the undergraduate and yet challenging to the specialist. All would have liked more space for notes in order to indicate where further material on their subject could be found. Our solution to the problem of length was to restrict full bibliographical references in the notes to each chapter to the secondary literature whose arguments were specifically alluded to, and to refer readers by author to additional titles listed in full in the bibliography at the end of the volume. In this way the notes to each chapter provide a compact source of references for those, particularly students, who want to read further on specific texts, while the main bibliography has become an extensive, and we hope useful, research tool for those engaged in longer-term scholarly work in these fields. Those interested in applying feminist critical methods to other canons will also find useful pointers in the bibliography.

We are immensely grateful to our contributors for their participation in this project, which involved not only producing the essays in this volume but also taking part in a two-day conference in November 2003 that gave us a very necessary opportunity to exchange ideas and approaches. We should like to acknowledge the generous support of the British Academy, which gave us a British Conference Grant of £2,000 towards the cost of bringing our US contributors to the UK for this event. We should also like to thank the Institute of Romance Studies and the Institute of Germanic Studies (at that time still separate institutes in the University of London's School of Advanced Studies) for providing two excellent venues for the conference and for their administrative support. Julie Crocker of the School of Modern Languages at the University of Exeter lent her computing skills to the task of formatting the chapters and bibliography, and the School also provided for the services of an indexer. Finally, we are grateful to the University of Exeter Press for the confidence they have shown in the project and the practical advice and professional support they have given us throughout.

Mary Orr
Lesley Sharpe
Exeter, December 2004

Contributors

Elizabeth Boa is Emeritus Professor of German, University of Nottingham. Her publications include *The Sexual Circus: Wedekind's Theatre of Subversion* (Blackwell, 1987), *Kafka: Gender, Class, Race in the Letters and Fictions* (OUP, 1996), 'Die Geschichte der O oder die (Ohn-)Macht der Frauen. *Die Wahlverwandtschaften* im Kontext des Geschlechterdiskurses um 1800', *Goethe-Jahrbuch* 118 (2001).

Gail K. Hart is Professor of German at the University of California, Irvine, where she also directs the Interdisciplinary Humanities Program. She has published books on Gottfried Keller's fiction and on German bourgeois tragedy and articles on German and comparative literature of the eighteenth and nineteenth century. Her new book, *Friedrich Schiller: Crime, Aesthetics, and the Poetics of Punishment*, appeared in 2005.

Robert C. Holub teaches in the German Department at the University of California at Berkeley. He has written numerous books and essays in the area of eighteenth- to twentieth-century literary, cultural, and intellectual history. His current research deals with Friedrich Nietzsche, situating his writings in the context of nineteenth-century scientific, social and political discourses.

Patricia Howe is Senior Lecturer in German at Queen Mary College, University of London. Her research interests are narrative fiction and travel writing in the nineteenth and early twentieth centuries. She has written on Fontane, Saar, Storm, Hofmannsthal and Schnitzler, and on women writers.

Ann Jefferson is Fellow and Tutor in French at New College, Oxford. Her publications include *Reading Realism in Stendhal* (CUP, 1988). She is currently working on a project entitled 'Writing Lives and Making Literature in France: 1750 to the present'.

Rosemary Lloyd is Rudy Professor of French at Indiana University, Bloomington. She has published translations of Baudelaire's letters, his novel *La Fanfarlo*, and his prose poems, and is the author of *Baudelaire et Hoffmann* (CUP, 1979), *Baudelaire's Literary Criticism* (CUP, 1981) and *Baudelaire's World* (Cornell UP, 2002).

Jann Matlock teaches at University College London. She is the author of *Scenes of Seduction: Prostitution, Hysteria, and Reading Difference in Nineteenth-Century France* (Columbia UP, 1994), and co-editor of *Media Spectacles* (Routledge, 1993). She is currently completing *Desires to Censor: Spectacles of the Body, Aesthetics, and Vision in Nineteenth-Century France.*

Mary Orr is Professor of French at the University of Southampton. Her most recent monographs are *Intertextuality: debates and contexts* (Polity, 2003) and *Flaubert: writing the masculine* (OUP, 2000). Her current research projects include a monograph project to re-map the history of ideas of nineteenth-century France through the lens of Flaubert's *La Tentation de Saint Antoine.*

Ricarda Schmidt is Professor of German at the University of Exeter and publishes in the fields of literature and culture of the nineteenth and twentieth century, focusing on E.T.A. Hoffmann, the relationship between literature, art and music, GDR literature, women writers and theories of intermediality and intertextuality.

Naomi Segal is Director of the Institute of Germanic and Romance Studies, University of London. She has published ten books, including two each on the French récit, the novel of adultery and Gide. She is currently writing a book on Didier Anzieu, gender, desire and the sense of touch, entitled *Consensuality.*

Lesley Sharpe is Professor of German at the University of Exeter. She is the author of *Friedrich Schiller: Drama, Thought and Politics* (CUP, 1991), *Schiller's Aesthetic Essays* (Camden House, 1995) and edited the *Cambridge Companion to Goethe* (CUP, 2002). She has also published on women writers of the eighteenth century and on the German theatre repertoire.

Judith Still is Professor of French at the University of Nottingham and is the author of *Justice and Difference in Rousseau* (CUP, 1993) and *Feminine Economies* (MUP, 1997). She is editor of *Men's Bodies* (Edinburgh UP, 2003) and co-editor of *Intertextuality* (MUP, 1990), *Textuality and Sexuality* (MUP, 1993), *Women and Representation* (Nottingham, 1995) and *Brazilian Feminisms* (Nottingham, 1999).

Introduction

Lesley Sharpe

Over the last thirty years or so, feminist criticism has transformed our consciousness of the literary landscapes and traditions of many countries. Feminist scholars have performed a massive task of recuperation in bringing to light and thus making available for new scrutiny the work of numerous women writers, whose disappearance from established literary history they have often accounted for with reference to the development of (male) standards of literary judgment and the emergence of a literary canon resting on those standards. This recuperation was the first stage in the emergence of a rival 'female' canon composed not only of women writers but of writers who experimented with genres such as autobiography, memoirs, diaries and letters, in other words with more personal forms of writing that had hitherto occupied the lower levels of the literary hierarchy. In addition, feminist theories of creativity and of writing have proposed radical, and of course often mutually incompatible, alternatives to the established traditions of aesthetics developed by and for male writers. 'Écriture féminine', for example, developed the notion of distinctively feminine writing strategies that challenge and overcome the binary oppositions of patriarchal logic and language. Thus feminist critics unsettled what had long been a fairly fixed picture of the giants and pygmies populating literary history, helped create a much sharper awareness of the immense diversity of writing and the variety of conditions of literary production by men and women, particularly from the eighteenth century onwards, and opened up the canon for reappraisal in the light of a wider-ranging and less normative aesthetics.

This collection of essays attempts to bridge a gap that we the editors as feminist scholars identified in the course of our own work on two of the great canonical writers of France and Germany, Flaubert and Schiller. We had noted that feminist insights and critical strategies often remained at the margins of the critical literature on canonical authors and were regarded as an optional extra to, rather than as an essential component of, the mainstream debates. This situation is in part the result of the overwhelming weight of scholarship that already exists on major writers, of which feminist studies are only a tiny part. But we sensed that this marginalization of feminist scholarship on canonical male authors (by contrast with the prominence of feminist scholarship on, for example, major women writers) might be attributable to a number of factors of approach and context. One is an older tendency in feminist work to concentrate on 'representations of women', which, though accessible as an introduction to feminist criticism, is necessarily limited and often static. A related factor is the practice of using a charge of misogyny as a stick to beat canonical writers with. A third factor arises from the rapidly changing academic environment, namely a growing disinclination on the part of younger scholars, male or female, to engage with major canonical authors, owing in part to the sheer volume of secondary literature on them and the plethora of different and often conflicting critical methods adopted.

The 'representations of women' and the 'uncovering misogyny' approaches of some feminist criticism of canonical writing were important stages in raising and sharpening awareness of the socio-historical context of these writers, and of the gender assumptions in art and their characteristic literary expressions. Canonical authors can be frightening monoliths. Feminist criticism has done something towards penetrating the aura surrounding them and exposing the chinks in their armour. The danger, however, is that rich works of literature emerge impoverished, less rather than more interesting, and that feminist criticism appears to lead into a cul-de-sac when its insights are not linked with wider critical debates of concern to the writer and his contemporaries or to the scholarly world today. Though canonicity itself is an issue raised by this present project, we do not start out by questioning the canonicity of the authors selected. We feel that it is historically beyond question and we also believe that our chosen authors have stood the test of time by demanding to be reread and reappraised by succeeding generations of critics. What we hope this volume will do is to contribute to a body of feminist scholarship that commands attention within the mainstream of critical debate on these writers because it engages with central aesthetic questions affecting them and our critical appraisal of them.

The third factor mentioned above—the changing academic environment—is the reason why we feel this project is particularly timely. There is, sadly, a rapidly progressing reduction of the curriculum in universities, with ever-increasing concentration on twentieth- and twenty-first-century studies. As a result of this, there are decreasing numbers of up-and-coming scholars who work on earlier periods and so there is still surprisingly little feminist work on many major literary figures—Heine is one example—whose writing would seem positively to invite it. We are convinced—and this collection of essays demonstrates—that feminist critical approaches offer new and exciting ways of re-engaging with major male writers. Less and less is the claim of these writers on scholars' and on students' time and effort taken for granted. This erosion of the notion of canonicity and of the centrality of the canon to literary studies as part of university education, is a particular challenge to those who want to incorporate feminist approaches in their work on major canonical authors. It requires a review of the aesthetic criteria underpinning the status of those canonical writers in the past and now. The result, as we hope this volume shows, is a demonstration of the ways in which feminist criticism not only brings new insights and perspectives to the interpretation of the most familiar texts but also opens up for fresh discussion the ways in which these works and their authors resist and challenge the boxes that literary historians have put them in.

The period we have chosen, 1770 to 1936, runs from the later Enlightenment to Modernism. Diverse though our authors are, they share a common European cultural heritage, grounded in the legacy of the Classical and Judeo-Christian traditions that formed the basis of Enlightenment humanism. We begin with a period in which the criteria for literary judgement are moving away from dependence on Classical authorities and on the notion of mimesis, and also from subservience to the belief that literature offers moral instruction, towards expressive theories and the Romantic notion of the artist as genius/leader/prophet, though also as outsider. We end with writers who challenge many of the standards of aesthetic judgment (for example, completeness, objectivity, representation) that were part of the Classical legacy and also underpinned Realist aesthetics through much of the later nineteenth century. What is common to our early and later writers, however diverse their writing, is a sense of the moral context of art as an engagement with and expression of human values and consciousness. We are not primarily concerned with identifying the rise of conceptions of art and creativity that excluded women (though in fact they usually did exclude women, and some of our writers contributed directly or indirectly to that exclusion). We are more concerned with the ways in which such things as our writers' theoretical positions and/or their experiments with genre and with traditional or avant-garde forms illuminate, when seen through the lens of feminist criticism, the dynamics of their writing. We believe that this concern with the underlying aesthetic issues, in addition to the new possibilities of interpretation of particular works, is one of the distinctive contributions of this volume. We see it as complementary to, and as finally dove-tailing with, the more familiar socio-historical feminist analyses, on which our contributors also draw in setting the context for their discussions. Crucially, we hope to demonstrate the flexibility and openness of feminist critical methods, which, though they draw on many of the strands of critical theory of the last thirty years, need not serve any overarching theory of, say, the undecidability of the text or any political or critical agenda, but can produce nuanced readings that stand on a broadly humanist understanding of literature.

The writers we have chosen for inclusion in this volume are all, as we have said, undisputed members of the canon of national, indeed arguably of world literature, though of course in their own day they received widely varying degrees of recognition by their contemporaries. Our choice was guided by a wish to cover our chosen period but also to draw in genres other than prose fiction, while recognizing that prose fiction would inevitably be an important focus. Hence we have regretfully excluded Balzac, although his contributions to the parameters of the Realist novel are discussed and contended in the chapters on Stendhal, Flaubert, Fontane and Zola. We also wanted to include writers on whom only a very limited amount of feminist scholarship exists and thus we excluded another obvious candidate, Kleist. We have kept the contributors' brief fairly flexible. No particular 'school' of feminist criticism was prescribed and each contributor uses the tools s/he finds most appropriate to the author and material concerned. All range beyond discussion of a single work, even if that is the centre piece, and the majority combine analysis of a prominent text with that of a less well-known one, so that the chapters offer something valuable to a wide academic readership, from undergraduates to advanced researchers.

The range of authors was restricted because although we could have easily filled a volume with either French or German contributions we chose to combine them, believing that the cross-disciplinary discussions would prove a particularly innovative and productive part of the project. The period under scrutiny was one of intense exchange between the literatures of both countries and most of our chosen writers exercised considerable influence on other writers and on literary developments in their neighbouring country: Rousseau on Goethe and Schiller, Hoffmann on French Romantics, Zola and Flaubert on German Realists, to name only the most obvious links, while Heine published his works in French as well as German during his twenty-five-year voluntary exile in Paris. What we are concerned with in this volume is not influence, however, but with the way in which feminist tools of criticism allow us to cut from earlier to later writers and across the national divide and back in order to examine from a variety of perspectives some of the central aesthetic issues and debates of the period. One is the status and image of the male artist, conceived by Goethe and Schiller, for example, and by the Romantic generation as an aloof prophet. Yet several of the contributions in this volume treat ways in which feminist critical questionings reveal highly ambivalent and ambiguous questionings of the artist's role, from Rousseau's unease with the host/guest relationship, to Hoffmann's explorations of creativity gone awry, to public perceptions of Zola as voyeur, to Gide's artist as pederast/pedagogue. Another recurring preoccupation is with issues of genre, with its traditions, boundaries and limits, from Schiller's attempt to propose a new approach to the definition of genre to Baudelaire's and Heine's experimentation with overt carnality expressed in traditional verse forms, to Stendhal's, Flaubert's and Fontane's explorations of the limits and limitations of the novel and the various aesthetic displacements that result from their attempts to avoid its gender-based clichés, to Kafka's conscious mixing of genre codes in a way that also unsettles gender codes. All these issues are linked to one of the central debates of the nineteenth century, the debate about Realism. Thus several of the essays expose ways in which, in theory and in practice, our chosen writers took issue with the claims of Realist theorists to objectivity and completeness and how the Realist novel, while superficially providing the ideal form in which to explore women's experience, had to be radically adapted by writers such as Stendhal, Flaubert, Zola, and Fontane if it was to escape its own deadening conventions, precisely with regard to the presentation of women.

In the process of completing this project the exchange of ideas among contributors and with the wider academic community was considered crucial. A conference was held at which draft chapters were read, and the ensuing discussions fed into the final contributions and into the Postscript that rounds off this volume and points forward to new feminist research possibilities. That Postscript also conveys something of the dynamic felt at the conference of work in progress on the literary canon. In the chapters that follow we invite participation in the shared sense of invigoration the contributors and their audience experienced, both through the rediscovery, via feminist readings, of the classic works by individual authors, and also through the challenge of reframing the aesthetic contexts of debates in France and Germany from 1770 to 1936.

1

Errant Strivings

Goethe, *Faust* and the Feminist Reader

Gail K. Hart

Johann Wolfgang von Goethe lived from 1749 to 1832, a long life that began in the Enlightenment under the vestiges of the Holy Roman Empire and extended through several revisions of the European political map and its intellectual climate zones. He not only lived through the era of petty German principalities and the Napoleonic wars, but he was also a participant in government as a state minister in the Duchy of Weimar and experienced some of the phases of war, including the Campaign of 1792, in which he accompanied the Prussian armies and his duke, Carl August, as they marched confidently into France.[1] The political world he inhabited, that of the French Revolution and its European aftermath and of petty absolutism in a dauntingly fragmented Germany, placed certain limitations on even the most prominent individuals, but it also provided a wealth of opportunity for an ambitious and active polymath. Goethe became a Privy Councillor (*Geheimrat*) and was actively engaged in all facets of the government in Weimar, where he enjoyed considerable celebrity for his literary achievements and learning. Goethe travelled somewhat within the continent, and met with the leading intellectuals of his day, as well as with heads of state, including Napoleon, who was a fan of *Die Leiden des jungen Werther* (The Sorrows of Young Werther). Though remembered primarily as a poet, he was active in politics, legislation, state bureaucracy, scientific research, publishing, and he also directed the court theatre at Weimar.

The literary world Goethe inherited was heavily determined by various efforts to establish an identifiably *German* literature, a body of work that was to be representative of the pre-national nationalism that emerged much more strongly in intellectual intercourse than in political affairs. Johann Christoph Gottsched (1700–66) had sought in 1730 in his *Versuch einer critischen Dichtkunst vor die Deutschen* (Attempt at a Critical Poetics for the Germans) to codify German literature and genre according to neo-classicist standards borrowed from the French. Gottsched, a writer and critic of considerable authority, had numerous French plays translated into German, largely for the sake of modelling tasteful dramatic composition. The debates about French influence and what should constitute a basic German cultural vocabulary continued into and intensified during Goethe's early youth and most of these debates centred on drama. Gotthold Ephraim Lessing (1729–81) was most conspicuously opposed to the principles laid down in Gottsched's theory and practice of the stage, and viewed his work as theatre critic at the Hamburg National Theatre as a contribution to the construction of a German nation—though this 'nation' still lacked political and geographical unity. That Gottsched, Lessing, and later Goethe and Schiller, engaged in varying degrees with the practical realm of theatre in their efforts to realize a German literature, indicates their faith in the potential of theatre to unite and motivate—fundamental prerequisites for nation formation. The heirs of Lessing, those who continued to seek 'the German' in reaction to 'the French', included Heinrich Wilhelm von Gerstenberg (1737–1823), Johann Georg Hamann (1730–88), and Johann Gottfried Herder (1744–1803), all of whom explored English models, specifically Shakespeare, as a guide to founding a culturally German literature. These thinkers felt closer to the English literary tradition and they frequently celebrated Shakespeare's lack of adherence to the compulsory figures of neoclassicist aesthetics.[2]

There was, however, little room at the foundational inn for Shakespeare's sisters, and almost no acknowledged female participation or consideration of women's issues in these attempts to realize a national identity through a characteristic body of literature. Luise Adelgunde Gottsched (1713–62) wrote and translated dramas that promoted her husband's rules for dramatic literature. Karoline Neuber (1697–1760), like many other professional actresses of the eighteenth and nineteenth centuries, composed plays and sketches for performance, though she was also dependent on Gottsched for a time. Sophie von La Roche (1730–1807) found success as a novelist, with the assistance of

Christoph Martin Wieland (1733–1813), her cousin and admirer, but women remained an appendage to the central movement of recorded literary history. Bourgeois and aristocratic women, and the occasional professional like Neuber or Johanna Sophie Albrecht (1757–1840), wrote letters, novels, short prose, poetry, dramas, translations, adaptations, history and autobiography, but, despite publication and impressive sales figures in some cases, German literary history has traditionally devoted very little space to these women's contributions. Literary judgement, editorial selection, and popular sentiment were largely controlled by the strong essentialist prejudice behind Schiller's well-known remark to Goethe in their correspondence (30 June 1797): 'It really surprises me how our women, in a purely dilettantish way, have been able to acquire a certain skill in writing that is nearly artistic.' The attribution of dilettantism—the near- but *not* artistic—to 'our women' derives from Goethe's and Schiller's common interest in the phenomenon, which they sought to analyze and describe in a joint project. They concluded: 'The dilettante is always only a half; he treats everything [artistic] as a game; as a way of passing time [. . .] of satisfying an inclination, of indulging a mood.'[3] The foundations of their study, which was never finished, show considerable overlap between their definitions of dilettantism and feminine stereotypes. Though the great pair praised women writers for testing their limits, the basic assumption was that women were not capable of genuinely artistic writing. Inasmuch as the category of artistic writing was implicitly defined to exclude them, this was indeed true. Since Goethe and Schiller both embodied and generated norms, it is not at all surprising that a women's German literary history, or even a balanced literary history involving both men's and women's writing, is an ongoing interventionist work of recovery.[4]

Goethe's adult life spanned a number of German literary-historical periods, including Sentimentalism, Rococo, Sturm und Drang, Classicism, and Romanticism. He participated in most of these stylistic movements and was, to an astonishing degree for a single individual, instrumental in or entirely responsible for the establishment of new literary styles and genres. Whereas Shakespeare and Dante are, like Goethe, arguably the premier writers of their nations/territories/languages, neither can be said to have determined the course of English or Italian literature. They 'merely' provided some of the highest examples of these national literatures and these examples were to some extent inimitable. Goethe, on the other hand, worked in the generic trenches and wrote exemplary pieces that in many cases were intended to create formal options and define German genre. His *Wilhelm Meister* novels established the *Bildungsroman*; his *Novelle*—originally titled *Die Jagd* (The Hunt)—was a bold attempt to determine the course of that developing form; *Hermann und Dorothea* was the prototype of the modern epic poem; earlier poems such as 'Mit einem gemalten Band' (With a Painted Ribbon) contributed to shaping the category of *Erlebnislyrik* (poetry of experience); dramas such as *Götz von Berlichingen* or *Iphigenie auf Tauris* outlined the stylistic features of the Sturm und Drang and German Classicism respectively. Goethe was thus actively *and consciously* involved in the founding and formation of modern German literature. He was furthermore instrumental in the formation of our standard understandings of German literary history, many of which were laid out in his autobiography *Dichtung und Wahrheit* (Poetry and Truth), 1811–33, and many of which persist, despite challenges, to this day. Though Goethe's popularity has waxed and waned in his native land—often in inverse proportion to that of Schiller—he was, is, and will most likely remain *the* principal German poet.[5]

How do feminist critics read and react to the monolith that is Goethe? How do they read his works, respond to his stature, assess the context for works and stature, and engage with his sheer ubiquity? Before I outline my understanding of 'feminist criticism' and its interactions with Goethe, I want to remark that there is not much critical literature addressing Goethe and his works that can be regarded as even remotely feminist. That is, given the massive proportions of Goethe criticism, the segment that explicitly represents or advances a feminist social or political agenda is rather small. Much of the work done by feminists on German literature in general consists in investigations of the few canonical women writers, and the discovery or rehabilitation of those women whose work was forgotten or dismissed by an almost radically mono-gendered literary historical tradition. Furthermore, because of the thoroughness of the literature on Goethe, very strong and tenacious standard readings and intellectual habits have emerged and challenges to that which we have *known* so well for so long may seem, both to reviewers and editors, to be simply crass or wrong. Finally, the hierarchical structure and politics of German universities are undoubtedly a factor in the dearth of feminist commentary on Goethe. Those who choose their topics with relative freedom are those who occupy professorships and, as a rule, those who occupy professorships tend to be neither feminists nor women.

There is, however, a restricted body of Goethe criticism that we can view as feminist. Within it, I would distinguish between two tendencies, namely the descriptive and the analytical. Though these are usually intertwined, it helps to regard them individually, as they employ different methods and address different agendas. Descriptive feminist writing on Goethe tends to review a text or texts from a feminist perspective, casting themes, events, and figures in another light and pointing out what are, from this perspective, skewed images of women's roles in social relations—often skewed by a kind of male narcissism that portrays women as helpers, hearth-tenders, self-sacrificing lovers, or disposable narrative/dramatic conveniences.[6] Goethe's status and his normative influence mandate (politically, practically, and personally) some critical feminist commentary on the basic configurations in his works and on the working out of those configurations. Descriptive treatment of fair and progressive representation of feminist issues—though conceivable—is rather rare in the literature on Goethe. A notable exception is Katharina Mommsen's portrayal of Goethe as an 'advocate for women' in her 'Goethe as a Precursor of Women's Emancipation',[7] but Mommsen's conclusions are, I believe, based on highly interested selections from the works, letters, and conversations.[8]

Analytical feminist criticism—or that subset of it that addresses Goethe and his works and his world—concerns itself less with the details of description, but rather concentrates on the possible motives behind or reasons for the qualities of the text in question, patterns of thought that underlie various aspects of the text, or the text's relatedness to theoretical or historical models. As noted, few essays are purely descriptive or purely analytical and my categorization necessarily oversimplifies by omitting all those forms of critical writing that are not text-bound or that do not centre on a given text—though there are a few such assessments of Goethe himself and his life, based on sophisticated biographical, social-historical, and psychoanalytical models.[9] These designations furthermore tend to imply a hierarchy that I do not want to invoke, namely the greater weight we assign to analysis over description, theoretical innovation over positivist deduction. There is a particular mode of description that underlies the best of feminist criticism and is perhaps inseparable from all feminist writing and that is the review/description of social relations, of literary texts, of law and established protocols for its enforcement, of so many aspects of gendered living, under feminist assumptions of equality or parity between the sexes or some manner of non-patriarchal model. Analytical contexts include models from Marxism and psychoanalysis to New Historical models, cultural studies, and social history, and examples in

Goethe criticism would be such strategies as Hannelore Schlaffer's examination of the situations in which Goethe may have served as a muse to women writers;[10] and W. Daniel Wilson's expansion on the common understandings of archival sources that see in the documentary evidence signs of a 'good' person with generally emancipatory leanings; or Barbara Becker-Cantarino's nuancing of the 'discourse of patriarchy' as the natural order in the *Wilhelm Meister* novels.[11]

I want to mention three areas of particular interest to feminist critics studying Goethe. The first is the proliferation of impressive and unusual female figures in his work, an oeuvre that includes the wild and athletic Eugenie of *Die natürliche Tochter* (The Natural Daughter), the steely and determined Klärchen of *Egmont*, *Götz von Berlichingen*'s politically strong and insidious Adelheid, and the free and independent Iphigenie who, far from being a human sacrifice, dictates to the ruler of Tauris and maintains that she was born as free as any man. These figures are by no means uniform and they are indeed unusual in their social context, suggestive of a creative imagination that was not bound by gender roles.[12] Goethe once remarked to Johann Peter Eckermann, that women

> are silver dishes into which we put golden apples. My idea of women is not abstracted from the phenomena of actual life; but has been born with me, or arisen in me, God knows how. The female characters I have drawn have therefore all turned out well; they are all better than could be found in reality.[13]

Whether Goethe's 'golden apples' are indeed better than the silver dishes they rest in cannot be verified, but his female figures are definitely his own and they have occupied critics of all stripes for two centuries.

The second area is that defined by the strong current of male narcisissm in some of the most prominent texts, something that almost runs counter to the creation of strong independent women, inasmuch as many of the women figures exist conspicuously and solely for the sake of the care and education of the hero.[14] Becker-Cantarino makes this tendency unmistakably explicit: 'All of Goethe's fictional heroines defined and derived their existence within the context of bondage and service to a male who himself was an independent and active individual.'[15] This is a very strong and inclusive statement and it poses a challenge to readers and critics, either to resist its sweeping universalism or to accept it and probe the context for the astounding consistency that Becker-Cantarino asserts. It should be noted that the imposing women mentioned above do fit her model, inasmuch as they are indeed bound to or in thrall to independent—if not always active—male figures. Even Iphigenie serves her brother's interests.

This current of 'bondage and service' is expressed in the recurring dyad of the innocent, youthful woman who is somehow associated with nature, and the wiser, mature woman more closely associated with culture, who tend to Goethean protagonists. *Stella*, for example, features a beautiful and childlike young woman (Stella) and an older, motherly woman (Cäcilie) who both love the male protagonist, Fernando, to the exclusion of most other thought and action. In the earlier version of the play (1776), they unite and enter into a polygamous relationship with Fernando, exclaiming, 'We are yours!' ('Wir sind dein!'; DK 4, 574). Faust experiences a similar pair of women, though consecutively, enjoying the company and devotion of Gretchen in Part I and acquiring Helen of Troy herself in Part II.

There is biographical support for such readings in Goethe's experience of the highly cultured Charlotte von Stein and his less educated and much younger common-law wife Christiane Vulpius, known to contemporaries and posterity as hyper-bodied and spiritually impoverished.[16] Helmut Fuhrmann has written at length on the dyad, casting Goethean protagonists as wavering Paris figures, uncertain whether the golden apple should go to Aphrodite or Athena.[17] Fuhrmann sees the roots of this dyad in Goethe's love for his mother (natural, happy, domestic, and paradoxically youthful) and his sister (highly educated, more serious and mature) (Fuhrmann, pp. 93–94). In Goethe's works, the competition reduces to that between a woman who is defined by her relation to home and family and one who has a more worldly set of interests and who shows independence. The question of independence is a vexed one since, as Becker-Cantarino asserts, most female figures, whether they favour beauty or brains, are somehow subordinated to the protagonists. Ultimately there is no typology that can account for the entire oeuvre, but one can see very clearly the trends that Fuhrmann and Becker-Cantarino elucidate.

A final area is Goethe's unusual representations of reproduction over the years in his work. The two-parent-and-child/ren family is a relative rarity and anyone reading the 'Prometheus' poem or drama fragment, or the Homunculus and Euphorion episodes in *Faust II* would be rather confused as to where babies come from. Prometheus builds his people in his own image from clay; Faust's famulus Wagner creates the beaker-bound Homunculus in his laboratory and announces triumphantly that

> Old-fashioned procreation
> is something we reject as folly
> [. . .]
> the beasts may still enjoy that sort of thing,
> but human beings, with their splendid talents,
> must henceforth have a higher, nobler source.[18]

Finally, Faust and Helen of Troy speak poetry to one another and somehow a 'child' is born of that artistic/intellectual union. The child Euphorion dies quickly, however, as he strives for adventure and mastery in war.

The occasional human children who do figure at all prominently in Goethe's writing tend to be of uncertain provenance and, like Otto in *Die Wahlverwandtschaften* (Elective Affinities) or Wilhelm Meister's Mignon, they do not survive. Götz's son is a great disappointment to his father and the spectator because he does not exhibit his father's courage and reacts to danger like the stereotypical girl. He is, however, replaced by a better son, Georg, who is not a blood relation, but who mirrors the temperament of his non-progenitor. Parents are relatively rare, children are endangered, and where we do have some sort of successful filial connection, it is, as in *Götz*, not through blood.[19] The avoidance of the standard methods of procreation that Wagner so archly disparages, has obvious applications for a theory of male poetic creativity that competes with and effaces women's reproductive role.

Like the great national poets Dante and Shakespeare, Goethe did produce something inimitable, something that cannot be classified convincingly in terms of genre or style, and that is *Faust*, on which he worked for almost all of his very long adult life and it is *Faust*, generically unclassifiable but called a tragedy by its author, that of all his works qualifies most easily as world literature.

When US university students read *Faust*, a not uncommon reaction to the eponymous protagonist is: 'Who does he think he is?' Students are usually appalled at what they read as Faust's arrogance and towering egotism. This applies not only to the titanic speeches of the early scenes, but also very much to his relations with or use of women. Students have great difficulty entering what they imagine is the historical space where this type of exploitation or subordination is more usual and less objectionable. Readers can, of course, make a wide variety of adjustments in order to enjoy (what has been presented to them as) great literature and one can indeed read over the passages that contradict one's values, suspending disbelief for the sake of cultural enrichment or entertainment. Still, Faust's supremacy remains almost as difficult to digest as Werther's sentimentality.

Faust is absolutely free of any strong independent, active female figure such as Klärchen or Eugenie, being rather populated by witches, mythological beauties, dark mysterious 'mother' shades and other exotica and erotica, and finally undergirded by the figure of a sweet young girl, whose utter devotion to the protagonist results in her demise and his redemption. Specifically, Faust uses and abuses and disposes of young Gretchen, who becomes pregnant, kills her baby, and is imprisoned and executed as an infanticide. In *Faust II*, which begins after Gretchen's execution in the first part, Faust falls in love with an image of Helen of Troy and then pursues the 'actual' mythological woman, with whom he enjoys brief happiness as her Nordic saviour (Menelaus is angry). Helen is an unstable figure, both pure representation and a woman Faust seeks to possess. Charles Grair complains that any subject-hood she may have had is lost or subordinated to her status as evidence and guarantee of Faust's power, as 'visual confirmation of his authority.'[20] Grair notes that '[f]or the patriarchal imagination, she represents a very desirable prize: a willing prisoner waiting to be seized, controlled, and assimilated' (105). The figure of Helen does bring out this aspect of Faust's ambition, demonstrating his/the patriarchal will to appropriate women as accessories of authority, but the flatness or bloodlessness of the portrayal ought to discourage rather than inspire advocacy.

Helen evaporates as Euphorion calls to her to join him in the realm of Persephone. Faust's exploitation of Gretchen and his appropriation of Helen as the embodiment of Beauty have not endeared him to our students. It will be the immodest aim of this undertaking to counter or temper the impressions I have attributed to these students and to suggest ways to bridge the gap of alienation that arises between *Faust* and the undergraduate, graduate, or professional reader who cannot reconcile the protagonist's titanism with his own twenty-first-century feminist leanings.

Unless the *Erdgeist* or earth spirit of the early scenes is female, we first encounter women as servant girls in the 'Outside of the City Gate' scene, an instant orientation to gender roles and exclusions that strikes me as not accidental. Then we see a witch in her kitchen, being dressed down by her master, Mephistopheles, as Faust drops by for some cosmetic sorcery to aid in his project of seducing women. The first target of this project to experience the world and its pleasures is Gretchen, and Faust, upon seeing her, imperiously orders the devil to procure her.[21] Since even the devil has to finesse certain situations, it will be up to Faust to seduce her, by declaring eternal love and fidelity. His great learning, lofty stature, and now-youthful appearance should do the rest. Mephistopheles then strikes a deal with the neighbour, Marthe, who asks only that they establish her status as a widow by falsely attesting to the death of her husband. Faust refuses to do this without determining for himself that the man is actually dead, insisting that he will not lie. Mephistopheles, while trying to persuade him, makes the devastating observation that Faust does indeed lie when it suits him and that he will presently tell Gretchen lies in order to seduce her. He will profess love and make the more or less mandatory claim that his love will endure:

> FAUST: Stop there! . . . When I am deeply moved
> and for the turbulence I feel
> vainly endeavor to find a name,
> yet range the world with all my senses
> and search for words sublime enough
> and call this ardor that consumes me
> infinite, endless, and eternal,
> is that some diabolical delusion?
> MEPHISTOPHELES: And yet I'm right!
> FAUST: Now listen and remember this,
> and please don't let me waste my breath:
> if someone claims he's right, and simply has a tongue,
> he's certain to be right.
> Now come, I'm sick of all this verbiage;
> and you are right—I have no other choice. (l. 3059–72/p. 78)

Faust's deception is calculated, described as a necessity, and justified both by this necessity and his near-acrobatic circumlocutions. Though he distinguishes between prevaricative discourses (the voluntary and the compulsory), it is clear that the crime of seducing and abandoning Gretchen is premeditated. This is furthermore affirmed by Faust in the 'Forest and Cave' scene where he laments that it was necessary to sacrifice her to his great designs. We then see Gretchen suffer loss and longing (Gretchen's Room), great remorse (At the Well, By the

Ramparts; Cathedral), the annihilating reproaches of her dying brother and incarceration in anticipation of execution for having killed her newborn infant. In the prison cell, the reality of her anguish is palpable as she cowers and hallucinates, and the reader has only the a priori knowledge of Faust's superior status to mediate the necessity of exacting this particular human sacrifice. This is an unpalatable offence against a human being, and a feminist issue inasmuch as Faust's enormous stature is maintained here by contrast to an inferior being, a woman/girl who is so deeply subordinated to a man as to be almost of another species—such that he can make his way to heaven over her dead body. Margaret P. Guenther identifies a 'double standard, providing separate, sexually segregated paths to salvation' in Faust's progress and asks, rhetorically, how a woman can even read *Faust*.[22]

I want to inject at this point another of Goethe's comments about women: 'Woman have no sense of irony, they cannot let themselves go [. . .] and they can't do this because they are needier and more dependent than men.'[23] Goethe's remark here is relevant to our discussion of feminist criticism because 'feminists' constitute a group that is disproportionately composed of women and widely rumoured to lack a sense of humour.[24] Feminists and feminist criticism evoke expectations of the high seriousness that is appropriate to the issues they address, but perhaps not always the most fruitful and flexible way to pursue these issues—at least one risks missing a great deal if one seeks direct validation of one's own cherished values in a text. Feminists, male and female, sometimes exhibit rigidities born of worthy political agendas that may interfere with disinterested contemplation or the appreciation of irony. My favourite piece of feminist criticism on Goethe's *Faust*, which I offer as a remedy to feminist seriousness, comes from a theatrical practitioner, Ruth Drexel, speaking in an interview with the writer, Anna Duennebier.[25] As a professional actress and director, Drexel has a depth of engagement with drama that few readers or critics can match. She explains to Duennebier that, though Goethe has a reputation as a 'Macho' (p. 62), she believes it is actually his interpreters who have created this impression with their readings and stagings of the play. It can be read differently, she insists, and she cites the 'Garden' scene conversation between Faust and Gretchen as her example. Here Faust, who is closing in on this young girl, asks her whether she is often home alone:

> GRETCHEN: Oh, yes, our household is a modest one,
> but still it has to be attended to.

> We have no maid; it's up to me to cook and sweep,
> to knit and sew, and to be always on my feet;
> and Mother is so fussy!
> [. . .]
> But now my days are mostly quiet;
> my brother is a soldier,
> my little sister's dead.
> She was a lot of trouble to be sure,
> but I'd be glad to have it all again,
> I loved the child so much.
> FAUST: An angel, if like you!
> GRETCHEN: I had the care of her, she loved me very much.
> When she was born, my father had already died.
> We gave my mother up for lost,
> she lay there in such misery,
> and she got better very slowly, bit by bit.
> That's why it was impossible for her to nurse the little mite herself,
> and so, all by myself, I raised her
> on milk and water; she became my child that way.
> Held in my arms, and lying on my lap,
> she smiled and kicked, began to grow.
> FAUST: You've truly known the purest form of happiness.
> GRETCHEN: But many a hard hour, truly, too. (l. 3109–14, 3118–37/p. 80)

Drexel reads the scene with its two competing discourses, Gretchen's account of her suffering vs. Faust's effusiveness, as a farce. Gretchen tells Faust of the hard reality of her life, of the work she must do, of the baby sister who became like her own, and of the death of this child—she speaks movingly of her very difficult life and of a grievous event that caused her great pain. Meanwhile Faust, who is completely absorbed in his contemplation of Gretchen, appears to be in another world, not hearing the content of her lines, but enthusing about her beauty and innocence—and looking rather foolish for his failure to apprehend the real young woman before him. Titanism inhibits perception and this in turn makes the titan look silly—and a silly titan is not much of a titan. One can easily imagine a staging that represents Drexel's perception of the farcical nature of the scene, that undermines Faust's authority or stature by examining his comic inadequacy as a listener. Such a staging could easily connect with numerous other passages, beginning in 'Faust's Study' where Faust could be portrayed as more of a bumbler and less of a titan than is often the case in the literature. Certainly there have been such stagings, but it is the nature of production to be ephemeral and of print to be eternal and, as academic readers and researchers, we are working mainly with the readings of scholars who reinforce the grand stature of Faust and those who react to this reinforcement. Ultimately, Faust is both highly accomplished, a matter of intense concern to God himself (are not the devil and the deity discussing his case as the play begins?), the centre of our play, *and* weak, delusional, and comical. His titanism entails a brittleness and his inflated stature invites the pin prick of an occasional comic reading. Within the farcical region or the ironic realm, where Faust and his primacy are called into question, male narcissism disperses and other issues and concerns emerge. The facts of Gretchen's life have a weight and solidity that overwhelm the doctor's less focused quest for diversions.

It should be noted that *Faust I* is a play that, while immersed in lofty matters ranging from origins to eschatology, also makes a very big fuss about the unhappy fate of a young woman. In fact, that part of the play is often referred to as the 'Gretchen Tragedy' and, if one looks at definitions of the tragic genre, which usually follows the fates of kings, Gretchen is a very unlikely tragic hero. Goethe conceived this part of the piece in the 1770s when 'bourgeois tragedy', generally understood as a drama about a young middle-class girl seduced by an aristocrat, was flourishing.[26] However, the centre of most bourgeois tragedies is the young girl's middle-class father and to all intents and purposes, it is he who is violated and disgraced. In *Faust I* (fatherless) Gretchen is the focus of the seduction tragedy and she matters in a way that few female figures before or since her have. That she gains such stature by playing her gender role well and loving the protagonist does not necessarily relegate her to the uniformity of tradition. This is neither emancipatory nor oppressive writing and Goethe did not, in any case, work along these particular axes. From one perspective, Faust is a demi-god and Gretchen is a sacrificial virgin. But there is much more material available here for students and critics to work with, beginning with the interesting detail that Gretchen is the subject of strong physical desire. She desires Faust, making this explicit in many of her solitary speeches, and accosts him physically when he tries to liberate her from her cell. This well-developed ardour on Gretchen's part certainly flatters the protagonist and perhaps those who identify with him, but it represents a new and unique subject position for such a figure—the female or feminine 'I' that expresses desire for pleasure and satisfaction.

Lessing's Emilia Galotti famously asks her father to kill her *lest* the desire she predicts she will feel for the prince should cause her to yield to him. But what Emilia predicts, Gretchen experiences.

One basic gender category that underlies much of the evaluation and theorizing of gendered literary figures is the male–female/active–passive opposition and it is precisely this opposition that Goethe repeatedly addresses and plays with in *Faust*, where, as we have seen, a ceaselessly striving protagonist lingers briefly with a young girl, who ultimately stakes out a static position in her cell, and submits to execution. She thus appears as the stationary object of abandonment juxtaposed to the moving, striving male subject. But Gretchen does not remain frozen in her cell and she is actually credited—in her heavenly excarnation—with *leading* Faust to his own salvation. Her leading function and Faust's tendency to follow bear greater scrutiny, and an early poem, 'Es schlug mein Herz' (My Heart Beat, 1771) and its revision, 'Willkomm und Abschied' (Welcome and Departure, 1789), illustrate the problem or the splendour of Goethean ambivalence that encompasses a certain 'both and', even as it presents an 'either-or.' The speaker in the original, a very active and passionate fellow, rides through the wild nocturnal landscape to visit his female beloved. When day dawns, they part: 'You left; I stayed and looked down at the ground/ and followed you with my tearful gaze.' ('Du giengst, ich stund und sah zur Erden,/ Und sah dir nach mit nassem Blick' (DK 1, 129)). Yet the revision of the poem several years later involves also a revision of the pronouns and seems to reverse the earlier tableau: 'I left; you stayed and looked down at the ground and followed me with your tearful gaze.' ('Ich ging, du standst und sahst zur Erden,/ Und sahst mir nach mit nassem Blick' (DK 1, 283)). The reversal of roles of the active leaver and the passive remainer and the flexibility (interchangeability?) suggested by the two versions foreshadows the dynamics of leading and following in *Faust*. Just as Drexel shifts our perspective on the weight of the Faust-Gretchen conversation, we can, by pursuing the instances of leading and following, identify an ambivalence about male activity vs. female passivity or suffering that undermines or complicates Faust's 'leadership'.[27]

Leading first becomes an issue in the 'Prologue in Heaven' section, when both God and the Devil indicate that they intend to lead Faust somewhere—obviously in two different directions. God proposes to lead him 'into clarity' and the devil, 'along my road'.[28] Thus both the heavenly and the diabolical plan involve *leading* Faust somewhere, and even before we encounter him blustering in his study, he is characterized as the designated follower. The German words for lead and seduce, *führen* and *verführen,* parallel the Latinate forms, using the same root and thus qualifying seduction as a form of *mis*leading. Faust begins to court Gretchen by approaching her on the street and offering to lead or escort her home:

> FAUST: My lovely young lady, may I perhaps venture
> to give you my arm and be your escort?
> GRETCHEN: I am not a young lady, or lovely either,
> and need no escort to get home. (l. 2605–08/p. 67)

Gretchen, who explicitly refuses to be led or escorted, never follows Faust, not here, not in their brief dalliance (he chases her to the garden house in 'A Summerhouse') and not when he pleads with her to follow him out of her cell and escape death. She returns in the final scene of the whole as 'A Penitent alias Gretchen' and asks the Mater Gloriosa, 'Grant me permission to instruct him/—he is still dazzled by the strange new light' (l. 2093/ p.305). Activity and passivity are, in *Faust,* actually gender-transitory qualities and this massive, encyclopaedic two-part tragedy-that-ends-happily shows us many aspects of the possibilities for human existence. Faust in his restless errant striving follows, but he follows what must be the projection of his own desires onto a leader figure—Mephistopheles as desire-laden leader is another case for consideration. *Faust* obscures boundaries, undermines polarities, and does not leave received ideas in their receptacles. The titanic stature of the professorial protagonist, beloved of the deity, is subordinated to that of a teenage girl and a demon, even as he abandons the former and cheats the latter.

Feminist criticism of *Faust* and of Goethe's work in general can find a great deal of interesting matter or spirit in the interstices between such gendered dualisms, and in the productive or reproductive anomalies we have considered here and will doubtless strive to lead us into greater clarity. In general, both readers and critics need to be aware of the flexibility and the possibility inherent in the writings of Germany's major poet. Such awareness might begin with the firm attention to the academic advice offered to a student by Mephistopheles as he impersonates a professor in Faust's study: 'Above all, learn to handle women' ('Besonders lernt die Weiber führen'; l. 2023/p. 51).

2

Hospitality and Sexual Difference in Rousseau's *Confessions*

Judith Still

Introduction: Literary life in the Enlightenment

This essay will focus on the intersection of hospitality and sexual difference in Rousseau's *Confessions*, the 'first' modern autobiography.[1] I shall begin with four introductory points. First, the importance and complexity of hospitality for Rousseau relate to financial necessity and power relations: it is very hard to make an honest living as a writer in the eighteenth century, and thus most writers either have their own resources or rely on wealthy patrons (or both). This is due to a number of well-known historical factors including the lack of secure copyright legislation and nightmarish problems of piracy. Rousseau has no significant independent means, and yet wishes to be independent and cannot bear being patronized. The understanding that he comes to of the potential importance of the role of the writer in any case entails rejecting it as a *métier* or trade. Importantly, Rousseau does not seem to regard his autobiographical texts—the work at stake in this essay—as *writing*, i.e. as part of his work as a *writer*. Autobiography has not yet been canonized as a literary genre.

The second point is that Rousseau is, and presents himself as, a stranger not only in terms of nationality, but also politically, socially, culturally, and intellectually. Hospitality is a key ethical and political relation for him, as well as a necessary support, but in his autobiographical writings he shows how being frequently a guest of *those with more means than himself* could be a very uncomfortable position for him. Classical models often imply that hospitality is either a relationship between peers (with the possibility of reciprocity over time) or a relationship between a master and a beggar.[2] The third point is that eighteenth-century society (the *ancien régime*) is apparently rigidly class bound, and yet the forces which will bring about its fall are already being felt; in other words, it is both profoundly inegalitarian and unstable. One feature of the class hierarchy is that it cuts across the sexual hierarchy. Women are both very constrained (for example, in law) and yet, in some cases, exceptionally free. While the Classical and Biblical models of hospitality are considered to refer primarily to relations between men, in Rousseau's world many important hosts are women. These *ladies* are often wealthy and powerful, and are certainly economically, politically and socially superior to Rousseau. Rousseau identifies with, and relates to, women very happily on an interpersonal level in many of the stories narrated in his *Confessions*; but his class-based argument against inequality entails, he asserts, a rejection of this aristocratic 'promiscuity' (the free, if not libertine, mingling of men and women), and hence promotion of an apparently misogynistic sexual separation of roles. This segregation implies the exclusion of women from the role of writer. At the same time, even men's writing is divided into virile productions produced alone or amongst men (good), and effeminate products, the fruit of spending too much time amongst women (bad). Perhaps unsurprisingly to a feminist and post-structuralist reader, none of these petulant (and repeated) assertions about sexual segregation in general, or sexed aesthetics in particular, *hold* in the detail of Rousseau's text.

Finally I wish to make a point concerning Rousseau as literary innovator, concerning the textual qualities of Rousseau's writing, the explicit drawing together of the personal and the political, and the passionate relationship with his implied reader, as well as the powerful content. All Rousseau's published work is innovative to some degree, but it is his autobiography that is most often hailed as inaugurating a new genre.[3] The gender politics of the genre of autobiography are instructive for anyone too optimistic about the forward march of history. Life-writing has proved *both* uniquely welcoming or welcome to women and other 'subalterns', *and* yet another case study of the power of the powerful to exclude others from legitimacy.

Reading responses to Rousseau

The history of readers' responses to any given author or text has to negotiate between the shifting socio-historical moments and conditions of reading, on the one hand, and the specificity of textual detail or authorial figuring on the other hand.[4] It is particularly important to bear in mind when attempting to distinguish a sexually differentiated readerly response, since the patterns of behaviour and discourse regarded as acceptable for each sex are historically variable. Male readers could comfortably weep over Rousseau's writing during his lifetime, but that particular fluid response has proved much harder for men to produce in more recent times. Some authors are particularly appealing to men and some to women, but Rousseau is unusual in the extent to which he has always cut across any gender line. While he makes some statements about women that can seem extraordinarily sexist to a modern eye or ear, it is obvious, particularly in his *Confessions*, that he loves women's company (and the company of many different kinds of women) at least as much as men's. There has been a strikingly bi-polar response to Rousseau from both male and female readers during his lifetime and up to the present day.[5] But if one were to make a gross generalization about sexual difference with respect to this polarity then one could say that male readers have been at their most passionate in vituperation. Voltaire's foaming invective and flights of fancy involve his attributing to Rousseau anything 'low' from venereal disease to a 'dog's life and death by a dog'; Conor Cruise O'Brien attempts to establish a genealogy leading directly from Rousseau to Hitler, Stalin and Pol Pot.[6] Male admiration, however, particularly in the twentieth and twenty-first centuries at least, has tended to be expressed as a solid rational admiration for the thinker. Women, however, have certainly expressed passionate love as well as reasoned admiration for Rousseau and his texts,[7] but their critique has tended to take a solid and rational form with far fewer hysterical touches than male critics have allowed themselves.

Feminist analysis of Rousseau's writing began almost immediately the work was published—perhaps because, rather than in spite of, the fact that his books and opera were so appealing to women. The most celebrated Enlightenment refutation of Rousseau's thinking on women by a woman is to be found in Mary Wollstonecraft's *A Vindication of the Rights of Woman*, first published in 1792.[8] Wollstonecraft concludes her trenchant analysis of Rousseau's treatise on education, *Émile*, and of the treatment of Sophie (Émile's bride) with the following: 'But all

Rousseau's errors in reasoning arose from sensibility, and sensibility to their charms women are very ready to forgive. When he should have reasoned he became impassioned, and reflection inflamed his imagination instead of enlightening his understanding' (p.189). In other words, according to the tenacious sexual stereotypes of the day (critiqued by Wollstonecraft) it is Rousseau's excessive femininity that made him both attractive to women and unable to present a reasonable account of women and women's education. Wollstonecraft also quotes Mme de Staël on Rousseau: 'Though Rousseau has endeavoured to prevent women from interfering in public affairs, and acting a brilliant part in the theatre of politics, yet in speaking of them, how much has he done it to their satisfaction' (p. 203).

Over the years feminists have continued Wollstonecraft's work to show up the misogynistic elements in Rousseau's texts and to analyse these.[9] This solid foundation has liberated his women readers, at least since the beginning of the 1980s, to be able to focus on other elements.[10] This essay is part of my own project to look at what in Rousseau invites and enables women *contra* the virile aesthetics he asserts. I have done this already via beneficence and the notion of (feminine) economies of the gift; the question of hospitality is closely related.[11] There is enormous scope for future study here in all three of Rousseau's autobiographical texts and related fragments,[12] but also beyond. *La Nouvelle Héloïse*, Rousseau's great love-story, much loved and wept over, is a novel of hospitality that explicitly sets itself up as demonstrating the possible constructing of a good home that will enable true hospitality. The good home is apparently a model of sexual distinction, and is set against the worldly and false hospitality of wealthy and promiscuous Parisians, apparently indifferent. However, distinction, difference, opposition, indifference and other ways of setting up relations between categories operate in a more complex way in this text than a first reading may suggest. The virile category of host as benign master of the house is as slippery and hard to sustain as is that of the modest woman who quietly tends the hearth; the arrival of a guest is an occasion for rejoicing but also a very dangerous moment.

Thus I am pursuing one particular set of tropes and realities through Rousseau. The structure of hospitality, of letting the stranger in, at once provides a model for textual and intertextual relations,[13] and also features repeatedly in Rousseau's narratives as a practical and emotional infrastructure. Hospitality enables Rousseau, the *stranger* par excellence, to write in a number of ways: he needs food, shelter, love and education; he needs to *please* and to establish a network of contacts. Rousseau presents himself as a foreigner both literally (in terms of nationality) and in terms of what we would nowadays call social class—both impacting on *language* (again in the broadest sense including codes of behaviour). He is unusual in presenting so clearly the problematic from the point of view of the guest. I shall now turn to the question: what is hospitality? And then to some specific examples from the *Confessions* where Rousseau's analysis (explicit or implicit) of hospitality lays bare something of the dynamics of power relations between the sexes.

The trope of hospitality

The Enlightenment has a particular place in shaping the parameters of many of the debates around, and practices of, hospitality in our own times. On the one hand, it saw the classic formulation in Adam Smith (as he is so often read), and many others, of an economic liberalism which is a powerful force today in relations between individuals as well as in the national debates around immigration, refugees, asylum seekers and so on. Smith's market exchange is conceptually antithetical to hospitality as understood here. On the other hand, in Kant's *Perpetual Peace: A Philosophical Sketch* (1795), the Enlightenment produced a key reference point for cosmopolitan theories of the need for nations to unite together and to offer hospitality to the citizens of other nations (even if Kant elsewhere expresses views we would regard as racist).[14] In Rousseau we find an early statement of an anthropological theory of 'man', in terms of the play of sameness and difference, that would permit hospitality between individuals of any race—even while we have a theory of the self-sufficient nation state which does not encourage cosmopolitanism.[15] Hospitality can be, and often is, treated without reference to sexual difference.[16] For example, Rousseau's model is often said to be Homeric hospitality and this is understood as the warm hospitality a male traveller receives from the master of the house.[17] My hypothesis is, however, that sexual difference is a critical element. Derrida writes of hospitality:

> This is a conjugal model, paternal and phallogocentric. It's the familial despot, the father, the spouse and the boss, the master of the house who lays down the laws of hospitality. He represents them and submits to them to submit the others to them in this violence of the power of hospitality, in this force of ipseity [. . .] the

> problem of hospitality [is] coextensive with the ethical problem. It is always about answering for a dwelling place, for one's identity, one's space, one's limits, for the *ethos* as abode, habitation, house, hearth, family, home.[18]

He goes on to focus on Biblical tales of sodomy and sexual difference, one of which (the tale of the Levite) has been retold by Rousseau in a 'prose poem' which is often taken to have considerable autobiographical purchase.[19]

Hospitality in the *Confessions*

There are many examples of the intersection of hospitality and sexual difference, even sexual violence to the point of rape and murder, in Rousseau's writings. Apart from the episodes in the *Confessions*, I would refer the reader to texts concerning Lucretia, the Levite of Ephraim, Sophie, and Milord Edouard.[20]

My first series of illustrations is that of the three cases of failed 'sodomy' in the *Confessions*. Rousseau frequently implies to his reader that he feels that he is feminized as a guest in situations where apparent hospitality, even asylum, masks a hierarchically imposed exchange. To be the object of male sexual desire is, for Rousseau, to experience a peculiarly pointed proximity to the situation of women. One episode from the second Book of the *Confessions* presents the notorious example of a male sexual advance in a Hospice for Converts in Turin, and of Rousseau's telling of the incident and its re-telling to him by the authorities. The hospice presents itself (and is presented by the Catholic Church) as asylum for the destitute Rousseau—from Protestant Geneva. But in fact it offers board, lodging, and 're-education' as part of a barely-veiled transaction. The earlier story of the Curé de Pontverre (Rousseau's first host after his flight from Geneva) has already given us this paradigm in a more delicate mode—including Rousseau's self-styled feminine flirtatiousness, a mode of behaviour that relates to his desire to be a good guest in this context. In exchange for apparent hospitality Rousseau must convert. When he innocently narrates the story of the approach made to him by a fellow (more or less professional) convert, and of the abject sticky white stuff projected from his admirer's body, the re-telling of the episode occasions a cold response from the authorities when yet more violence is done to the young Rousseau's innocence (*OC* I, 66–69; *The Confessions*, p. 72). The casual explanation, by one of the principals of the hospice, of the mechanics of homosex (which Rousseau is presumed already to understand on one level, but perhaps misunderstand on another in that he may fear that it would hurt) is itself experienced by Rousseau as a kind of rape, or, at least, violation of innocence. It also converts the earlier episode into attempted rape whereas previously it had been experienced as an inexplicable malady on the part of an over-eager friend. Rousseau tells us that this gives him special insight into the position that women can be put in.

On two other occasions, presented as a kind of pair in Book IV, the young Rousseau, sleeping rough in Lyons, is approached by men with propositions. The first calmly suggests that they masturbate together (*OC* I, 165–66; *The Confessions*, p. 161); the second (a priest) suggests that they share a bed, an offer that the impoverished youth accepts, assuming that it carries no conditions. He had refused a similar offer from his admirer in the Turin hospice only because the man was dirty and stank of chewing tobacco. When the priest begins to caress him, Rousseau talks his way out of the situation, he tells us, by re-telling the story of the Jewish (or 'Moorish') convert in Turin (*OC* I, 167; *The Confessions*, p. 162). On this occasion his 'petit récit' (little tale) has the desired effect—as it so often will when his host/hostess has a tender heart. The male object of male desire need not of course be 'feminized' by this desire. However, Rousseau, whose representation of his own androgyny is almost as notorious as his advocacy of sexual difference and separation, presents the succession of stories in this light, and it is a key element in the reader's response to these tales of abuse of power within hospitality.

My second set of illustrations concerns the male host who does not treat Rousseau as sexually desirable, but rather as a virile companion in sexual desire. In both cases there is a measure of equality or reciprocity between the host and guest. The first occurs in Venice when a ship's captain (Olivet), whom Rousseau has helped, invites him to dinner on board ship (*OC* I, 318; *The Confessions*, p. 298) and then procures a high-class prostitute for him. The second takes place in Paris when Rousseau has, for the first time (thanks to the generosity of M. de Francueil and Mme Dupin), been able to set himself up in his own home with Thérèse, his final life-long companion, and thus entertain friends to dinner. It involves the Minister Klupfell who returns Rousseau's hospitality by inviting him and Grimm for dinner, and pushes the hospitality to the point of inviting each of them in turn to share his mistress, described by Rousseau as 'la pauvre petite' (*OC* I, 355, translated rather lamely as 'the little girl'; *The Confessions*, p. 331).

Rousseau thus lays bare one of the classic structures within hospitality. He shows us, with some discomfort, how homosocial bonding between equivalent *hôtes* (host and guest) is achieved by the mediation of a female object.

Finally, and very importantly for Rousseau, we have female hosts. (I should like to reserve the term 'hostess' for the wife who entertains on her husband's behalf and use 'host' for someone who entertains of her independent will, although this is not always possible without ambiguity.) The most important by far is of course Mme de Warens who offers Rousseau everything—not only food, shelter, education, sex, but also the possibility of being himself and of regarding her house as his home. But to suggest that this exceptional woman is not exceptional in being the subject or object of erotic desire on the part of her male guests, I shall give two other rather different examples—and note that this desire is so usual that Rousseau often feels the need to inform us on the rare occasions that he has failed to fall in love with his female hosts (for example, *OC* I, 158; *The Confessions*, p. 153). My first example, which I shall not analyse in detail here, is that of Mlle de Graffenried and Mlle Galley, who treat Rousseau to an improvised dinner at Thônes (*OC* I, 135ff; *The Confessions*, pp. 133ff). The episode is suffused with innocent eroticism. Rousseau tells us that in his youthful imagination he always falls in love with the daughter of the house, he needs 'young ladies' if not princesses in castles. In fact, the reader might note that this pattern does not occur very frequently in his autobiography; he usually falls in love with the woman/wife rather than the daughter of the house, as is the case with Mme de Warens (whom he names 'Mamma'). And Thérèse (whom he calls 'aunt') is positioned more ambiguously—almost the servant of the house. The second example is Mme Dupin who receives Rousseau at her toilette. He takes to dining with her two or three times a week, finally declaring his passion in a letter (*OC* I, 291–92; *The Confessions*, pp. 274–75) since he finds her too intimidating to speak to directly. With Mme Dupin we enter the subject of the particular hospitality which was of crucial importance to the would-be writer in the eighteenth century. Beyond the need for food and shelter, the writer or artist needed patrons and contacts and hence needed to please in the sparkling world of aristocratic and high bourgeois literary salons. When these powerful patrons are women, Rousseau's relation to them is complex, involving desire, affection and fear as well as the sometimes biting political and social analysis which is a recurrent feature of the *Confessions*. These complexities must be set alongside his assertions of the necessity for separate spheres for men and women in order both for literal procreation to take place on the requisite scale and for literary creation to take place of a properly virile kind.

The writer and the salons

When Rousseau first comes to Paris he attempts to make a career, and one of the things he must do is to shine in conversation at the table and in the salon. But even the reader of the autobiography who knows nothing about Rousseau has already been informed (in Book III) that Rousseau cannot bear the 'unbearable constraint' of society gatherings (*OC* I, 115; *The Confessions*, p. 114). Rather than benefiting as a guest, it *costs* him when he is obliged to entertain his hosts and his fellow guests. When Rousseau is entertained informally and without luxury or ceremony (most of all by Mme de Warens, but also by Mlle Galley and others), he has a huge appetite, chats[21] and laughs freely, as well as enjoying a relaxed silence. In society gatherings, usually presided over by fine ladies, he cannot enjoy his food, cannot speak, or says things he regrets. He also suffers from an acute need to urinate at uncomfortably frequent intervals. Rousseau's anecdotes of getting it wrong in polite society are often complicated and carry a sexual undertone. This is true of his first emblematic tale in Book III in which he claims that he insulted his hostess by inadvertently suggesting that she might have needed to consult a doctor famed for treatment of venereal disease.

At times it seems as if writing will provide a solution to this: in Book VII Rousseau relates how, in early days in Paris, he was invited to dine with Mme de Beuzenval, and only belatedly realizes that she intends him to sit with the servants. As he makes his excuses and prepares to leave rather than be positioned as a servant, her daughter-in-law, Mme de Broglie, apparently saves the day by making it clear that he should instead join them and their close friend M. Lamoignon at table. But he does not feel at home in that place either: the conversation is much too 'Parisian' for him to be able to join in. He 'takes his revenge' after the meal by reading them a poetic epistle (to Parisot) he has written, and 'je les fis pleurer tous trois', slightly less marked in the English 'I moved all three to tears' (*OC* I, 290; *The Confessions*, p. 273). Making people weep in this way is always a particular satisfaction to Rousseau—as we see in his account of the first performance of *Le Devin du village* (The Village Seer) when he would like to drink the tears falling from the eyes of the many beautiful female spectators. I should emphasize, however, that these tears are sentimental and thus semi-pleasurable, not the product of cruelty and pain. Instead of dry and combative wit, like the *épée* a mark of nobility and a weapon to maintain your social place, his gift is *sensibilité*, the natural outpouring of the sensitive soul. It is not hard to see that these episodes play upon sexual difference, but the game is a very complicated one. Rousseau is ready to accuse Parisian society of sexual indifference: men who are too feminine and women who are too masculine. His solution, as a guest who does not want his female host to place him in the kitchen and yet finds social repartee at table difficult, is to arouse emotion. Weeping in response to the appropriate stimuli is not, for Rousseau, effeminate but natural—and thus closer to both real masculinity and real femininity than social markers of gender. Although he enjoys recurrent, if brief, moments of similar triumph after his self-styled 'moral reform', when he abandons any attempt to carry an *épée* or indeed a watch, Rousseau comes to realize that his writing only has true merit (as *instruction*) if he is free of all social obligation, including obligation to his paying public of readers. He therefore forsakes high society and attempts to support himself by copying music (*OC* I, 362–63; *The Confessions*, pp. 337–39). Hospitality will nevertheless remain a material and emotional support for writing (food, shelter, affection), but no longer a support for self-promotion or the networking which necessitates pleasing (*plaire*).[22]

Autobiography

In telling his tale, Rousseau inaugurates a genre, a genre that, for him, is so far removed from his version of virile early-modern aesthetics that it is barely to be considered 'writing' at all. Autobiography proves to be in fact potentially very powerful for subaltern groups—which is where he, as stranger, might place himself, even as he does not wish *to be placed* amongst the servants. In some ways it is his inability and unwillingness to fit the social norm as he sees it that fuels his autobiographical narrative. African-Americans are just one more recent example of a subaltern group who have turned to forms of autobiography as a means of finding a voice and telling their (side of the) story.[23] And yet once canon formation gets under way it is white men (often bourgeois to boot) who predominate. One of the most important, if not the most important, theorist of autobiography is Philippe Lejeune. His *Le Pacte autobiographique* deals primarily with Rousseau, and then with Gide, Sartre and Leiris.[24] He has also published books specifically on Gide and Leiris as autobiographers. This focus on the white man is typical of books on autobiography—unless they proclaim themselves specifically as dealing with women's writing, race or 'gender'.[25]

While Rousseau himself is hostile to women writers, and to the influence of women's salons, many women novelists and dramatists are very popular in his period. It is nineteenth-century critics who are the most successful in their attempts to condemn these eighteenth-century women writers to oblivion; they begin to be resurrected only thanks to the efforts of feminists in the last third of the twentieth century. Women's life writing cannot be tracked in terms of a history of publication and responses in quite this way since autobiography itself (in spite of the *Confessions*) only achieves canonical status as a genre in the 1950s. When critics do turn their attention to autobiography as a genre, then subaltern groups begin to be excluded by them *de facto* if not indeed *de iure* or *by definition*. Susan Stanford Friedman argues that George Gusdorf's seminal essay 'Conditions and Limits of Autobiography' (1956) defines autobiography in such a way as to make it less likely that texts by women, minority or non-Western writers would be included.[26] He refers to a certain individualistic 'consciousness of self' which is, he argues, quite historically specific. Friedman claims that this creates a critical bias since self, self-creation and self-consciousness are understood differently by those who have particular culturally-imposed group identities. She also claims, following Sheila Rowbotham and Nancy Chodorow, that women are differently socialized—in interaction rather than isolation.

Rousseau, who sees himself as an outsider and was indeed an outsider in his day, thus inaugurates a genre that seems hospitable to a range of diverse voices. It was certainly not his avowed intention to give women this kind of voice; but women have responded vocally and repeatedly to Rousseau and his work, rationally and emotionally, enthusiastically or angrily. Many female and working-class writers, many writers of colour, have followed his example in turning to life-writing—no doubt an over-determined choice. Heroes or important men can easily write or have their stories told whether or not they sign the text and have it termed autobiography rather than biography. But the potential that life-writing has held out since Rousseau is for someone not deemed heroic or socially or politically important by their contemporaries to tell their tale and be the 'hero' of their own text.[27] However, within life-writing there is a hierarchy, and what are deemed journals or memoirs, for example, are downgraded. Even where women's writing about themselves is accepted as autobiography it is rarely presented as a master-piece.[28] Women's writing moreover is often studied principally by women, and the consequent impact on their careers as researchers of definitionally 'minor' authors is not straightforward. Rousseau praises hospitality but was often uncomfortable as a guest—that very lack of comfort no doubt fuelling the sharpness of his analysis in his writing. His writing is, I would argue, unusually hospitable to many readers, including women, in spite of his many anti-feminist pronouncements. Regardless of these, his writings inspire writing. Yet almost two and a half centuries later, feminists, women, are still not at home in writing. The split in Rousseau's writing between explicit anti-feminist pronouncements and an affective and effective encouragement of women is simply reversed today when lip-service is paid to an equality and diversity that enables real inequalities to continue to flourish.

This essay was completed while I was the recipient of a Major Research Fellowship funded by the Leverhulme Trust.

3

Gender and Genre

Schiller's Drama and Aesthetics

Lesley Sharpe

Perhaps no German poet has enjoyed the adulation of his fellow Germans as much as Friedrich Schiller. Even if, since the 1960s in particular, younger generations have felt estranged from his high-sounding idealism and no longer read more of his works than the shrinking number still to be found in the school curriculum, his cultural and literary legacy have been enormous. His stage works and poems helped create a German literary and dramatic language. His theories of poetry gave powerful impetus to German and other European Romantic thinkers. He succeeded as no other dramatist of his age did in recreating tragedy in the grand manner, but infused with a modern consciousness and intricately linked to the public concerns of his day. His struggles against the tyrannies of eighteenth-century absolutism and with his own physical illnesses made him even to his contemporaries a heroic, almost Christ-like figure.[1] After his death the liberal sentiments in his work (often crassly lifted from their context and misrepresented) made him the spokesman for a nineteenth-century bourgeoisie struggling for the liberalization of German society.

Because of this moral role ascribed to him in the nineteenth century, Schiller's poetry was committed to memory by generations of school-children. Among his poems we find some strong reinforcements of the gender stereotypes developing in the later decades of the eighteenth century. His most popular poem, 'Das Lied von der Glocke' (The Song of the Bell), celebrates the traditional German housewife, never resting, holding the family together, while the father confronts the world outside the home. In 'Würde der Frauen' (Dignity of Women) we find a reflection of the contemporary idealization of women as guardians of 'nature', their harmony, repose and spontaneous, unreflective goodness contrasting with male striving for unreachable goals. These poems reflect contemporary notions of gender relations and also in particular Schiller's discussions in the mid-1790s with his friend Wilhelm von Humboldt, whose essay 'Über den Geschlechtsunterschied und dessen Wirkung auf die organische Natur' (On Sexual Difference and its Effect on Organic Nature) interprets nature as a reciprocal process of creativity (identified with the masculine) and receptivity (identified with the feminine). Schiller shared the prejudices of his day against women who tried to transcend this paradigm of passivity. His most notorious comment on the emerging phenomenon of the woman writer is his poem 'Die berühmte Frau' (The Famous Woman), in which the husband of a woman writer complains that his wife is thus displayed for all to see and can be bought by the whole world.[2] Particularly alienating for the modern reader is the association of writing by women for publication with prostitution. The poem is meant to be comic but not to the extent of invalidating the husband's complaint.

Goethe and Schiller formed a friendship and literary alliance that lasted from 1794 until Schiller's early death in 1805. Their project was to supply the German-speaking world with the exemplary works of literature that up to then, with a few exceptions, it had failed to produce. These works were to be inspired by the two writers' reflection on the Classical legacy, which both, after their youthful *avant-garde* phase, had increasingly come to see as the yardstick for contemporary writing, albeit adapted to the modern situation. The results were works such as (from Goethe) the first part of *Faust* and the epic poem *Hermann und Dorothea* and (from Schiller) *Wallenstein* and his later dramas. They shared with the majority of men at the time the belief that women could not aspire to the heights of true artistic achievement: women lacked the necessary education and scholarship as a foundation and the spark of creativity that, as Humboldt's theory illustrates, was regarded as being vouchsafed only to men. Schiller's own portrait of the artist, as exemplified by Letter 9 of his *Briefe über die ästhetische Erziehung des Menschen* (Letters on the Aesthetic Education of Humanity), is of one who has the independence and authority of a prophet. He must be 'raised under a distant Greek sky' (that is, his aesthetic sense formed by contemplation of the Ancients), returning 'terrible like Agamemnon's son' to purify his homeland.[3] This elevation of the artist figure is at the start of a long Romantic tradition that restricted women's talents to the production of ephemeral works for popular consumption.[4] Yet in practice Schiller was more generous to women's writing than such attitudes suggest, a generosity that sprang in part from his activities as an editor, grateful for poems from women to fill his annual volume of poetry, the *Musenalmanach* (The Muses' Almanach). His own sister-in-law, Caroline von Wolzogen, wrote a successful novel, *Agnes von Lilien* (1796/97), which, on appearing anonymously in *Die Horen*, gave rise to speculation that its author was Goethe himself. Schiller encouraged her writing and got her into print, though he did not think her work was of lasting artistic merit.[5]

Feminist approaches to Schiller at first focused strongly on these exemplary expressions in poetry of the essentialist view of passive/intuitive/intellectually limited femininity, linking them to the bourgeois elements in his conception of female dramatic characters and to the gendering of the aesthetic categories (feminine beauty and masculine sublimity) he developed for his theoretical discussions of art and poetry.[6] It has, however, long been recognized that Schiller's female dramatic figures are anything but mere incarnations of conventional bourgeois femininity. The majority are figures in historical dramas and are faced with challenges outside the scope of the experience of the conventional bourgeois housewife and mother. Even when dealing with contemporary women such as Amalia in *Die Räuber* (The Robbers) and Luise in *Kabale und Liebe* (Intrigue and Love) Schiller gives them heroic qualities and a desire to assert their autonomy in the face of coercion. Where he might have presented a simple suffering girl, he makes of Thekla in *Wallenstein* a resolute and independent woman, who in spite of her cloistered existence has a sure sense of when she is being manipulated and knows how to resist.

Of Schiller's plays *Maria Stuart* (Mary Stuart) has attracted perhaps the greatest number of feminist interpretations because it features two strong and diametrically opposed female main characters, Elisabeth and Maria, who are locked in an insoluble personal and political conflict. Traditional scholarly and popular understanding of the play focused until the 1960s on the title figure. Her death as a self-styled Catholic martyr and victim of a judicial murder tended to be interpreted in the light of Schiller's aesthetic writings and dramatic theory. She was considered a demonstration of the sublime, as expounded in Schiller's treatises *Über das Pathetische* (On Tragic Pity) and *Über das Erhabene* (On the Sublime), because she transcends physical destruction morally by accepting her unjust execution and thus mediates to the audience the exhilaration that springs from an imaginative experience of the human capacity for freedom. Alternatively, she was seen as a 'beautiful soul', a type defined in Schiller's treatise *Über Anmut und Würde* (On Grace and Dignity), in whom duty and inclination, the moral and the natural, are perfectly harmonized. The traditional emphasis on Maria's final triumph tended to limit the perception of the importance of Elisabeth's role. She was seen as a negative foil, an example of the female consumed by unfeminine lust for power, who thus fails as a ruler and as a woman and stands condemned at the end of the play.[7] In line with this interpretation, the political dimension of the work was frequently regarded as a demonstration of the irredeemable wickedness of the world, from which the exemplary Maria teaches us to turn away. The emergence of some feminist debate on the play from the late 1970s onwards, however, coincided with a greater emphasis in general on the play as historical and political drama.[8] *Maria Stuart* is very frequently performed in Germany, where its popularity with audiences and its contemporary resonance rest on the continued fascination with the question of how women respond to and exercise power. An important impetus to feminist interpretation was given in 1979 by Gert Sautermeister, who emphasized the psychological dependence of the two queens on norms of femininity embedded in the attitudes around them and the resulting conflict between their public and private roles.[9] Helmut Fuhrmann and Hans-Peter and Martina Herrmann elaborated on this theme, emphasizing discontinuities between the traditional conceptions of femininity and the action of the play.[10] All these critics highlight Schiller's insight into the conflicts arising from the intersection of power politics and sexual politics.

In this essay I shall combine discussion of *Maria Stuart* with *Über naïve und sentimentalische Dichtung* (On naïve and sentimental poetry) in an attempt to show how a feminist approach to both these works results in a clearer understanding of the tension within Schiller between the ambition to create exemplary works reflecting a Classical aesthetic and his realization that the modern writer must seek a new aesthetic. In *Maria Stuart* the challenge is tragic form and he produces his sparest, most economical plot to date. But it is a play with two tragic heroines, in which the action cuts from the sphere of the one to the sphere of the other, apart from a brief but fateful meeting in the third act. This is therefore an expansion of and an experiment with Classical tragic form. As his central characters Schiller takes two women who might be linked with the notions of tradition (Maria) and experiment (Elisabeth) in two senses. Maria is a Catholic (ex-)monarch who holds to the old idea of the ruler as God's anointed, whereas Elisabeth, a Protestant and, to Catholics, illegitimate, is forced to find a new way of ruling and of maintaining her position by popular assent.[11] And as a tragic figure Maria can style herself finally as a Catholic martyr, embracing a revered and ready-made role, while Elisabeth is left alone and deserted at the end of the play, not, I would argue, as a sign of her punishment but as an acknowledgement of the complexity of her situation, in which there is no ready-made role for her to assume.

At the heart of the play is the tragic incompatibility of morality and politics, a dilemma illuminated by its gender discourse. Elisabeth has used judicial murder to get rid of her rival. To cover up her involvement she has banished the men she wishes the world to hold responsible, Burleigh and Davison, and now she turns to Shrewsbury, the voice of justice and mercy. He tells her he has not been able to save her 'better part' and prefers retirement to the task of putting the seal on the deeds she will in future perform (now, by implication, that she has rejected justice and given in to the temptation of tyranny; see l. 4023–28). Shrewsbury has always been regarded as an unequivocally positive figure in the play, a counterweight to the ruthless Burleigh, the advocate of *Realpolitik*. He, it is held, is the voice of conscience to Elisabeth and a kind of surrogate father. I argue that Schiller gives us a more complex moral-political discourse than that simple contrast suggests. The gender assumptions of the characters help to highlight this complexity and indicate that the play as a whole calls Shrewsbury's standpoint into question.

Burleigh believes that it is his duty to secure the peaceful future of the realm. That future depends on the cultivation of allies (France), the production of heirs (through Elisabeth's marriage) and the elimination of the threat of uprising and usurpation. Hence he believes Maria's death is necessary. Without it there will always be the danger of assassination, religious strife and civil unrest. Thus he urges Elisabeth to think not of the ease of her conscience but of her people (l. 1254–94). Clearly he has had a major role in securing the guilty verdict against Maria for conspiracy in the Babington plot and now, in Act II, he wants to bring Elisabeth to the point of decision.

Shrewsbury, by contrast, urges Elisabeth to do what is morally right and to trust that the consequences will take care of themselves. He denies the jurisdiction of the court set up to judge Maria, and if the court cannot judge her then Elisabeth must judge and, Shrewsbury implies, must be merciful to her (l. 1316–19; 1340–47). Such an approach to decision-making in the political world rests on a belief that good flows from good and evil from evil. Shrewsbury's view of the relation of politics to morality has much in common with that of Kant. His late essay of 1795, *Zum ewigen Frieden* (Perpetual Peace), is a consideration of the conditions for peace in Europe in the French Revolutionary era. In the first section of the appendix, he denies that there is a discord between morality and politics. For Kant politics is the practice of the doctrines of law, and morality, based as it is on the same fundamental principles, must be in harmony with the law:

> The god of morality does not give way to Jupiter (the god of violence); for the latter is still under the rule of Fate, in other words reason is not enlightened enough to survey the series of predetermining causes that allow one to predict with certainty in accord with the processes of nature the happy or unhappy outcome of human actions.[12]

Kant distinguishes between the moral politician, who understands the principles of statesmanship in such a way that they can coexist with morality, and the political moralist, who fashions a morality to the advantage of the statesman. The former may make many mistakes but may learn from experience, but the latter, by denying the capacity of human beings to exhibit goodness, makes improvement impossible and thus perpetuates crimes against the rule of law.

Kant's distinctions are echoed but with a different emphasis and interpretation in the sociologist Max Weber's famous essay 'Politics as a Vocation'. It was written in the immediate aftermath of World War One, when a defeated Germany was struggling with political upheaval and ideological conflict. Weber's analysis of this same question—the relationship between politics and morality—was written with a consciousness of the Kantian tradition of political thought but is a rejection of it. Weber's starting point is the knowledge that politics is about power backed up by the possibility of violence. He distinguishes between an 'ethic of responsibility' and an 'ethic of ultimate ends'. The politician pursuing the former course believes that certain consequences are foreseeable as the result of certain actions and that these foreseeable consequences must form part of any responsible decision about how to act. The politician pursuing ultimate ends believes that the morally right decision must be made regardless of any foreseeable consequences. But, as Weber points out, experience does not support such confidence in the triumph of the right. To ignore immediate and foreseeable consequences suggests a blind trust in providence that is irresponsible:

> He who lets himself in for politics, that is, for power and force as means, contracts with diabolical powers and for his action it is not true that good can follow only from good and evil only from evil, but that often the opposite is true. Anyone who fails to see this is, indeed, a political infant.[13]

Weber took it as axiomatic that different spheres of life demand different principles of action and that to aim to preserve perfect moral purity is disastrously naive in the world of politics.

Schiller's dramatic presentation of the dilemma is more evenly balanced than Weber's but it is not an endorsement of the Kantian position, as is often assumed. Far from proposing that pure moral action is the way forward in politics he suggests rather that the worlds of politics and morality are tragically unbridgeable. To argue that Schiller puts into Shrewsbury's mouth a Kantian advocacy of the categorical imperative as a gauge of political action is to presume an allegiance on Schiller's part to the Kantian moral position that is not justified by the play.[14] Rather than using Shrewsbury to heighten by contrast Elisabeth's failure to follow her conscience, Schiller exposes the inadequacy of the Kantian categorical imperative as a political ethic as much as he does the moral shortcomings of Burleigh's *Realpolitik*. It is clear that Elisabeth pays a great cost in terms of her own humanity by failing to have the courage to own up to the way she has inwardly chosen all along. But neither is Shrewsbury vindicated. He condemns her in the final scene but his disappointment may be taken as a warning rather than as a prediction directed at the audience. We are not entitled to assume that Elisabeth's reign will henceforth be marked by tyranny.[15] We simply do not know what happens politically after the end of the play. Schiller takes care not to allow us to know the longer-term outcome of the decision so that we concentrate on the drama of the decision and share the characters' uncertainty about the possible consequences. Arguably, Elisabeth stands condemned in the audience's eyes not primarily because she signs the death warrant—she has after all that very day been the object of an assassination attempt that has brought home to her how vulnerable she is, even in her innermost circle—but because she will not acknowledge what she has done. The fact that she will not is linked to the gender discourse of the play.

Burleigh and Shrewsbury treat Elisabeth very differently as a woman. Burleigh fears her wish to avoid decision but does not otherwise impute womanly weakness to her. He sees it as his duty to manoeuvre her into marriage but less to make her fulfil a preconceived notion of her 'destiny' as a woman than to ensure an heir to the throne. Under his influence Elisabeth has attempted to rule, as she says, 'like a man and like a king' (l. 1171). By contrast with Burleigh, Shrewsbury specifically appeals to his vision of femininity to persuade Elisabeth to spare Maria:

> Do not refuse to hear the voice of mercy.
> God did not make severity the stuff
> Of woman's heart; and those who made the law
> That England's throne should not be barred to woman
> Proved that severity should never be
> The test of virtue in this kingdom's rulers. (l. 1342–47)[16]

Shrewsbury knows that Elisabeth wants to appear just. He uses an essentialist argument about the nature of woman as gentle and combines it with hints at the possibility of a better future for the country that is looking to its queen for mercy. She therefore has a special duty to give that lead. Shrewsbury then continues to plead Maria's sad condition, even excusing her marriage to her husband's murderer, Bothwell, on the grounds that it occurred in dark times:

> Who knows by what black arts she was beguiled?
> For woman is a frail and feeble creature. (l. 1372–73; p. 45)

Elisabeth's vigorous rebuttal of that last assertion is sometimes taken as a sign of her own suppressed frustration but actually Shrewsbury's words here are tactless in the extreme. He has to be interrupted again after his next speech (l. 1377–97) because of his eulogies to Maria's beauty. This is not therefore the voice of wisdom but of someone who combines a demand that Elisabeth act from pure motives regardless of the consequences to herself and others with an attachment to his sentimental view of femininity, a view in fact more typical of Schiller's own day than of the sixteenth century. The gender discourse that is woven into the moral/political dilemma thus serves to expose the danger of a sentimentalized view of the feminine and underscores how Schiller dignifies his women in *Maria Stuart* with the power of moral discrimination without making the ensuing decisions any easier for them. They are conscious of men's expectations of them and of the pressure of gender assumptions but that consciousness exists alongside an obligation to face up to the same ethical dilemmas as men.

Maria makes sense of her unjust execution by accepting it as a way of atoning for her complicity in the murder of her second husband,

Darnley. Her dignified death is conventionally interpreted by critics as an example of Schiller's theory of the sublime as developed in his essays on tragedy. According to this theory, the sublime is an aesthetic response in which the audience witnesses the physical destruction of the protagonist while gaining a sense that there is a moral freedom in human beings to accept and thereby transcend even physical destruction. Schiller developed this sophisticated reinterpretation of Aristotle's catharsis on the basis of Kant's notion of the sublime as expounded in the *Critique of Judgement* § 28: human beings, standing at a safe distance, may be overwhelmed by the knowledge of their vulnerability in the face of the force of nature but rise above that first response through the realisation that as creatures possessing reason (*Vernunft*) they participate in the noumenal realm, which is indestructible. The existence of this long-lived tradition of interpreting the play as an example of the sublime is an example of the gender-blindness of older criticism. For at several points in Schiller's aesthetic writings (though not specifically in the short essays on tragedy) the notion of the sublime is gendered, as is the related concept 'dignity' in *Über Anmut und Würde.* Schiller always centres his arguments on contrasting and complementary terms: the beautiful and the sublime, the naïve and the sentimental, grace and dignity, in which the first term of the pair is associated with the feminine and the second with the masculine. In *Über naive und sentimentalische Dichtung*, there are even hints that Schiller, in this respect also a follower of Kant, believes that women do not possess reason in the full sense in which men possess it and thus by definition cannot be vehicles of the sublime. Yet in the play that seems more than any other to exemplify and mediate what he means by the sublime, the tragic figure is not a man but a woman. While Schiller may transcend his own gender boundaries here, he is at the same time showing Maria casting herself in the traditional role of Catholic martyr, drawing on a long tradition of women showing serene transcendence in death. She contrasts with his experimental tragic figure, Elisabeth, and it is she, not Maria, who closes the play. The double tragedy looks back to the old traditions of drama and of female heroines and forward to an expansion of tragic form and of the aesthetic possibilities of the tragic heroine.[17]

Schiller's main treatise on poetics, *Über naive und sentimentalische Dichtung,* is another product of his intensive dialogue with the Classical tradition in the 1790s. It has attracted only very limited attention from feminist critics, and, where it has, it has been used as proof that Schiller denied women any place in poetry and cultural progress (Bovenschen, pp. 244–56). Yet it demonstrates Schiller's remarkable awareness of the changes in aesthetic sensibility and the need to develop a more flexible and dynamic approach to criticism as a response to that changing consciousness.

In the treatise, written in 1795, Schiller is asking: what kinds of poetry are there? what kind of poet am I? what is the future of poetry? He categorizes all poets according to two types of poetic consciousness. Either the poet has an immediate and apparently unreflective relationship to external reality or he stands in an indirect relationship with that reality and his work mediates an underlying tension between his perception of external reality and the ideal. The former, the naïve poet, is more characteristic of the ancient world, while the latter, the sentimental poet, is the norm in the modern world. Sentimental poetry, in Schiller's sense, is incapable of achieving the simple perfection of the works of the Ancients but it embraces greater intellectual complexity and range. The sentimental poet is embarked on an infinite quest to recapture the singleness of vision of the naïve under the conditions of his modern divided consciousness.

Schiller begins his treatise not with poetry but with a general framing anthropological argument. He identifies a common response to natural scenes or objects on the part of modern observers: somehow they move us because they remind us of a harmony we have lost: '*They are what we were*; they are what *we should again become*. We were nature just as they, and our culture, by means of reason and freedom, should lead us back to nature.'[18] He contrasts this response to nature with the objective depiction of external reality typical of the Ancients, who do not show this longing for nature because they had not entered a stage of civilization in which culture had created a gulf between human society and nature. And to express this sense of separation from a happier past Schiller uses a telling set of images:

> We then see in irrational nature only a happier sister who remained in our mother's house, out of which we impetuously fled abroad abroad in the arrogance of our freedom. With painful nostalgia we long to return as soon as we have begun to experience the pressure of civilization and hear in the remote lands of art [i.e. artifice] our mother's tender voice. (NA 20, 427; p. 188)

The use of the metaphors of mother and sister is symptomatic of the association in the treatise of women with nature and hence with the naïve.

In her groundbreaking study *Die imaginierte Weiblichkeit*, Bovenschen was perhaps the first feminist critic to discuss systematically in relation to German literature how this conception of femininity served to justify the exclusion of women from any independent contribution to cultural progress.[19] Schiller sets his argument about poetry within a speculative three-stage history of civilization. Human beings exist first in a state of primal unity, through sophistication they become estranged from nature and thus inwardly divided, but by an arduous process of striving for the ideal, which is a construct of reason, they can regain the harmony they have lost, but regain it on a higher level. But women, identified with nature and with the naïve, seem thus by implication excluded from this journey. They seem to act only as a visible symbol of that lost harmony for the men who observe them and who by virtue of reason are the ones who carry civilization forward.

Bovenschen's claim about Schiller's exclusion of women can, however, be modified and extended in the light of the whole argument of the treatise and of his very idiosyncratic way of conducting aesthetic arguments in general. First of all, the function of the framework is not to exclude women, though one might see this as an implication. The function of the framework is to establish the centrality of art to human development (and thus assert a moral core to art) and to provide a utopian perspective on the discussion of poetry that guarantees art's continuous change, progression and open-endedness. Secondly, Schiller's aesthetic writings are all attempts to see how far aspects of Kantian thought can be used to solve some of his practical problems as a writer. For Schiller the Kantian, reason (as shown in the brief discussion of the theory of tragedy above) is a key concept. His characteristic arguing through contrasting and seemingly mutually exclusive pairs of concepts—the naïve and the sentimental, grace and dignity, the beautiful and the sublime—gives reason the vital pivotal role. The second term of each cognate pair arises through the introduction of reason, so whereas the first term is characterized by harmony, the second is characterized by struggle and transcendence. Schiller's association of women with the naïve, with grace and with beauty, as noted above, casts doubt on his according to women the capacity of reason, the prerequisite of moral autonomy, at least in the measure it is accorded to men.

Through all Schiller's aesthetic writings there runs a fundamental tension, however. He wants to affirm the harmony of beauty as the perfect union of sense and spirit but in fact feels that its repose, its self-sufficiency, its lack of internal struggle, its very materiality are in some way suspect and that the conflict and transcendence that produce dignity and the sublime are somehow superior.[20] In order to have his cake and eat it he always postulates a reconciliation of his two terms in a higher synthesis, though in fact this manoeuvre is always a logical impossibility because the two terms are originally set up as mutually exclusive. At the root of these apparently impenetrable arguments is a profound mistrust of nature, in the sense of the material world, and thus a profound mistrust of his own models of harmony, which imply an affirmation of the material world. As a result, his writings on aesthetics are full of images of conflict that express his sense of the need for the mind to subdue the material. In the association of women with nature and the naïve we can see Schiller's ambivalence towards them. On the one hand they are idealized and yet on the other their association with the material world makes them threatening. This ambivalence is evidence of the enduring power, even in a secular context, of the models of thought deriving from the Christian appropriation of Neo-Platonic traditions, in which woman is identified with a fallen creation.

Yet Schiller's belief in the superiority of struggle and transcendence is linked to a profound nostalgia and longing for repose. By gendering the terms naïve and sentimental, at least in the anthropological framework of his argument, Schiller says less about women than about men. For in the images of struggle and the longing for repose we catch a glimpse of the strain of the kind of masculinity that is the necessary result of gender polarization. In this construction of masculinity men have all creative, proactive functions, sole access to reason and thus control of all rational discourse. Thus they can escape imprisonment by the material feminine. Yet at the same time one detects in the longing for nature a weariness of this perpetual control and conflict. Schiller's use of the Neo-Platonic paradigm of exile and return in his three-part speculative history of humanity arguably suggests a wish to give value to the suppressed feminine and yet his mythologization of women bars the way to his giving them any real content. One perhaps can suggest that in creative writing he is able to give women the content he denies them here.

Crucially, Bovenschen points out that when he reaches the central discussion of poetry, Schiller's terms are no longer gendered (pp. 251–52). For *Über naive und sentimentalische Dichtung* is a work notorious for the shifts in the meaning of its key terms. The speculative history into which Schiller places his discussion of poetry turns out to be only one discourse of the work, while the actual discussion of poetry rests on rather different meanings of the key terms *nature* and *naïve*. For example, at the beginning of the treatise the naïve is defined with reference to the general experience of sophisticated people recognising a kind of uncorrupted and unconscious innocence in others. But by the time we get to the naïve poet, the more general and familiar anthropological definitions of the naïve have disappeared and the term denotes a kind of singleness of vision with no connotation of the primitive, spontaneous or rough-hewn at all.

The fact that Schiller has changed the terms of his argument must be significant and one may justifiably ask whether the poetological argument has different gender implications from the speculative historical framework. When it comes to poetry, the naïve and the sentimental are both discussed only in relation to men. But nothing in the argument itself specifically excludes women and perhaps it is legitimate to detach his practical thoughts on literature from what we may happen to know about his presuppositions in order to see how they might be fruitful in feminist context. He is asking himself what the appropriate ways of categorizing modern literature are. Rather than doing so on the basis of genre, he uses the concept of *Empfindungsweisen* or 'modes of feeling'. He argues that while the naïve poet stands in one necessary relationship to external reality, the sentimental poet, being separated by self-consciousness from an unreflective relation to them, can choose the standpoint from which to view them. If he wants to stress the inadequacy of the real in relation to the ideal he will write in the satiric mode and if he wants to emphasize the feeling of regret at the passing of the ideal he will adopt the elegiac mode of feeling. Schiller gives the terms *satire*, *elegy* and *idyll* his own specific meanings. Particularly, he emphasizes that he is not talking about genre, even though he is using established terms with long genre traditions behind them. To push the point further home, he stresses that a writer can move from one mode of feeling to another and back again in the course of the same work. By using the concept of modes of feeling Schiller recognizes that traditional concepts of genre, deriving as they do mainly from classical models, are not adequate to help us identify the distinctiveness of modern writing or at least that there are other ways of analysing literary works, ones that challenge the boundaries of genre and that embrace the notion of experiment implicit in Schiller's concept of the modern. For the sentimental poet can never reach his goal. All he can do is set out on an infinite quest to approach by degrees an unreachable perfection.

This challenge, however understated in Schiller's treatise, to the usefulness of traditional notions of genre in understanding and judging modern writing is a progressive strategy for women writers and critics, for it indicates, perhaps even requires, the decline of the hierarchy of genres. One of the prejudices against women writers in Schiller's day was that they were not capable of creating or appreciating poetry in the highest-ranking genres such as tragedy. They lacked, it was held, the educational background, the intellectual rigour and the capacity for sustained effort to be able to create high art.[21] And even in the lesser genres such as prose fiction women writers constantly had to present their work as being didactic, useful and hence justifiable as an activity that took them away from their true calling, the home, even at a time when the idea of the autonomy of art, its liberation from subservience to moral purposes, was otherwise gaining ground. Schiller's theory is anti-didactic and requires experimentation and openness to new forms and types of literary expression, even though women's actual creative scope and opportunities at the time still lagged far behind such theoretical insights.

Of course, elsewhere Schiller is anything but indifferent to traditional genre definitions. He spent a great deal of time in the early 1790s theorizing about tragedy and later discussing with Goethe his own tragedies as he was writing them. Jointly they wrote the short essay 'Über epische und dramatische Dichtung' (On Epic and Dramatic Poetry; 1797). In fact Goethe records Schiller's ambition at one stage in the life of the Weimar theatre to have a building devoted to the staging of tragedies and once a week to restrict attendance to men.[22] In *Über naive und sentimentalische Dichtung*, however, he inserts into the discussion of satire two remarkable paragraphs arguing the respective merits of comedy and tragedy and, surprisingly, it is comedy that prevails as the more significant form of literature. For the aesthetic effect of comedy, he claims, is to allow us to glimpse an ideal state in which we can look at life with sovereign imperturbability. Thus Schiller reverses his usual dramatic hierarchy and in doing so also implicitly undermines the gender ideology that sustains tragedy at the top of the hierarchy.

If the sentimental writer, as Schiller claims, always writes from an awareness of tension between real and ideal, the notion of his objectivity is an illusion. It is the naïve poet in his scheme who is characterized by the capacity for realist writing, for only he has the singleness of vision to ensure objectivity. If we take Schiller's notion of the tension between ideal and real and reformulate it in broader terms as a tension between the writer's vision of the underlying determinants of external reality and its surface manifestations, we can see that he anticipates some of the aesthetic debates and problems arising from nineteenth-century Realism and highlighted by analysis of the presentation of women.[23] In particular he anticipates the difficulty Realist novelists will have in depicting more than the obvious social conventions acting on women's lives and therefore moving beyond the clichés that quickly limited their fictional expression. This problem is explored in the essays on Stendhal, Flaubert and Fontane in this volume, which uncover the aesthetic strategies employed by these writers to escape these clichés while showing female subjectivity as inevitably conditioned by convention and language.

In the introduction to this chapter I mentioned Schiller's portrait of the artist in his *Ästhetische Briefe* and it is inescapably true that he was one of the writers responsible for a deepening of the perception of the gulf between high art and mere writing, dilettantism, as he called it. *Über naive und sentimentalische Dichtung* presents us with an alternative portrait of the literary artist, a portrait of himself, not as the serene Olympian he was often taken for by later generations, through association with Goethe, but as a restless, self-questioning spirit. This is someone who feels separated from a secure tradition and so longs on one level to feel part of it, someone who cannot simply appropriate the criteria and forms of the past but has to be prepared to strike out on new paths, knowing that they will take an infinite time to explore, someone who sees that experiment is the only way to find a language and forms that express with honesty a complex vision.

4

Male Foibles, Female Critique and Narrative Capriciousness

On the Function of Gender in Conceptions of Art and Subjectivity in E.T.A. Hoffmann

Ricarda Schmidt

E.T.A. Hoffmann (1776–1822) began to carve out a literary career only when key figures of the first generation of Romantic writers were already dead (Novalis, Wilhelm Heinrich Wackenroder) or had moved on to Catholicism (Friedrich Schlegel, Clemens Brentano). Yet Romantic writers—particularly Novalis, Wackenroder, Ludwig Tieck, August Wilhelm Schlegel, Adalbert von Chamisso and Friedrich de la Motte-Fouqué—continued to be important literary reference points for Hoffmann. Like the earlier Romantics, Hoffmann assumed that art was autonomous. But it was, for him as for them, an autonomy within a moral context where art was practised and supposed to be received with religious fervour, not the kind of autonomy of the twenty-first century which sees art as having no social function. Like the early Romantics, Hoffmann thought of the artist not as copying from nature, but as creating something new: the artist as genius. But he developed his concept of the artist both in continuity with and in distinction from early Romanticism. He held on to early Romantic idealism and its concern with the role of the artist in developing a vision of an ideal beyond the status quo. However, he never conceived of the ideal as imminently realizable, nor to be realized in a symbolic union of the artist-protagonist with an idealized woman, as Novalis, Tieck, and Friedrich Schlegel had.

Hoffmann was open to a variety of, sometimes incongruent, aesthetic values, ranging from Romanticism to the Gothic novel, from classical music to Gozzi's revival of the *commedia dell'arte*, from Nazarene painting to grotesque and fantastic art, from Schiller's impassioned seriousness to Sterne's ironic sentimentalism, from Rousseau's earnest sensibility[1] to Cervantes's comic debunking of idealism. The Romantic aesthetics of ordered chaos, striving for the sublime, self-reflectivity, irony, fragmentariness and symbolic indirectness he developed further into highly complex and consciously crafted narratives with changing focalization and perspectivization in an interlocking web of unreliable narrators. This absence of a central narrative perspective in many of his works, together with imperceptible transitions from a vividly depicted contemporary reality to the realm of the fantastic, and a rapid shifting in tone from the sublime to ironic mockery, make his texts appear to many readers as lacking cohesion. The obsession with dark, sometimes gory, actions in Hoffmann's texts, and his interest in externalizations of psychic processes, betray the influence of the Gothic novel. On the other hand, the serious thematic concern throughout Hoffmann's texts with music as the realm of the sublime, as well as the adaptation of technical musical features to literature—like the use of *Leitmotiv* and variation, the contrasting of different voices and the counterpoint-like technique in his prose, the tendency to express meaning through the structural organization of the material rather than through explicit commentary—point to Hoffmann's admiration for the classical composers Gluck, Haydn, Mozart and Beethoven, whose work he reviewed for professional musical journals. Hoffmann's predilection for the grotesque can be traced back to his interest in the *commedia dell'arte*, as mediated by Jacques Callot's etchings and Carlo Gozzi's fairy tales. This contrasts with his longing for the re-creation of positive ideals, which is reflected in his admiration for an early nineteenth-century school of German painters in Rome, called 'The Nazarenes' ('Die Nazarener'), and their, to modern eyes, epigonal and saccharine style of religious and mythical painting.

Although Hoffmann published many of his stories in collections which were aimed primarily at female readers, and although he acted in his legal capacity for the writer Helmina von Chézy, he is not known for having absorbed any female literary influence; he even disliked the work of his friend's wife, Caroline von Fouqué. He was receptive to women's aesthetic creative powers only with regard to singers and actresses. Not only did his singing student Julia Marc leave a deep impression on his writing, but he also valued professional singers such as Johanna Eunicke for the depth of their expression of feeling.

Hoffmann's diverse aesthetic techniques have given rise to wildly differing interpretations of his stories and novels to this day. Different feminist readings arrive at diametrically opposed conclusions concerning the nature of the same protagonist's desire and Hoffmann's stance on gender.[2] On the other hand, interpreters of very different theoretical persuasions sometimes arrive at surprisingly similar conclusions. Thus feminist and anti-feminist readings of Hoffmann end up as strange bed-fellows in their negative view of Clara in 'Der Sandmann' (The Sandman);[3] a pre-feminist reading anticipates many of the findings of a feminist reading;[4] and nineteenth-century critics who bemoan an absence of positive ideals in Hoffmann are oddly echoed in their findings, which are, however, evaluated in a diametrically opposite way, by twentieth-century deconstructionists who celebrate the dispersal of meaning and the dissolution of identity in Hoffmann's texts.[5]

Feminist criticism of Hoffmann's work has not formed a distinct and homogeneous school of Hoffmann interpretation. Rather it has participated in the different critical tendencies of the last three decades, when focusing on the feminist topics of the representation of women in Hoffmann's work and, primarily, on the function of woman in the constitution of the male subject and of the work of art. Feminist critics have predominantly read Hoffmann's texts as proto-feminist, rather than criticizing them for patriarchal tendencies. Hoffmann's famous night piece 'Der Sandmann' has been the work most frequently chosen for analysis, and it shall be my main focus in this discussion of feminist readings of Hoffmann.

The earliest feminist reading of Hoffmann stems from Hélène Cixous. It set a trend which has been dominant in literary criticism of many different schools to this day: to try to find manifestations of modern theoretical positions already positively realized in historical texts, and to claim them as precursors of the latest fashion. In 1974 Cixous argued that not only contemporary avant-garde literature, but already literature of the past couple of centuries, has been working at the subversion of what she calls the 'masculine libidinal economy'. This term signifies for Cixous not a biological but a cultural concept, comprising notions of logocentrism, the unity of the subject, and phallogocentrism; it designates a kind of desire that is characterized by castration, death, calculation, conservation, property, and power. Cixous sets this masculine libidinal economy evaluatively in binary opposition to a 'feminine libidinal economy'. The latter she understands as based on the knowledge of the multiplicity of the subject, aiming for intensity of experience rather than the conservation of energies, for endless seduction rather than possession, for ecstasy rather than continuity. According to Cixous, Nathanael's desire in Hoffmann's story 'Der Sandmann' demonstrates such a feminine libidinal economy:

> Nathanael's entire being is contained in this impetus into which he is absorbed and disappears: nothing holds him back in a self, which never attracts his gaze. He does not turn back on himself, he projects himself, his gaze enamoured of the void which his desire constitutes as an absolute eye.[6] (Cixous, p. 42-43)

Nathanael's 'feminine' desire, in turn, is said to shape the structure of the text with its achronological, decentred, digressive, intense form of narration—all features which for Cixous comprise *l'écriture féminine.* Moreover, Cixous sees the pillars of phallogocentrism shaken in 'Der Sandmann' by the slippage, in respect of the signification of femininity, of the differences between alive and dead and between metaphor and reality—a conclusion I criticize in an earlier essay for isolating certain elements of the text without examining them in the context of the narrative concept or of literary history.[7] For many of the technical narrative features Cixous lists as examples of *l'écriture féminine* are to be found in mainstream literature by male authors who hold conventional views on gender. Nathanael's allegedly feminine desire for the automaton, on the other hand, looked at from the perspective of object-relations theory rather than of Cixous's Lacanian libidinal economy, appears to be in line with the quite traditionally masculine one of wanting to use woman as a mirror to reflect man twice his natural size. Cixous identifies in her reading exclusively with the protagonist Nathanael and follows him in devaluing Clara as an automaton, thus disregarding the vital distinction between internal and external focalization and the narrator's shifting allegiances to his characters. It is perhaps a telling irony that, quite unintentionally, Cixous's explicitly feminist reading comes close to Raimund Belgardt's 'blame-the-woman' type of interpretation, which also fails to take into account perspectivization and narrative context. We hear in Cixous's confirmation that Clara is '—we shall see—and Nathanael is not mistaken, reductionist, immobilizing, chilling, in opposition to the feverish effect which the sight of Olimpia produces' (Cixous, p. 71) an echo of Belgardt's evaluation of Clara. Using a decontextualized, and thus distorted, quotation from the story, he generalizes that Clara is characterized by a 'a mental sleepiness which cannot be overcome' (Belgardt, pp. 690, 694, 697). Belgardt sees her mind directed 'only to utilitarian values' (Belgardt, p. 694), and argues that Clara represents a social environment, characterized by mental barrenness and lack of understanding, which destroys the isolated artist.

A decade later, Susanne Asche explores the function of the mirror-image in relation to femininity in Hoffmann's work. She is also working within a poststructuralist framework, but without knowledge of Cixous's work on Hoffmann or of Luce Irigaray's feminist adaptation in *Speculum de l'autre femme* (Speculum of the other woman)[8] of post-structuralist tenets. While her findings converge with Cixous's as far as the dissolution of the identity of the literary subject, not only as a problem to be explored but as Hoffmann's positive aim, is concerned (according to Asche, Hoffmann shows in his texts, 'that an identical self cannot be constructed in the mode of literary speech' (Asche, p. 157)), they differ with regard to the role of gender. While Cixous saw in Nathanael a manifestation of feminine desire, Asche argues, on the contrary, that Hoffmann shows the female beloved again and again in his work as the male artist's dream or mirror-image, which must not be touched if the male artist's precarious sense of self and the flow of his artistic production are not to be destroyed. Taking the texts with a fatal ending as displaying the almost unavoidable consequence of a constitution of the male subject which requires the exclusion of the female one, Asche generalizes that Hoffmann 'narrates the mechanisms of exclusion and the erection of borders which are the precondition for a literature centring on the reflexive self' (Asche, p. 169). That is, she considers Hoffmann not as the producer of an image of femininity, but rather as the critical narrator of the sacrifices which a commonly accepted type of cultural production of images and its resultant constitution of the masculine subject demands. Asche takes up key arguments which Peter von Matt formulated in his influential 1971 study of Hoffmann: that women in Hoffmann's work are the 'concretized projection of the inner being' (von Matt, p. 64) of the artist, and that 'the re-transformation [of the female beloved] into the image' (von Matt, p. 52) is necessary in order to avoid 'as a last consequence, murder as its perverted opposite form' (von Matt, p. 69). But while von Matt classed these features as reflections of Hoffmann's 'autistic experience of being' (von Matt, p. 74), Asche turns them round as Hoffmann's conscious exposure (and, by implication, rejection) of the mechanisms of exclusion which make possible a literature that is centred on the reflexive subject (see Asche, p. 169)—that is, male literature.

In contrast to Cixous's ahistorical projection of late twentieth-century convictions of an ultimately clichéd and conservative 'feminine libidinal economy' onto Hoffmann's male protagonist, and also in contrast to Asche's claim that Hoffmann's texts critically demonstrate the violence of what in the late twentieth century came to be termed 'the constitution of the male subject', Margarete Kohlenbach tries to set Hoffmann's work in a multi-faceted relationship to concepts of femininity in early Romanticism. Kohlenbach aims to show a 'divergence between Hoffmann's texts and Kreisler's stance with respect to the early Romantic philosophy of love' (Kohlenbach, p. 660). In this triangulation of (a) Hoffmann's *œuvre* as a whole, (b) one of his fictional characters, and (c) early Romanticism, she situates Hoffmann's concept of love and femininity historically in relation to early Romanticism, in terms which take account simultaneously of both progression and regression. She concludes that Hoffmann's depiction of love falls short of Friedrich Schlegel's revolutionary attempt in *Lucinde* to unite spiritual and sensual love, and independence and union, in femininity, but that it points out the danger inherent in the early Romantic idealizing of femininity, namely that idealization 'can coincide with denying to women a life of their own' (Kohlenbach, p. 673). Furthermore, she shows heterogeneity, contradiction and duplicity within Hoffmann's fiction, and consequently the futility of any attempt to deduce clear authorial intentions from isolated sections of the text. Kohlenbach makes this point by contrasting Kreisler's pronouncements on the asexual love of the artist in *Die Lebens-Ansichten des Katers Murr* (The Life and Opinions of Tomcat Murr, 1819–21) both with other textual evidence from that novel (which hints at the fact that the reader is not to take Kreisler's pronouncements at face value), and with Hoffmann's treatment of the loving artist in the rest of his oeuvre, particularly 'Der Sandmann'. Kohlenbach reads, achronologically, the earlier story as a satirical critique of the main weakness of the protagonist in the later novel and, moreover, of *the* Romantic poet in early Romantic discourse on femininity, in particular of his 'failure to engage in a passionate relationship with an independent person' (Kohlenbach, p. 665). However, judging Clara against the intentions of Romantic writing as voiced by the narrator of 'Der Sandmann', Kohlenbach argues that Clara is criticized for falling short of the Romantic ideal. Thus Kohlenbach arrives at the irritating conclusion not only that Hoffmann works within the parameters of Romantic poetics while satirizing *the* Romantic poet, but also that 'Der Sandmann' 'leads to the negation of what it affirms when read as a satire on Kreislerian attitudes and beliefs' (Kohlenbach, p. 668).

Despite these troubling contradictions, Kohlenbach's reading provides valuable insights. In principle, the combination of a narratological and a historical analysis, as practised by Kohlenbach, allows for a more complex and nuanced understanding of the relationship of a text to the cultural tradition and to the modern reader than the eye-catching attempts to claim simultaneously, on the one hand, a seamless continuity from a historical author to a contemporary theoretical position and, on the other hand, a radical rupture between a text and its historical context.[9] However, Kohlenbach's impasses show that more attention needs to be paid to two points. First, the historical development of Hoffmann's central themes needs to be taken more into account, as it is not quite convincing to read a later text as being satirized by an earlier one. Furthermore, Hoffmann's relationship to his cultural and aesthetic context should be examined in more detail, in order to define more precisely the aim of his satire, rather than claiming that each feature that differs from early Romantic texts makes Hoffmann a parodist of Romanticism *tout court*.[10]

Hoffmann's best known texts are stories which were often first published in journals or almanacs, and later put together in three collections (with some of the stories being written specifically for the collection): *Fantasiestücke in Callot's Manier* (Fantasy Pieces in the Style of Callot, 1814–15), *Nachtstücke* (Night Pieces, 1816–17) and *Die Serapions-Brüder* (The Serapion Brethren, 1819–21). For this last collection Hoffmann added a communicative frame in which a group of friends discuss the stories told by the group members. These discussions, as well as the poetological dialogue *Seltsame Leiden eines Theater-Direktors* (Strange Sufferings of a Theatre Director, 1818), are an important source for any examination of Hoffmann's poetics. Hoffmann's stories are particularly notable, first, for their fusion of the real and the fantastic; second, for the exploration of unconscious processes, above all of imagination, madness and split identity;[11] third, for their complex narrative form, which leaves much to the reader to work out;[12] and fourth, for centring on art, including questions of artistic inspiration, aim and failure, the social function of art, the relationship between artist and society.[13] These features and themes are also shared by the longer texts which appeared independently in book form: the novels *Die Elixiere des Teufels* (The Elixirs of the Devil,

1825–16), and, incomplete, *Die Lebens-Ansichten des Katers Murr*; the fairy tales *Klein Zaches genannt Zinnober* (Little Zaches, Called Zinnober, 1819) and *Meister Floh* (Master Flea, 1822); the capriccio *Prinzessin Brambilla* (Princess Brambilla, 1820). Furthermore, Hoffmann published musical reviews, and he composed and published operas, liturgical music, songs, ballets, and chamber music.

While some critics maintain that Hoffmann's *œuvre* and his concept of art undergo no development at all,[14] others posit a radical change. Claudia Liebrand argues that Hoffmann's 'art-theoretical creed'[15] develops from a negative aesthetics (by which Liebrand understands an antagonistic relationship of mutual exclusion between life and art, and the extinction of life before art can take place), via a number of intermediate positions, such as an aesthetics of affirmation and one of utopian reconciliation, to an aesthetics of positivity (which dissolves the separation between art and life by showing reality as staged, and the staged show becoming reality). Since Liebrand sees each of these positions as both posited and subverted in the same text, her categories lack convincing delimitation. I cannot criticize her categories in detail here;[16] but I want to take up from Liebrand the idea of a development in Hoffmann's concept of art, and, focusing on the relationship between artist and beloved, I want to examine the function of gender in conceptions of art and subjectivity in Hoffmann.

Although Hoffmann is frequently thought of as the writer who bemoans the sad fate of the artistic genius driven to despair, even madness, by a hostile environment (as is indeed the case in many of the *Fantasiestücke*), not all his fictional artists are conceived of as great. Comically incompetent, Kater Murr, Amandus von Nebelstern (from 'Die Königsbraut' (The King's Bride)), the eponymous Baron von B., and Abbate Chiari (from *Prinzessin Brambilla*) immediately spring to mind as parodies of artistic ambition. There are also those with some real talent which they fail to bring to fruition, like Nathanael in 'Der Sandmann', the eponymous Rat Krespel (Councillor Krespel), and the painter Berthold in 'Die Jesuiterkirche in G.' (The Jesuit Church in G.). In short, lack of recognition, which Hoffmann's artists so often suffer, is not always presented as an indictment of a philistine environment unable to recognize greatness. Some of Hoffmann's artists are ironically presented as self-centred, conceited, vainglorious, with sometimes only a mediocre or small talent, or one that never blossoms because of internal and external circumstances. Needless to say, apart from Mademoiselle de Scuderi, Hoffmann's creative artists are primarily male, with only a few female singers (the singer of Donna Anna in 'Don

Juan', Julia in *Kater Murr*, Antonie and her mother in 'Rat Krespel', the Italian singers in 'Die Fermate' (The Pause), Bettina and Zulema in 'Das Sanctus' (The Sanctus)) and a self-taught actress breaking this concentration on the male subject as the representative of the human condition. In Hoffmann's work women have above all a supporting function, both, as muses, in spurring male artists on to greatness, but also in revealing their weaknesses to the reader.

With regard to the traditional role of women as muses, Hoffmann frequently does not follow the early Romantic model of uniting the artist and his muse for a utopian ending, and of presenting this union as one of body and soul, of the real and the ideal. Rather, he drives a wedge between the real and the ideal. Hoffmann's response to his personal trauma in 1812—the impossibility of realizing his love for his sixteen-year-old singing student Julia Marc—found expression in a number of fictional constellations in which the male protagonist has to learn that he can never physically possess the ideal he has projected onto the beloved, but must distinguish between the real woman and his ideal. That the latter continues to serve as the guiding star for his art, or for the development of his ideal self, makes the loss of the real woman easier to bear. This preservation of idealism also marks the difference between Hoffmann's late Romantic position and Postmodernism. If the artist is unable to make the distinction between the real woman and his ideal (as is the protagonist in Mozart's opera *Don Giovanni*, according to the narrator's interpretation in 'Don Juan'; Berthold in 'Die Jesuiterkirche in G.'; Nathanael in 'Der Sandmann'), he meets a catastrophic end. It has often been argued that Hoffmann's artists are required to renounce sexuality in favour of an ascetic, incorporeal concept of art. However, while the earlier texts indeed put more emphasis on the need for separation between the real and the ideal (see 'Don Juan', *Die Elixiere des Teufels*, 'Die Abenteuer der Sylvester-Nacht' (The Adventures of New Year's Eve)), Hoffmann soon moves to an exploration of different ways in which the real and the ideal can co-exist without fusion. This occurs in 'Der Artushof' (King Arthur's Court) in a banal doubling of the beloved woman (Felicitas, the ideal, is renounced and Dorina, the look-alike real woman, is married). Frequently, the co-existence of the real and the ideal is split and they are associated with two different artists, one of whom unites with his beloved while the other pursues artistic celibacy (as in 'Meister Martin der Küfner und seine Gesellen' (Master Martin the Cooper and his Craftsmen), 'Der Kampf der Sänger' (The Singers' Fight), and 'Signor Formica'). But the relationship between the real and the ideal is dealt with in most complex form in *Prinzessin Brambilla*, which enacts an education towards a recognition of the co-existence of the real and the ideal for both the male artist and his beloved—who, in the process of this education, also becomes an artist.

Having outlined the general development of the changing role of woman for the artist in Hoffmann's work, I will now explore it in more detail in 'Der Sandmann' and in *Prinzessin Brambilla*. While paying attention to the cultural context of Hoffmann's work, I will combine a narratological analysis with an analysis of the constitution of the subject in the male protagonist, following Judith Butler's notion of the subject as both an effect of subjection and as the presupposition of agency.[17]

Whereas Hoffmann's lively re-writing of Goethe's carnival report and the discovery of Hoffmann's parody of Goethe's acting style[18] in *Prinzessin Brambilla*, led to the impression that Hoffmann rejected Goethe (and all values of Classicism) wholesale, it is worth pointing out that both 'Der Sandmann' and *Prinzessin Brambilla* draw on a motif from Goethe in an assenting way, though far surpassing the literary merits of Goethe's minor text. Developing the motif in different directions thematically and aesthetically, both texts share Goethe's critique of false sentiment in his satire *Triumpf der Empfindsamkeit* (Triumph of Sensibility, 1778), in which he mocks excessive sensibility (including his own in *Werther*) in a lover preferring a doll over a real woman—a doll whose hollow inside is stuffed with the literature of sensibility.[19]

In 'Der Sandmann', the question of how to distinguish between a subjective and an objective perspective on experience is dealt with in shifting focalizations with such mastery that uncertainty, fear and terror are evoked in the reader. But it is clear that the protagonist's artistic talent suffers from his preoccupation with the dark power which he supposes has re-entered his life in the shape of Coppola. The narrator vouches for Nathanael's decline as a poet in the externally focalized comment:

> Formerly he was particularly good at gracious, lively stories, which he wrote down and which Clara listened to with the utmost pleasure; now his poetry was dark, incomprehensible, formless, so that, even though for his sake Clara did not say it, he nevertheless felt how little it appealed to her [. . .] Nathanael's poetry was indeed very boring. (H3, 30)[20]

In addition to this response via unconscious body language, Clara comments verbally when Nathanael reads to her his poem, which foretells in gruesome images 'a terrible fate destroying their love' (H3, 32) and which pictures Clara as the cause of Nathanael's death. The narrator has already hinted ironically at the unreasonableness of Nathanael's expectation of eliciting an enthusiastic response to this poem from the very person whose loss of a lover it portrays (see H3, 31-32). Thus Clara's critical rejection of the poem has been prepared for by the narrator as entirely foreseeable by everyone but the egotistic poet. Clara's verbal rejection of the poem coincides, moreover, with her physical embrace of the poet: 'Clara pressed him gently to her breast and said quietly, but very slowly and seriously: Nathanael—my dearest Nathanael!—throw the wild—terrible—mad fairy tale into the fire' (H3, 32). But Nathanael is unable to differentiate between Clara's love for him and her understandable dislike for the content of this poem, and he replies to her request by swearing at her, and by running away from his critic. His self-centred refusal to engage with another viewpoint paves the way for his infatuation with a mechanical doll which can never answer him back, a doll which only his gaze animates and whose main attraction is its imagined confirmation of Nathanael's artistic talent. Even if there is a supernatural power at work in Nathanael's demise (and the text skilfully leaves this possibility, as well as that of a childhood trauma as the cause of his terrifying end, in the air), it is clear that his narcissistic refusal to listen to anyone with a different perspective on life from his own is the other main factor. Nathanael's very insistence on not bowing to anyone's entreaties, on setting his insight above everyone else's, and on following his fantasies without rational restraint (all of which is in opposition to the attitude of Theodor in this story's twin narrative 'Das öde Haus', H3, 163–98), prevents his functioning as a subject. In this sense, Judith Butler's observation (p. 11) that 'No individual becomes a subject without first becoming subjected or undergoing "subjectivation" (a translation of the French *assujetissement*)' applies to him. But while this night piece criticizes the lack of rationality and social interaction in the male poet (who, as I argue elsewhere, is not to be read as a parody of early Romanticism, but rather of creativity gone awry),[21] Nathanael's female critic does not simply emerge as the positive model for the reader to identify with. As so many critics have noted, the narrator's sympathies seem to be withdrawn from her when her conventional happy ending is told. She is rational, and also sensitive enough to function as the muse for architects, painters, musicians, and poets, and as the interpreter of Nathanael's strange psychological processes to the reader, but she undergoes no significant conflict or development herself and thus, while intellectually superior to Nathanael, she is of limited interest to the reader.

It has often been argued that Clara is closer to the mechanical Olimpia than the reader might suspect, because both are described as 'images' and 'automata' (see Annuß, Belgardt, Cixous, Ellis). However, since it is primarily Nathanael who applies these dehumanizing epithets of an artefact to Clara, while attributing superhuman divinity to the manufactured doll-woman Olimpia, we have to regard them as an ironic expression of his inability to distinguish between the real and the imaginary, and as a sign of his desire to fix Clara in the position of his ideal.

'Der Sandmann' is also remarkable in one other respect. While in the *Fantasiestücke* an abyss is portrayed between the gifted artist and an uncomprehending and unappreciative society which the narrator tries to bridge with his stories, in 'Der Sandmann' society allegedly recognizes itself in the artist's fateful love for the doll Olimpia. The narrator reports:

> In order to become quite convinced that they did not love a wooden doll, it was demanded by several lovers that their beloved should sing and dance a little unrhythmically, that while being read to she should embroider, knit, play with the little lap dog etc., but above all that she should not only listen, but also speak sometimes in *such* a way that this speaking presupposed thinking and feeling. (H3, 46-47)

Thus Nathanael's infatuation with an automaton is ironically presented as a social malaise, and any gap between this artist and society is closed. Yet while this ironic comment stands in contrast to the presentation in many of the *Fantasiestücke* of the artist as seer and superior genius, the continuity alleged here between attitudes held by society at large and by a talented, but failed, artist is merely stated by the narrator, not demonstrated in the story. On the contrary, the story is remarkable for showing that those whom Nathanael denounces as cold and philistine are immune to Olimpia's charm. It is not the poet, but the unpoetic rest of society, who find her stiff and regulated movements 'unpleasant' (H3, 38); who laugh at Nathanael's exaggerated enthusiasm for her singing, who fail to want to dance with her, who laugh at her (see H3, 39). The general post-party discussion is scathing about Olimpia: 'above all everybody attacked the deadly rigid, mute Olimpia, to whom they wanted to attribute, despite her beautiful appearance, complete dullness' (H3, 41). Nathanael's friend Siegmund dismisses Olimpia as 'wax face', 'wooden doll', 'rigid and soulless' (H3, 41) and stresses that this view is shared by many. The narrator's report on the social reaction to the discovery of Olimpia's true being is therefore not based on anything depicted in the story. Rather, while having shown that in relation to Olimpia it was primarily Nathanael (following Goethe's doll lover, Prince Oronaro) who was duped by an excessive imagination unchecked by reason, the narrator now simply supplements the implicit critique of the artist *manqué* with a narratologically unmotivated explicit critique of a social ideal of femininity in general, presented as the common ground between the would-be-artist Nathanael and the bourgeoisie he despises—perhaps with the intention of enabling the average reader to feel Nathanael's fate as a closer possibility.

In *Prinzessin Brambilla*, the artist-protagonist is also far from being an ideal artist. Giglio is introduced, in far more negative terms than Nathanael, as 'a somewhat vain actor whose merits are not held to be too high' (H3, 775). His beloved, the seamstress Giacinta, lashes out at his poor tragic acting with a quick tongue: '"Don't be silly [lit.: a hare] . . . and save your antics for the next few days!"' (H3, 776). She condemns his 'damned lachrymose emotionalism' (H3, 843) and his habit of becoming ecstatic about anything and everything, which causes him to walk about like 'a permanent boring tragedy' (H3, 845). So familiar is she with his set pieces that when, during an argument with her, he 'fell into the awful desperation-monologue of some tragedy by Abbate Chiari' (H3, 847), she prompts him when he forgets his lines and thus comically deflates his desperation.

In both my chosen texts, the artists' girlfriends function as the first critics of their work, and the women's critical powers are highly developed—mainly quiet, sensitive and serious in Clara; witty, passionate and capricious in Giacinta. Although the narrative focus is not on them, their supportive roles are complex, allowing them the intellectual edge over their male lovers and a great deal of emotional independence. Both male lovers feel threatened by the women's intellect. Nathanael complains to Lothar of his displeasure that Clara can 'distinguish in such a clever and masterly way [. . .] You probably read lectures in logic to her so that she learns to examine and separate everything nicely.—Don't do it!' (H3, 24). And Giglio is full of 'annoyance and fury' (H3, 846) that Giacinta '[has] become clever in a miraculous way. You philosophize about yourself in a way that astonishes me' (H3, 846).

Both Nathanael and Giglio turn away from their critical girlfriends in pursuit of a muse onto whom they project their ideal of femininity. In 'Der Sandmann', Nathanael's ideal is implicitly criticized as egocentric because it turns out to be embodied by an automaton. Nathanael's inability to rebuild a bond with a living woman leads ultimately to his madness and death. Giglio, by contrast, successfully undergoes a process of education. A master of ceremonies, the charlatan Celionati, directs Giglio's learning programme in which psychological processes are externalized in theatrical, fairy-tale-like and carnivalesque actions. The narrative switches to and fro, as if it were a hall of mirrors, between reality, dream, the theatrical stage of tragedy and of *commedia dell'arte*, carnival, and myth.

Rather than portraying the development of the male artist and his craft in relation to two different types of women in a triangle, as in 'Der Sandmann', *Prinzessin Brambilla* multiplies the interrelationships into a cross of four, where each person has to relate to three other manifestations of self and other. For both Giglio and Giacinta have a double, that is, an ideal self or dream self, dressed up in carnival costume as Prince Cornelio di Chiapperi and Princess Brambilla. Both Giglio and Giacinta pursue their ideal beloved for a long time, without recognizing that Giacinta and Brambilla as well as Giglio and Chiapperi are merely the everyday self and the ideal self of the same person. Celionati's education, which is directed primarily at Giglio, aims at two, apparently contradictory, things. First, Giglio is required to accomplish a carnivalesque debasement of his false ideas of grandeur. Second, both Giglio and Giacinta are encouraged to aim for the sublime. 'Remember your dream image!' (H3, 802) is given as a motto to them both (see H3, 845). This means that Giglio's subjection is not simply a Bakhtinian carnivalesque denigration in which the lower bodily functions assert themselves. Hoffmann's distance from the Bakhtinian position is to be clearly seen in his choice of the eight etchings from the twenty-four plates by Callot which formed the basis of this tale: all the obscene images have been left out.[22] What Hoffmann is concerned with is not only the dizzying challenge to simplistic notions of order and identity, but also the regaining of a complex and artful balance (see the voices given to the dancers and their props, the tambourine and the sword, in chapter six, H3, 870–72). Accordingly, Giglio recognizes that his ideal self is embodied in the carnival Prince Cornelio di Chiapperi, and that the mythic King Ophioch, an allegory of philogenetic development, is his mirror-image. The same dizzying complexity of juggling with different roles as aspects of the self is achieved by both Giglio and Giacinta. Both recognize in themselves and in the other the coexistence of a sublime ideal and comical bathos. This enables the capriccio to have a happy ending, with both of them acting as equal partners in *commedia dell'arte* performances and ruling happily supreme in the land of art. But before Giglio achieves this balance, he has to embrace a series of comic and capricious humiliations: wearing utterly unsexy *commedia dell'arte* costumes, being locked up in a cage like a bird for his vanity, being forced to be bled, being laughed at and criticized for his acting. He has to kill his former conceited self in a mock duel—the old self is revealed as a hollow puppet stuffed with literature, just as Prince Oronaro's female beloved in Goethe's satire—and to change from a tragic to a *commedia dell'arte* actor. The subjection of his former self is completed when, as Capitan Pantalon, he kneels at the feet of his ideal, Princess Brambilla, and in recognition of her rule he kisses her slipper (see H3, 902). It is this symbolic subjection of Giglio which is the precondition for his finally ruling supreme as a subject, for, as Judith Butler puts it: 'If there is no formation of the subject without a passionate attachment to those by whom she or he is subordinated, then subordination proves central to the becoming of the subject' (Butler, p. 7). Giglio's repeated subjection forces him to assimilate other perspectives on himself. It forms the basis on which he can develop enough critical distance from himself to juggle the different facets of his self successfully, and thus to become a fuller subject, and to be able to act as a sovereign agent both on stage and in life.

In 'Der Sandmann', the male and the female protagonist each remain flawed and incomplete while it is the narrator who implicitly embodies the balance between enthusiasm and critical distance; this balance is for Hoffmann the *sine qua non* of the true artist. In 'Der Sandmann', women's eyes function as a mirror for the artist. In *Prinzessin Brambilla* it is the lake in Urdargarten that serves as the mirror of insight for both male and female protagonists, who learn to combine critical self-denigration with the striving for the sublime. It is this insistence on the sublime *and* the ridiculous, on idealism *and* the comical critique of the delusions of idealism (in other words, an unwillingness to renounce the ideal while yet exploring its dangers), which distinguishes Hoffmann from Postmodernism. That this balance between idealism and its critique also coincides with a remarkable gender balance in *Prinzessin Brambilla* is achieved at the cost of lowering the artistic medium: from poetry (or music or painting in other stories) to acting. Drawing on the *commedia dell'arte* tradition with its intelligent female protagonists, as well as on his own admiration for opera singers and actresses, Hoffmann succeeds in creating with Giacinta a multi-faceted female character on a par with the male protagonist, and in overcoming some of his own earlier gender stereotyping. It has to be said, however, that, contrary to the appropriating feminist readings of Hoffmann by Cixous and Asche, questions of femininity were for Hoffmann always subordinate to his concern with the problems of art. But although for Hoffmann, in accordance with the gender norms of his time, the male artist was the prime model of the human condition, within these limitations his depiction of femininity ranges from the stereotypical to the complex and subtle. At the latter end it depicts femininity, both on the level of plot and on that of narration, as an intellectual and emotional power on a par with the male artist. However, this equality is one that is driven purely by the requirements of art, specifically to find an image for the balance and complexity which art in Hoffmann's view ought to achieve. It co-exists with the patriarchal prejudice of viewing women's acting merely as a 'natural' talent that does not require study (see *Seltsame Leiden*, H3, 473). Hoffmann's texts do not set out to challenge the gender stereotypes of his time (see his depiction of the disaster to which the attempt to educate a woman out of her 'natural' gender leads in 'Die Marquise de la Pivardière', H3, 730–65). But within the given range of gender stereotypes, Hoffmann's purpose of exploring the relationship between the real and the ideal for an artist extended the gender boundaries of his age: in some of his best texts, he created female characters of remarkable intelligence, wit, and independence of mind.

5

Varieties of Female Agency in Stendhal

Ann Jefferson

> The Goddess within the novel (any novel) stands for that which is, as it were, 'bigger'.[1]

French Realist fiction is a predominantly male affair. It is male novelists who portray and analyse social reality, while their women contemporaries are marginalized in forms of writing, such as idealist or sentimental fiction, which carry considerably less status.[2] Yet at a time when the credentials for all fiction remained less than wholly secure, even for Realist writers, the ability to portray women was regularly played as a trump card. Balzac boasts in the 'Avant-propos' to the *Comédie humaine* that his great scheme will contain 'men, women and things'. And this achievement will be all the greater for the fact that, unlike the natural world, 'in Society, women do not always turn out to be the female of the male'.[3] In other words, the accurate portrayal of women will be a measure of attainment in a sphere designated—at least in France—as that of the male writer.

Stendhal is rather less triumphalist than Balzac in his approach both to mimesis and to women. One of his first books, *De l'Amour* (1822), is a largely femino-centric account of love from a culturally relative viewpoint; and it is based on the assumption—first articulated by Mme de Staël—that the degree of civilization of any given society can be gauged by the position it accords to women, and by the state of relations between the sexes.[4] The book contains a sequence of chapters on the education of women in France at the time, which quite explicitly condemn the educational impoverishment of women and the consequent waste of female talent: 'The present education of girls is a product of chance and the stupidest form of pride. And as a result, their most shining qualities, holding the richest promise of happiness, both for themselves and for us, are left idle.'[5] In short, a description of the female condition is used as material for a social critique, and not simply as a token of realist mastery. Stendhal's autobiography, the *Vie de Henry Brulard* (The Life of Henry Brulard) is equally femino-centric, but in a different perspective. As he begins to cast his mind back over his life, Stendhal claims that his entire existence can be summed up by a list of the women he has loved, and he portrays himself scratching their initials in the dust as he gives himself over to recollection. His role in relation to these women, he says, has been that of unhappy and often unrequited lover, and each is recalled in her difference, rather than being notched up as another conquest in some Don Juan-esque tally. There are no ambitions to any *mille e tre* here. As a novelist, too, Stendhal gives a major place to his female characters. Three of his five novels have two heroines of near-equal stature to a single male hero-protagonist. He also depicts a huge variety of secondary female characters, with the result that there is no single female essence in Stendhal, and no recourse to standard female stereotypes. The title of his first novel, *Armance* (1827), refers to its heroine, as does his last, unfinished novel, *Lamiel*, which, in addition, presents an astonishingly energetic and unconventional female figure. In fact, all of Stendhal's heroines are striking for the degree of initiative they display, and, aside from Lamiel, the most memorable of these figures are generally considered to be Mathilde de la Mole in *Le Rouge et le Noir* (The Red and the Black) of 1830 and the Duchesse Sanseverina in *La Chartreuse de Parme* (The Charterhouse of Parma) of 1839.

Over and above the female characters and roles that Stendhal invents for his fiction, he also places his writing in a femino-centric literary context. This he does by citing the example of Mme de Lafayette's *La Princesse de Clèves* (The Princess of Cleves) and her portrayal of the movements of the soul as preferable to Walter Scott's dutiful inventory of the material reality of the Middle Ages in his novels.[6] He also regularly invokes women as his ideal readers and as the litmus test of his success as a writer. The autobiography appears as a project worth undertaking when he considers that 'I run the chance of being read in 1900 by the souls I love, the Mme Rolands, the Mélanie Guilberts'.[7] (Mme Roland was a Girondin supporter during the Revolution and wrote her Memoirs in prison while she awaited execution. Mélanie Guilbert was an actress and Stendhal's first mistress. Her initials appear in the list of women who marked out his life at the beginning of his autobiography.)[8] And in the notes that he jotted in the margins of *La Chartreuse de Parme* when he was considering revising the text, Stendhal reminds himself that the book needs to appeal to 'thirty-year old women of wit'.[9]

On all these counts, then, Stendhal would appear to be a promising candidate for a feminist reading, and indeed the feminist reception of his work to date broadly endorses this upbeat picture. This reception chimes with the aspects of Stendhal's presentation of women in his work which I have just outlined, in the sense that as a critical corpus, it lends itself to being considered under three main heads which I shall provisionally call (1) woman as agent, (2) the psycho-sexual perspective, and (3) women as writers. Between them, they review Stendhal's portrayal of women from the point of view of action, the psyche and of language. I shall begin with action.

This is the area in which Stendhal first drew plaudits from feminist critics. Writing in the journal *Confluences* in 1944, Clara Malraux declared Stendhal's heroines to be amongst the few free women in three centuries of French literature.[10] This view is picked up and developed in terms of unqualified endorsement by Simone de Beauvoir in *Le Deuxième Sexe* (*The Second Sex*) published in 1949. She singles out Stendhal for his portrayal of women, which she finds 'a relief' after that of many twentieth-century writers, because he does not present his female characters in terms of some constraining 'feminine essence'. They are creatures of flesh and blood, who are human beings before they are women. For Stendhal 'woman is not pure alterity: she is a subject in her own right. Stendhal never limits himself to describing his heroines as functions of his heroes: he gives them a destiny of their own.'[11] Beauvoir praises his critically enlightened portrayal of the way that nineteenth-century French society stifles and stunts the talents of women, and notes that Stendhal does not just defend women's freedom, but their right to self-fulfilment and individual happiness (DS 377; p. 255).

This emphasis on Stendhal's presentation of women as autonomous subjects has been continued in recent years, and has led to particular attention being given to *Lamiel*, notably in two full-length critical studies devoted to this unfinished work.[12] It has also been treated in a slightly more oblique and complex way by Naomi Schor, who argues that realist writing is unable to accommodate the freedom and autonomy of women which Simone de Beauvoir had so unproblematically identified in Stendhal's fiction: 'What seals the degradation of the feminine in nineteenth-century French fiction is the devastating fact that the post-Revolutionary female protagonist is consistently deprived of the minimal attribute of subjecthood, which is not, or not merely the faculty of speech, the capacity to produce signs, but rather the power of locomotion, the right to move about freely.'[13] She tracks the recurrent motif of Lamiel's socially inappropriate 'loping gait' throughout Stendhal's unfinished novel; and she interprets the fact that the text existed only in the form of a number of incomplete versions, as tacit acknowledgment on Stendhal's part that Lamiel's energies and initiatives must inevitably stall the writing that seeks to represent them. This approach leaves female autonomy unscathed as one of Stendhal's aspirations, but the Realist novel compromised as the means of its representation.

The second strand in feminist criticism of Stendhal has focussed on his psycho-sexual dynamic, and on the roles he ascribes to women in his own internal world. In a chapter on Stendhal in her *Histoires d'amour*, Julia Kristeva explores Stendhal's investment in powerful female figures in light of the question: 'Stendhal, fut-il feministe?' (Was Stendhal a feminist?). She answers by arguing that in attributing such power to his female figures, Stendhal is constituting a kind of female idolatry whose main purpose is to function as an antidote to established religion. And she concludes that, 'If there is a Stendhalian feminism, it consists precisely in the worship that suggests that feminism is perhaps our last religion, that of the woman with authority.'[14] In other words, for Kristeva, there is something a little self-serving in Stendhal's portrayal of powerful women which turns out to be harnessed to another agenda altogether.

Carol Mossman's study of gender differences in *Le Rouge et le Noir* is less specifically concerned with Stendhal's own individual psychic make-up, and instead explores the issue in terms of two differently gendered dimensions in the structure of the novel. She distinguishes here between the patrilinear plot, which carries the action of the novel forward, and a cyclical and spatial dimension of the text, which is maternal in essence. Unlike the narratable patrilinear component, this maternal dimension, while thoroughly informing the text, does not lend itself to direct representation. Like Schor's account of female energy, this picture has consequences for the form of novel which, in accommodating both male and female, ceases to be monologic, and no longer operates according to a single principle. In this case, the psyche which construes gender differences in such terms is a collective and cultural one, rather than a specific and authorial one.[15]

When it comes to the question of his treatment of women as subjects of language, however, Stendhal has emerged rather badly from feminist critique. There have been two recent studies which each examine Stendhal as part of a wider contemporary literary phenomenon: the literary representation of the *mal du siècle* in the case of Margaret Waller, and sentimental fiction in the case of Margaret Cohen.[16] In Margaret Waller's account of the *mal du siècle*, which she dubs the male malady, she argues that male writers of the early nineteenth century presented a feminized image of men which had as its counterpart the annexing of a traditionally female cultural domain. Waller concentrates principally on *Armance* which, without any acknowledgement of its source, rewrites *Olivier ou le secret* (Oliver or the secret) whose author was a woman, the Duchesse de Duras.[17] Margaret Cohen takes up a similar theme when she claims that the male Realists expropriated the genre of the novel itself from women, whose chief means of expression was the sentimental novel, and one of whose best-known exponents was the same Duchesse de Duras. Cohen argues that Realism emerged by suppressing a whole tradition of writing in the nineteenth century, which was largely by and for women; and she claims that the legacy of Realism has left us with a blind spot about all forms of fiction which did not adopt its implicitly masculine presuppositions and principles. Where, in Schor's account, Realism was incapable of presenting women as subjects of action, in Cohen's and Waller's histories, Realism blanks out the possibility of seeing women as writers by suppressing the genres with which they were principally associated. So, when it comes to seeing women as writers, as subjects of language, these recent readings by feminist critics come up with a resounding 'Non' to Kristeva's question: 'Stendhal fut-il féministe?'

The question then is: What are we to make of these disparities in the various feminist accounts of Stendhal? Can we put them down to a naivety born of the optimism of early French feminism, which more sophisticated and alert forms of criticism have subsequently tempered? Or are there other questions to be asked? It seems to me that we need to address the issue of the particular forms of agency which feminist critics might wish to identify. And we need, moreover, to ask whether these forms are interchangeable, or whether one inevitably trumps the others. If the key concern of feminist criticism can be taken to be the ways in which female subjectivity is constituted, recognized or denied, then it would seem to be important to be able to distinguish between the different domains in which this subjectivity emerges. In the case of Stendhal, female agency appears as unproblematically positive when women are the subjects of action, but the picture becomes less straightforward when women are viewed as subjects of writing. I shall devote the remainder of this essay to looking in more detail at Stendhal's portrayal of women as subjects in each of these domains, and will go on to consider whether, in addition to the spheres of action and language, Stendhal might be identifying further versions of female agency.

First, however, a little more needs to be said about the social and literary context of Stendhal's writing, and in particular of *Le Rouge et le Noir*.[18] It was published in 1830, the year of the July Revolution which resulted in the Bourgeois Monarchy of Louis-Philippe. During the 1820s, under the Restoration, Stendhal had more to say about the need for a literary revolution which would be a counterpart of 1789 in the world of letters, than about further political revolution. In one of the 'Letters from Paris, by Grimm's Grandson' which he wrote for *The London Magazine* in 1825, he announces (in French) that '*La Revolution commence en la litterature*' [sic], and he predicts that within two or three years the Revolution of 1789 would finally 'produce its effect upon literature'.[19] He does not spell out a precise programme for this literary revolution, but it can be inferred from his comments about many of the books he reviews, that an accurate description of contemporary social reality would be the key to it. He complains repeatedly that most social portraits in the books he reads are anachronistic, and are often at least twenty-five years out of date. It must be said that he includes a number of women writers—such as Sophie Gay in her three-volume novel *Les Malheurs d'un amant heureux* (The Misfortunes of a Happy Lover)—amongst those who he claims are guilty of this time-lag. Part and parcel of this complaint about the inability of contemporary writers accurately to portray contemporary society, is Stendhal's denunciation of the willingness of writers to comply with the terms and the frames used by a society which imposed conformity in all spheres. This is an objection that Stendhal lays at the door of the Duchesse de Duras's *Édouard* when he accuses her of withholding 'the expression of a touch of feeling, because she did not find an appropriate form of words, invented or sanctioned by some female and fashionable writer'. He goes on to suggest that this is a problem to which women writers of the time are particularly prone: 'literary prudery is a great stumbling block to our poor authoresses'.[20] Nevertheless men writers are also occasionally guilty of this failing, and Stendhal does not hesitate to accuse Alfred de Vigny's *Cinq-Mars* (1826) of a non-Realist 'affectation'. In short, what Stendhal requires of writers—male and female alike—is an accurate portrayal of social reality in terms which express that reality as directly as possible, against the grain of a society which has every interest in masking social truths and in gagging their expression.

Censorship was a political fact under the Restoration and could lead to court sentences for those who were deemed to have breached its prescriptions. Stendhal alludes to this political reality, but he also presents his potential readers as liable to take offence at the mirror which a mimetic portrayal would hold up to them. It is the vanity of the French public which is ultimately blamed for literary censorship: 'In making the portrait of the society of 1829 (the time this novel was written), the author was laying himself open to displeasing the ugly faces whose likeness he was drawing, and those ugly faces who were all-powerful at the time could easily have him up in court and send him to the galleys for thirteen months.'[21] It is anticipation of such responses that prompts Stendhal to attribute his invocation of 'The truth, the harsh truth' to Danton in his epigraph to Book 1 of *Le Rouge et le Noir*, thus announcing his long-awaited literary Revolution at the outset of a novel which styles itself as a 'Chronicle of 1830'.

This harsh truth may be something that social demands make it especially hard for women to articulate, but it is one whose test entails the accurate portrayal of women, and of their position in a society which places them under such pressures. The seditious potential of the portrait of Mathilde is conveyed by Stendhal when he depicts his male readers refusing to acknowledge it as true. In the staged conversation between author and reader in Book 2, Chapter 19 of *Le Rouge et le Noir*, the author offers mock reassurance to his ticklish male reader that Mathilde is 'wholly imaginary', and that her character 'is impossible in our age, no less prudent than virtuous' (RN 556; pp. 341–2). In short, Stendhal is claiming that a subversively accurate view of French society will be one that faithfully represents the women who live in it, but which, precisely because of the position that society places them in, is not one that women themselves are likely to be able to produce. In other words, it is beginning to look as though Stendhal's revolutionary Realism will portray women in books written by men in a manner which positions women differently according to whether they are subjects of action or of writing.

It is time now to examine *Le Rouge et le Noir* in more detail and to explore the ways it presents women and constructs female subjectivity. As we have already seen, among the various credentials that the Realist novel claims for itself as regards its topicality, the depiction of women is prominent. In a projected review of his own novel, Stendhal repeatedly comments on the accuracy of the novel's social portraiture, and singles out the figures of its two heroines, Mathilde de la Mole and Mme de Rênal. Mathilde incarnates the phenomenon of 'Parisian love' which he claims is 'absolutely new' ('Projet', p. 712). Her character was based in part on the real case of one Méry de Neuville who eloped to London with a social inferior; and (genuine) reviewers also commented positively on Stendhal's achievement in capturing this new type: 'The character of Mathilde has brought about a complete reform amongst heroines of fiction. Such a creation amounts to an entire revolution. There is more real boldness and novelty in it than in all the supposed romantic characters in whom innovation never went beyond epithets.'[22]

The case of Mme de Rênal is less immediately striking, but in Stendhal's account, just as much of an achievement: 'This new provincial life which has overrun France since 1800, is extremely boring and full of suspicion, but it has produced a charming type of woman who was impossible in the merry way of life which reigned from 1715 to 1790' ('Projet', pp. 719–20). He also states in the novel that most members of Parisian society of the time would have been incapable of perceiving her true nature, and it takes the revolutionary Realist to see the women of post-Revolutionary society for what they really are: 'Madame de Rênal was one of those women to be found in the provinces whom one may easily take to be fools until one has known them for a fortnight.' This is because she is the product of the isolation and lack of education inflicted on provincial women at the time. Such women have no access to the language used by the society which has created them: 'She had no experience of life and made no effort at conversation [ne se souciait pas de parler]' (RN 40; p. 250). However, these limitations are, paradoxically, what enable Mme de Rênal to act: in her ignorance she misreads her situation with regard to Julien until it is too late to retreat, and discounts the warnings of her more worldly friend, Mme Derville. Through her invisibility to herself and her unawareness of her own image in the eyes of those around her—both of which are consequences of her social illiteracy—Mme de Rênal finds herself in love with Julien and compromisingly intimate with him. For the same reason, she also proves highly resourceful in dealing with the threat of the affair being denounced, as when she devises anonymous letters to throw her husband off the scent by incriminating Valenod. Similarly, when Julien is imprisoned after the famous shooting, she knows only that she will now forever be 'a heroine of anecdotes' (RN 465; p. 684); but the language of these anecdotes is sufficiently far removed from her own (limited) repertoire that she is not deterred by thoughts of how she must appear to the outside world from visiting

Julien in prison and from acting on the love that she feels for him. Stendhal's picture of his society does not just include topical portraits of its women: through those portraits it also highlights the languages in which the subjectivity of contemporary women is constructed. And he shows how this particular woman (Mme de Rênal), as a product of the society which uses that language, eludes its effects by virtue of the very restrictions that her social position imposes on her.

Most of the other women in the novel, however, do not escape that language so easily, and indeed do not seem to want to. This is clearest in the case of the secondary characters, such as Mme Valenod, who is wholly preoccupied with her newly acquired bourgeois property, and who, during a dinner party, ignominiously berates a servant for breaking a wineglass and '*spoil[ing] one of her sets*' (RN 138; p. 351); or Mme de la Mole, who presides over a salon in which it is forbidden to speak of politics or to make a joke; or Mme Derville, who is appalled to see her friend fall in love with a man she can only view as a calculating social climber; and Mme de Fervacques, whose rigid moral constitution is easily manipulated by Julien with the programmatic love-letters he borrows from Prince Korassoff. All these women, in their different spheres, exhibit a powerfully coded sense of propriety which is nothing less than the language of the social worlds that they live in, and which they have to a large degree adopted as their own. Society has constituted them as subjects whose programme it dictates in advance.

The other apparent exception to this is Mathilde; but unlike Mme de Rênal, she is only too aware of this logic, and is capable of analysing it in shrewd and extremely illuminating ways. She sees that even the life-and-death occasion of a duel has become nothing more than a formality where 'Everything is known beforehand, even what a man is to say when he falls' (RN 314; p. 528). Her solution to this pre-determined tedium is, like the one that Stendhal himself imagines: escape. The trouble is that the escape routes which she envisages are themselves equally coded, whether it be the example of her ancestor's mistress Marguerite de Navarre, the idea of Julien as a potential Danton and herself as Mme Roland, or the pursuit of forbidden sex as described by the novels she is not supposed to read. However socially disreputable the code, it is still a code. The intractable problem with all encoded forms of action—including the actions that Mathilde undertakes as the most extreme forms of escape from convention—is that its subjects remain just as powerfully constituted by society's languages as those whose predicament they are seeking to avoid. 'Her spirit, haughty enough but saturated with all that dry prudence which passes in society as a faithful portrayal of the human heart, was not made to understand in a moment the joy of defying all prudence which can be so keen a joy to an ardent soul' (RN 442; p. 661). Prudence is just another word for fidelity to the social text, and in her own way Mathilde has internalized the languages that society deploys, just as much as the women whom her own example might otherwise invite us to scorn.

There is, moreover, a further complication highlighted here by Mathilde's recourse to language as a means of escape from social constraint. It is that such language has a way of turning people—and women especially—into objects of social vision. Mme de Rênal is able to shrug off the prospect of being a heroine of public anecdote, but Mathilde cannot help rising to the prospect of cutting a figure in the public eye through her socially defiant display of passionate devotion to her plebeian lover. Her heroism is fuelled by the fact that '[her] proud spirit must always entertain the idea of a public, *of what people would say*. In the midst of all her anguish, of all her fears for the life of this lover, whom she was determined not to outlive, she had a secret longing to astonish the public by the intensity of her love and the sublimity of her actions' (RN 444; p. 663). Mathilde positively revels in being an object in the public eye, and the object of its language (a point which Scott-Moncrieff's translation foregrounds here in the italicized phrase). Indeed, for all its apparent unconventionality, her mourning for Julien follows prescription through and through: she repeats the actions of her ancestress in taking and burying Julien's decapitated head, and she follows the lavish dictates of Restoration taste by organizing an Office of the Dead attended by twenty priests, and by ordering some extremely expensive marble sculptures from Italy to decorate the mountain cave in which she sets up a memorial to him. In view of all this, it is plausible to suppose that it is an awareness of the effects of the objectifying logic of language on those who set themselves up as its subjects which lies behind Julien's injunction that Mathilde should never speak of him to their son.

This discussion of Stendhal's women in *Le Rouge et le Noir* has ended up demonstrating that, despite apparent differences, language and action are inextricably linked in Stendhal's picture of the social sphere, especially as regards women. Insofar as the two can be separated, language seems to the more pernicious because of the way it constitutes women as certain kinds of social subject: if Mme de Rênal escapes to a certain degree, this is because of her linguistic limitations; but if Mathilde, for all her attempts to do so, eventually fails, it is precisely because of her fatal mastery of social languages. This logic would seem to apply with a particular vengeance to women writers in Stendhal's world. In another one of his 'Letters from Paris' in the *London Magazine*, Stendhal describes an occasion where Delphine Gay, the poet-daughter of the novelist Sophie Gay, declaimed some of her work in the cupola of the recently reconsecrated Panthéon. This episode is portrayed by Stendhal as one of vulgar theatricality, in which performer and public each confirm the other in the image to which they aspire:

> A fortnight ago Mdlle. Delphine Gay, having carefully arranged all the parts of her little drama, in concert with the Ultra fanatic priests of Sainte Geneviève, invited two hundred persons, who ascended into the cupola (five hundred and fifty-two steps). There, mounted upon the painter's scaffold, which was left standing [by the artist Gros], and consequently within the walls of the Sacred edifice, Mdlle. Gay, with wildness in her looks, and her fierce eyes starting from their sockets, recited two hundred lines. Never was a Pythoness inspired by a more ardent flame, and never, assuredly, did a young girl, or even a married woman, in France, commit a more extravagant impropriety.[23]

As far as the rest of the audience were concerned, the performance was rated a great success: the priests rushed up to congratulate Mlle Gay, and her friends threw themselves at her feet as if in a swoon. Stendhal was alone in being horrified, but the impropriety he condemns is the complicity between performer and public which reinforces the inauthenticity of the society in which the event took place. Delphine Gay may be portrayed by Stendhal as making a particular ass of herself here; nevertheless, in ridiculing her pretensions, he is not condemning a single woman writer, nor even all women who have ambitions to write, but a whole society and a whole literature: 'Charlatanism [. . .] is the great curse of French literature' (ibid.). Writers, it would seem, are no exception to the rule whereby all speakers of language in this society—men and women alike—are susceptible to becoming its objects.

Stendhal's own language here could be said to be a part of this process, since, as he sketches the scene in which she acts out her speaking part, it constructs the 'poetess-pythoness' in a particularly objectified and unflattering manner. There is, however, one important fact about Stendhal's account, and this is that it is addressed to a public outside France: the English readers of the *London Magazine*. As far as

Stendhal is concerned, it is just such a readership—outside the here and now of his contemporary France—that has the best chance of providing the elusive means of escape from the pernicious effects of contemporary French society. It is foreign readers, and readers of the future, and even readers from the past (such as Mme Roland), who offer the possibility of establishing a bypass to the lure of collusion with the social codes of contemporary French society.

In the last part of this essay I want to examine this readerly dimension to Stendhal's writing, and to consider the role he ascribes to women as readers rather than as writers, and as subjects of a gaze, rather than as its quasi-inevitable object. In Stendhal's world, looking and reading offer modes of subjectivity other than those of action and of language. He envisaged multiple readerships for his work, male readers and female readers, real readers and ideal readers (such as the 'happy few' to whom *La Chartreuse de Parme* is dedicated), readers of his own day, and readers of the future (1880, 1900, 1930, and so forth). The reader who takes offence at the portrait of Mathilde in *Le Rouge et le Noir* is portrayed and addressed as a man: 'Ah, Sir, a novel is a mirror carried along a high road' (RN 557; p. 663). But Stendhal also portrays contemporary readers as women, and on this he has much to say. The 'Projet' attributes the existence of a female readership in large part to the nature of contemporary society. The large numbers of women readers are above all a symptom of the fact that nineteenth-century France has become a social desert in which women are driven to fill their time by reading ('Projet', pp. 700–1). Stendhal goes on to describe two main generic trends within fiction, each associated with a different, but female, readership: '*le roman pour les femmes de chambre*' (the novel for chambermaids) which has few literary pretensions, tends towards the stereotype ('the hero is always perfect and ravishingly handsome'), and is mostly read in the provinces by readers whose only demand of the novel is 'extraordinary scenes which reduce them all to tears' ('Projet', pp. 714–15). (These chambermaids may include Mme de Rênal's maid, Elisa, who is deputed to sign up to the local *cabinet de lecture* as a cover for Julien's own reading habits.) The other group of readers described by Stendhal are 'the ladies of Paris' who are much more demanding of their authors, and tend to be suspicious of any literary contrivance designed to show off the hero in his best light. Whatever the detail of Stendhal's analysis of the readership of contemporary fiction, he is not alone in characterizing the novel in terms of a (potentially subversive) female readership. As Hugo said in his *Les Contemplations* (1856): 'The Revolution/ [. . .] is in the novel which murmurs quietly to women.'[24] Mathilde and Lamiel are both great readers. But as we have already seen, and despite Hugo's optimism about the revolutionary potential of the novel, it is Mathilde's subversive reading (she smuggles books out of her father's library) that allows her to deceive herself about the possibility of exemption from the social charlatanism which she so astutely identifies. In the case of Lamiel, her insatiable and equally secretive reading either cannot be put into action at all, or else must be acted out as crime. Moreover, it should be noted that Mme de Rênal is not (or barely) a reader. Since novels are portrayed as purveyors of the social languages in which subjects become ensnared, reading does not automatically, in and of itself, offer Stendhal's contemporary women readers a subject position that might offer the much-needed possibility of escape.

However, when he envisages his ideal readers, Stendhal imagines them as belonging to another era, perhaps to another place, and very often as being female. He may have had limited expectations of his English readers in 1825 as his postulated interlocutors, but, as we saw in his musings and hopes concerning the readers of *Henry Brulard*, Stendhal's ideal readers include quite precisely identified women, Mme Roland and Mélanie Guilbert. Such readers are the living embodiment of an 'elsewhere', and hold out the possibility of escape to Stendhal as the subject of his own writing. Their appeal—and it is a very powerful appeal—is that they do not have any dealings with the conventions and expectations of the world in which Stendhal lives. This is not the sole prerogative of women readers, and Stendhal also speaks of writing his memoirs 'like a letter to a [male] friend [un ami]' whom he places in the future: 'What will that friend's ideas be in 1880? Very different from our own!' (VHB 536; p. 7). It is this difference which provides the possibility of immunity from social conformism: 'This is new for me: to speak to people of whose cast of mind, whose style of education, whose prejudices and religion I am wholly ignorant! What an encouragement to be *truthful* and nothing but *truthful*, that's all that counts' (VHB 537; p. 8, Stendhal's italics). If Stendhal's goal is to describe accurately the world of 1830, it is with a readership fifty or a hundred years distant as its horizon.

There is, nevertheless, a case for giving women the edge over men in this role of distant reader, and it comes from Stendhal's description of many of the female figures that he discusses in his *Histoire de la peinture en Italie* (History of Painting in Italy) and in other writings on painting. (Published in 1817, the history had been on the stocks since 1811 and was his first major work.) There are many reasons why Stendhal regarded both Italy and the Renaissance (the main period of painting discussed in his history) as supreme incarnations of Western civilization and therefore as an ideal environment for women. But he regularly homes in on paintings of women in his commentary: Madonnas and Holy Families in great numbers, but also more active and ferocious figures such as Diana, Judith, Herodias, and Beatrice Cenci (ferocious because she was a parricide). Clearly, these women figures are the object of the spectator's gaze, including that of Stendhal. And since painting is regarded here as a representation of the soul, of emotion and the inner life, where the ultimate object of representation is in a sense invisible, that gaze is a particularly searching activity.[25]

Over and above their position as objects of the spectator's scrutiny, however, Stendhal's accounts of these female figures frequently draw attention to their eyes, and present them as subjects of a gaze of their own. Indeed, it is this very subjectivity which contributes to making these figures resistant to the spectator's visual enquiry. For example, writing in his journal in the year that he embarked on his *Histoire de la peinture en Italie*, Stendhal describes one of Volterrano's sibyls as having the eyes 'of a great soul' and as 'speaking to God with a gentle confidence'.[26] This figure is presented neither as simply enduring the painter's representation of her, nor as colluding with the social values of the spectator, but as a powerful quantity in her own right with no hesitation about engaging the Divinity in direct dialogue. Another kind of gaze is evoked in Stendhal's description of Raphael's *Holy Family*, where the Virgin Mary is entirely caught up in her own thoughts as she gazes into a middle distance beyond the painting. Within the depicted scene, the infant Jesus is turning to meet Joseph's glance, but Mary remains bound up in her own world, whose focus is once again outside the painting itself (*Musée*, p. 139). A third form of subjectivity in relation to the gaze is illustrated in Stendhal's comments about Raphael's *Madonna of the Chair*. Here, a beautifully attired Madonna looks directly back at the viewer: '[this Virgin] is looking at the spectator: others do not look at anything and even have a slight squint' (*Musée*, p. 105). Although the unusual care with which she is dressed implies an expectation of being looked at, this Madonna is protected against the potentially harmful complicities with the world by her ability to look back at it from inside the picture. In all these paintings, then, the woman is described as the subject of her own gaze whose focus, in one way or another, leads out of the painting to another world. It breaks open the frame and creates the possibility for the spectator to escape in turn into another dimension.

When Stendhal imagines his ideal women readers (Mme Roland or Mélanie Guilbert) it is as addressees of a writing to which they respond as subjects of this kind of gaze focused on a *beyond*. These women readers offer an escape route from a society which otherwise severely limits the sphere of female action, and subjects its female members to its objectivizing discourses. This kind of (ideal) reading is understood by Stendhal as active response, and not as a mere distraction from the tedium of Restoration society. In *Le Rouge et le Noir*, it is Mme de Rênal (though she actually reads very little), rather than Mathilde (though she reads a great deal), who is most likely to be capable of this kind of reading. The difference turns on the way each is positioned in relation to the gaze. Mathilde must always be its object, while Mme de Rênal belongs to the class of Stendhalian heroine who is marked out by her position as source of a gaze—as is Mme de Chasteller when she looks down from her window with its parrot-green blind in *Lucien Leuwen*, or Clélia when she looks across to Fabrice's prison cell at the top of the Tour Farnèse in *La Chartreuse de Parme*.[27]

It is these figures—Mme de Rênal, Mme de Chasteller, Clélia—who open up the novel to the possibility of an outside, to a dimension beyond, which Stendhal's contemporary French society conspired to ignore. Neither action nor writing can achieve this on their own. Writing requires the counterpart of reading, or at least of a certain kind of reading which I have here identified as feminine, to achieve its end. Stendhal's account of women in their various guises needs to be understood in the context of his analysis of that society whose workings meant that action and language could not be the most propitious forms of intervention for its subjects, whether male or female. It is for this reason that it matters to distinguish between different forms of intervention, different kinds of agency and the different possibilities contained in the various subject positions he outlines: action, language and writing, looking and reading. The tendency to privilege action and writing in modern feminist criticism might need to be modified to take account of different social or cultural circumstances. The circumstances evoked in Stendhal's fiction are such that his own writing requires a certain kind of reading if it is to open up its hard-won portrayal to a world outside itself. Stendhal anticipated his writing being inflected according to the figures it found itself in dialogue with (the friend of 1880, or Mme Roland). And so too, feminist criticism might find that its dialogue with Stendhal has as much to contribute to its own practices and assumptions, as feminist critics have to offer in creating fresh perspectives on the French Realist canon.

6

Heine's 'Mädchen und Frauen'

Women and Emancipation in the Writings of Heinrich Heine

Robert C. Holub

Heinrich Heine lived through times of turbulence and change. Born in 1797 into an assimilated Jewish family, he experienced the Napoleonic conquest of Germany as well as the liberation from French rule during his childhood. After a brief stint in business, he studied at the universities of Bonn, Göttingen, and Berlin, eventually earning a degree in law in 1825. During this year he also converted to Protestantism, less out of conviction than out of a sense, common among the Jewish population, that conversion would bring with it a fuller integration into a Christian, German society. Like most young German men during the initial decades of the nineteenth century Heine was drawn toward nationalism, but already in the 1820s he recognized its anti-Semitic and non-democratic tendencies, and for the rest of his life he became a critic of patriotic excesses. His earliest works consisted mostly of lyric poetry, which have become famous in part owing to their frequent use in songs by German composers, but toward the end of the 1820s and throughout much of his life, he engaged in a journalistically informed prose, characterized by a fierce wit and liberal attitude. In the 1830s, seeing no future for himself in a repressive and apolitical Germany, Heine immigrated to Paris, where he remained until his death in 1856. During the 1840s, like many other German writers, he became radicalized, and for a time he consorted with socialists and leftists: he was acquainted with Karl Marx in Paris and contributed to the same radical journals that contained the writings of the left Hegelians. In the 1850s, suffering from a debilitating illness and disappointed by the failed revolution, Heine turned to a private religion but never wavered in his struggle for justice and emancipation.

Controversy followed Heine in almost every aspect of his writings. Indeed, to a certain extent he himself invited this controversy, nurtured it, and took pleasure in its blossoming into a public event. His remarks about German nationalism, for example, were designed to provoke a response from the conservative, patriotic drum-beaters for German unity, and his embrace of a cosmopolitan, liberationist worldview made him the target of contemporaries whose narrow horizon and traditionalist views made Heine a traitor to their Teutomaniacal outlook. Such attitudes plagued Heine during his life, but also, and sometimes more tenaciously and with more disastrous consequences, in his reception. The diatribes against Heine after his death often centred on his disloyalty to his fatherland, which he putatively abandoned for the frivolity of Paris and the French in 1831. Tied to this controversy around Heine were his religious views, which always included a rejection of Christian orthodoxy and, especially in the period prior to his debilitating illness, an espousal of sensualism, pantheism, and Hellenism. Closely connected to these challenges to conventional religious dogma was a perception that Heine advocated a violation of accepted moral codes. Heine cultivated the image of a worldly Don Juan who did not hesitate to break with the norms of a Biedermeier social order and its social restrictions. These positions on religion and morality were propounded in part to arouse the ire of more conventional thinkers, and we find Heine criticized for his views both during his lifetime and in subsequent decades. A less welcome ramification of Heine's penchant for controversy are the attacks on him for his Jewishness. From 1825, when the first Judeophobic critique appeared in the press, through the more vehement assaults of rabid anti-Semites in the late nineteenth century to Heine's removal from the German literary canon by National Socialists, Heine and his reputation have repeatedly suffered owing to the religion of his birth. Controversy, in short, with regard to religion, politics, religious affiliation, and morality, have accompanied Heine and Heine criticism from his initial writings to the present day.

Given this continuous history of contestation, it is all the more astonishing that Heine's views on women and women's emancipation have seldom come under scrutiny. It is symptomatic of this neglect that

George Peters, in a monograph treating the secondary works on Heine from his earliest years until the most recent German unification, devotes only a single paragraph to feminist criticism. 'Feminist theory', Peters writes, 'has been slow to come to Heine, somewhat surprisingly, since gender issues, particularly the role of woman as both saint and sinner, play a central part in Heine's work.'[1] Of the three books cited by Peters two were written by men who criticize Heine for his womanizing.[2] Only the third work, *Heinrich Heines Frauen*, composed by Ingrid Straube for the small publishing house Rimbaud in Aachen, contains a critical vantage point that one can readily identify as feminist.[3] Straube's pamphlet—it is a mere twenty-two pages in length—is hardly a conventional piece of scholarship. It comprises rather a bitter and polemical personal invective against Heine and his writings, often employing the rhetorical device of directly addressing the dead poet and accusing him of various types of misogynist behavior. As far as I can tell, it received no echo at all in Heine scholarship, no review in the annual *Heine Yearbook,* and no imitators utilizing a more scholarly and less personal tone. Indeed, I found to my astonishment that if I plug the words Heinrich Heine and feminism into a Google search, the talk that is the foundation for this essay is cited as the fourth entry. In the three entries above my talk the association between Heine and feminism was a coincidence of verbal proximity, not a serious consideration of the topic. Historically, women have been silent on Heine's treatment of women as well. Absent from the record are critical comments from the various emancipated women Heine knew during his lifetime, for example, the German Jewess Rahel von Varnhagen, the noted French writer George Sand, or Christina, Principessa di Belgiojoso-Trivulzio, an ardent supporter of Italian freedom.[4] Heine offended many contemporaries with his views, and since his death he has been accused of many offences by his detractors. With few exceptions, however, feminists have not chosen to criticize and analyse his writings, despite the fact that women play a central role in many of his texts, particularly those of the 1820s and 1830s, and despite prima facie evidence that he resorts, as Peters contends, to the typical male stereotypes of women drawn from a long tradition of patriarchal thought.

The cause of this reticence is itself an interesting topic for speculation. It appears that one factor involved with Heine's neglect by feminists is his credentials as one of the few outstanding, progressive intellectuals in the early nineteenth century. Women in his time and ours may have been reluctant to chastise a writer who otherwise represents a liberal direction in German letters. Heine's own assaults on the church and religion, on social conventions and middle-class behaviour, on political repression and the denial of human rights all imply an enlightened attitude toward social issues that have been important for the women's movement; to criticize one of the few German standard bearers of emancipation would seem unwarranted, even if Heine's depiction of women might lag behind his other social views. We find a similar phenomenon in Brecht studies, which held sway until John Fuegi's book, *Brecht and Company: Sex, Politics, and the Making of Modern Drama*,[5] stirred a huge controversy by exposing some of Brecht's anti-feminist practices. Heine is perhaps even more invulnerable since he himself belonged to a minority (at least until 1825), and it is quite possible that his Jewish origins play a role, in the German world at least, in the absence of criticism about his depiction of women and his dealings with women's emancipation. As an outsider himself, as a writer constantly castigated by conservatives and nationalist critics, as a target for vituperative and prejudicial remarks during his own lifetime and for decades thereafter, Heine probably had developed a partial immunity from criticism for his views on women and their subjugation in a patriarchal society. Straube's text indicates as much, since she assumes the role of a disappointed student, whose attacks are sharpened because she had been told by her teachers that Heine was a paradigm of humanity, a fighter for enlightenment, and a keen observer of injustices in the social order. Like many products of a sudden conversion, her break from the prevailing orthodoxy surrounding Heine is accordingly an acerbic and personal confession.

Perhaps one of the problems in approaching Heine's views on women and women's emancipation is the absence of a standard. In evaluating a writer's position on sensitive political and social issues critics and scholars tend to apply two methods. The first subjects the writer to the standards that prevail in the present. Thus the gauge for anti-Semitism in an author from the past, for example, will be based on the views that have been established today for these matters, and we find in German criticism quite often that writers from the past are condemned because of remarks that strike us today as offensive, but in their own context were commonplace. Such a procedure is especially perilous because the values we embrace today and the language we employ about issues relating to race, religion, and gender are different from what was within the bounds of acceptability for other eras. And while it is for us self-evident that racism and sexism are never to be tolerated and never appropriate, other epochs had different issues and modes of expression that make them incommensurable—to a certain degree—with our own measures. It is not a question of their being right and our being wrong, or vice versa, or of providing an excuse for past prejudice, but simply of recognizing the social and historical embeddedness of values, language, and action. The second way of evaluating a writer's stance on these sensitive issues is to contextualize so that we arrive at an understanding of what the writer could possibly have known, or of how he or she measures up against a retroactively established 'scale of enlightenment' on a set of controversial issues. In this case the author is measured not against our standards, but against the social norms prevailing in a past era. In this way one could find an author severely wanting with regard to contemporary values, but within the acceptable range of his or her own times. An obvious difficulty here is how to contextualize: do we consider what the norm was for the hypothetical 'average person' in a given social order, or do we search for the most 'advanced' authorities and draw the comparison with them in mind? In Heine's case, do we opt for setting his views against those developed by the feminist movement that has prevailed in western societies since the 1970s, condemning him perhaps for falling short of this standard of enlightened thought, or do we view him against the prevailing views of the 1820s and 1830s? If we prefer the latter procedure, is Heine to be compared with Franz Grillparzer, Heinrich von Kleist, or Georg Büchner? Or is he to be judged for his failure to recognize the writings of Betty Gleim, Amalia Holst, and Mary Wollstonecraft?

I would like to suggest a somewhat different way of approaching Heine and his texts. Rarely do the ways I have outlined achieve very much differentiation in their evaluation. The procedure is motivated and directed by a desire to reach a conclusion, usually a thumbs up or thumbs down on a writer's treatment of women and feminism, and I believe for most male writers of the nineteenth century, and many in the twentieth century, it would be very easy to justify the latter. It strikes me, however, that the reason we are interested in past authors, male or female, is because they are complex beings whose writings and views do not always fit neatly into one preordained category or another. Not only are they complex, they also change or modify their views with time. In Heine's case the complexity and change are rather obvious: no one would confuse the deceptively simple verses in his *Buch der Lieder* (Book of Songs, 1827) with the sensual and often risqué lyrics of *Verschiedene* (Variae, 1833, 1844) or the humorous, combative poems of the 1840s, especially those found in the *Zeitgedichte* (Poems of the Times, 1844). Indeed, even during a more restrictively defined span of years Heine was known for assuming various masks or poses, and it would be misleading to identify any of these various personae with the poet Heine *tout court*. I would like to suggest examining Heine in two of his most prominent personae during the 1820s and 1830s, and focusing in this examination on the portrayal of women and women's emancipation in his writings. These personae were not developed specifically to deal with issues surrounding women and their subjugation in the nineteenth century, but rather to explore the nature of relationships between the persona and one or more women, or between men and women in general. The results of this brief investigation may not lead us to any startling conclusions about Heine's feminist sensitivities, but it should provide us with some insight into why the reduction of Heine's views to a single evaluation does justice to neither the elusiveness of his positions nor the intricacy of his thought.

Let us begin with the pose that Heine assumes in his earliest sustained works, the early poetry. For the most part we can view him in the first half of the 1820s, when he composed most of the verse that eventually found its way into the *Buch der Lieder*, as the poet of unrequited love. In poem after poem Heine's male persona has been scorned by a woman who loves another, who disdains his advances, or who simply does not return the feelings he has for her. Biographical accounts have tended to identify this pose with an actual experience Heine had in his early life, specifically with the rejection he putatively suffered at the hands of his two rich cousins from Hamburg, Amalie and Therese, the daughters of wealthy Uncle Salomon. But there is really no need to find an objective correlative for these poems, since the experience described in them is a common one for almost all young men at one point in their lives, and since the literary tradition is replete with lyric poetry dealing with this very topic. The question that presents itself for us is how does Heine represent the women who break the young poet's heart? Although a woman is addressed or referred to in the vast majority of the poems included in the *Buch der Lieder*, the answer to this question is not very easy. Certainly one of her outstanding features is that she remains for the most part unnamed and described in only the most general and stereotypical terms: she possesses red or ruby lips, lily fingers, violet eyes, a white bosom, and golden hair. We frequently encounter the tendency toward demonization and beatification that one finds so often censured in feminist criticism as part of the male Madonna–whore complex, and Straube similarly takes Heine to task for this dichotomous vision of women. Perhaps the worst one can say about the various anonymous women that populate these poems is that they remain props for the poet, clichéd and two-dimensional cardboard figures without real personalities or individuality. They exist merely for the poet-persona, as a way for him to rejoice, or suffer, always a means for him to explore his own emotional state, which is the primary focus for the poetry, never an end.

Examples of this attitude abound in the *Buch der Lieder*. I have selected one illustration that stands for many, poem number XXIII in the section 'Lyrisches Intermezzo' (Lyrical Intermezzo)

> Then why are all the roses so pale,
> Oh speak, my love, oh why?
> Then why, in a green and verdant vale,
> Do the violets mutely sigh?
>
> Then why does even the lark in air
> Sing a song of gloom?
> Why hangs above the balsams there
> The odor of a tomb?
>
> Why has the sun no more today
> The glory that once it gave?
> Why is the earth so gaunt und gray
> And lonely as a grave
>
> And why am I so pale and so bleak?
> O tell me, my love, my own!
> Tell me, my darling, my sweetheart—speak,
> Why did you leave me alone? (DHA 1/1, 154; p. 59)[6]

The outstanding characteristic of this poem, similar to most in this collection, is the use of stock images and motifs from the Romantic tradition. The roses, the green grass, the blue violets, the lark, the balsams, the sun are all part of the tradition that Heine appropriates and plays with in his early verse. Here we have the familiar notion that nature is itself in harmony with the poet's mood; the usual symbols of blossoming love refuse to cooperate: roses are not red and blooming, but pale; the green grass is not the site of happiness and burgeoning springtime, but of violets that do not partake in the song of springtime: they are mute. The lark sings a mournful tune; the normally sweet balsams exude a death-like odour. Nature has obviously been perverted by some catastrophic occurrence, or else the poet imagines that nature reinforces his own moroseness. The anaphoral structure of the poem, which comes across more strongly in the German, where 'warum' (why) begins every other line except in the final stanza, than in the English rendition, sets a structure of unanswered questions, or perhaps queries that have no answers because the answers are too obvious. The rhetorical conceits around which the poem is built do not quite produce rhetorical questions: the whys have an answer, and this answer is implicit in the poet's final query. The sole voice we hear is the plaintive song of the poet, whose own feelings are projected onto his surroundings, and whose reasons for composing his verse remain—in typical Heinesque fashion—undisclosed until the final line, although most readers could easily guess them long before reaching the conclusion. What we have, then, in this poem and in much of the *Buch der Lieder*, is more an experiment with various forms and building blocks of Romantic verse than a genuine expression of emotion, a thoroughly composed and controlled lyric that foregrounds for its readers its own compositional components.

Where does the woman appear amid this experiment in romantic motifs? How is she accounted for and what does she represent? The answer is that she, like other elements Heine uses, is a cliché drawn from tradition and situated among the other romantic images. She is a prop, as it were, a convention that has as little physical reality as the lark and the grass invoked by the poet. She is directly addressed, of course, in the very first line, but her appearance here serves only to remind us of her ultimate connection with the very phenomena that the poet is describing. Although the poet is the only one uttering words, she is implored to speak, but, like the violets that bloom in the green grass, she remains silent throughout. Indeed, as the poet proceeds on his gloomy accounting of his natural surroundings, she recedes into the background, appearing again only in the final strophe, evoked more powerfully by the fourfold repetition of one or another form of love (Liebe) combined with the possessive pronoun 'my': 'Mein liebes Liebchen', 'mein herzallerliebstes Lieb'. We have no description of her, no physical attributes, no hint of her personality. We learn of only one act on her part: that she has left the poet, and this act then forms the emotional foundation for the entire rhetorical and symbolic structure. In some sense, however, it is unfair to see the woman in this and in other poems as a reflection of Heine's views on women any more than it is to see his views on nature or ecology reflected in his reference to grass or balsam or larks. For the early Heine women appear as one element, albeit a central and necessary element, from the romantic warehouse of imagery. They form part of the mosaics or tapestries that we call his early verse, but their relationship to any real women, or even their ability to propagate a view of women, is severely limited.

There are other poems in the *Buch der Lieder* that occasionally give us a slightly different insight into Heine's attitude toward women, or at least the relationship between the sexes, providing us with evidence that he was not indifferent to the plight of women, even and perhaps especially in the middle- and upper-class society he often frequented. Poem L from 'Lyrisches Intermezzo' is one of Heine's most humorous and artful accomplishments:

> They talked of love and devotion
> Over the tea and the sweets—
> The ladies, of tender emotion
> The men talked like aesthetes.
>
> 'True love must be platonic,'
> A wizened old councillor cried.
> His wife, with a smile ironic,
> Bent down her head and sighed.
>
> The canon opened his fat face:
> 'Love must not be coarse, you know,
> It's bad for the health in that case.'
> A young girl lisped, 'Why so?'
>
> The countess sadly dissented:
> 'Oh, love must be wild and free!'
> And graciously presented
> The baron a cup of tea.
>
> You should have been there, my treasure;
> An empty chair stood near.
> You'd talk of love and its pleasure
> So charmingly, my dear. (DHA 1/1, 183–84; pp. 68–69)

From this poem we clearly see Heine's recognition that the frustration surrounding the convention of love and marriage in proper society was not solely of male provenance. The women in this poem have an idea of love that differs vastly from their male counterparts'. Significantly, most of the women are either silent or terse about their views: the men are more expansive about love and its attendant feelings, monopolizing the conversation. But the women have somewhat the upper hand, since Heine allows them in most cases to deliver the ironic comment to the men's brash—and decidedly unaesthetic, despite the claim to the contrary—pronouncements. Are the women really any better characterized by 'tender feelings', as the first strophe maintains? It appears that they are more passionate, or at least longing for a passion that exceeds what we normally associate with tenderness. In any event women in this poem are consistently portrayed as sensuous beings, compelled by their restrictive social surroundings to repress their needs and even their expression, while the males are simply windbags whose utterances—and not only their utterances—leave the women unsatisfied. While the *Buch der Lieder* in most cases presents the reader with the stereotypical view of male frustration at a social order that does not lead to fulfilment in love, at times, quite obviously, Heine demonstrates that women are not really better served by the moral codes common to bourgeois society in contemporary Germany. The idealized love sought by the poet suffering from heartbreak as well as the passionate longing for romance are both apt to be dashed hopes in the increasingly mundane world of the nineteenth century.

There is one further element in this particular poem that merits comment: the poet's woman friend who is absent from the intimate tea party. Indeed, in a typical fashion the last strophe lends the entire poem an air of ambiguity and uncertainty, leaving more questions unanswered and forcing the reader to wonder what point Heine is trying to make. Why is the poet's lover not at the tea party? Was she perhaps not invited? And if so, was she not invited because she did not possess the requisite social status? Was she expected to attend, as indicated by the place at the table reserved for her? And if this is the case, why has she not come, what has prevented her from appearing with her lover? Has she, like the typical women in the other poems of the *Buch der Lieder*, abandoned the poet-persona? And finally, what does Heine mean when he writes that she would have told about her love in such a pretty fashion? Does he mean *their* love or only *her* love? Would she have reinforced the sensuousness implied in the responses of the other women? Or would she have revealed that her lover, unlike the men around the table, shares the passion here attributed to women? None of these questions is answered, and the way in which we interpret the final stanza has the potential to force radically divergent views of Heine, his attitude toward women, and his depiction of the relationship between the sexes. The thrice repeated diminutives in the final strophe (Plätzchen, Liebchen, Schätzchen) may suggest condescension from the poet; or they may be genuine expressions of endearment. As usual with Heine, we have no way of knowing for certain. The poet-persona may be suggesting that theirs is a model love, different from the frustrated loves and muted discord apparent in the other couples. Or he may be condemned to what the *Buch der Lieder* establishes as the common fate of bourgeois society: love as an eternal mismatch between man and woman.

Let me turn now to another pose that Heine assumes at a slightly later period of time. By the 1830s Heine was no longer writing poetry that adopted the Petrarchan traditions of a supplicant male longing for an unattainable woman. With his voluntary exile in the French capital came the advent of a new era and a new approach to the relations between the sexes, and we find Heine assuming the persona of a street-wise poet thoroughly acquainted with the Parisian pleasures of the night. The poems in *Verschiedene*, which were written and began to appear in the early 1830s, thus marked a turning point in Heine's depiction of women and their emancipation. The title of each section of *Verschiedene* is the name of a woman or women; the common theme is an erotic encounter with a woman less proper than those who rejected the poet so cold-heartedly in the *Buch der Lieder*. In this collection of verse Heine does not place himself in nature or in the middle-class parlour; here he is in an urban setting, on the streets of the metropolis, at the theatre, and above all in the bedroom. Although today these poems would hardly strike us as scandalous, the reactions of critics in Heine's day provide clear evidence that he was successful in his endeavour to affront bourgeois sensibilities. The *Blätter für die literarische Unterhaltung*, for example, wrote: 'Heine's debauched plaints of love are evidence of a horrible degeneration of his temperament' (DHA 2, 411).[7] All the criticism that Heine received for this collection, however, was formulated with the male persona in mind. The concern of commentators was the putative validation of a dissolute male life style, the flouting of moral codes, and the rejection of conventional religious wisdom. The critical perspective of the nineteenth century did not include a judgment of what this verse meant for the image of women, or how it contributed to or detracted from the emancipation of women. The focus in every attack from German periodicals of the era is the shocking licentiousness of the poet rather than the situation of the women with whom he consorts.

Corresponding to the sexually satiated poet, however, is the image of a woman quite different from the proper middle-class women, or even the frustrated upper-class women, of the 1820s. For one thing these women receive names, and although they too are often characterized in terms that make them anonymous or interchangeable, Heine pays much closer attention to physical attributes. Diana, for example, is described as something of an amazon by her cautiously apprehensive and fascinated lover:

> Oh, this maid of mass dimensions,
> Giant hulk of womanhood,
> Makes it plainly understood
> That she has no chaste intentions.
>
> If I should—through overheating—
> Put myself into her power,
> Lordy, would I rue the hour!
> Yes, indeed, I'd take a beating.
>
> What a throat and bosom—splendid!
> (Higher up it's all a blur.)
> Ere I trust myself to her,
> Be my soul to God commended. (DHA 2, 42; p. 339)

In contrast to the young ladies of the *Buch der Lieder*, who rejected the poet, remaining aloof and proper, women like Diana are a match—sometimes more than a match—for the poet's own desires. They enjoy the sensuality of love-making and the physical pleasures of the boudoir. These women are actresses or courtesans; in any case, they occupy the lower end of the socio-economic spectrum. In this regard they are not the equal of the poet in intelligence and learning: they are, after all, the object of his desire, not the companion on his life's journey, so that they match him only in their thirst for carnal pleasures. To some degree, therefore, they also disclose the mismatch that exists in middle-class life, the hypocrisy of its moral values, and the dishonesty of the bourgeois institution of marriage. While the poet of the 1820s was unable to find a woman from the middle class who would respond in kind to his affection and desires, thus forcing him into the pose of troubadour repeatedly rebuffed and disappointed, the poet of the 1830s is able to find physical satisfaction in brief encounters with women of somewhat less reputable status, but still cannot find a relationship that will afford him continuous love, companionship, and pleasure.[8] The key to Heine's women, we begin to realize, is that they are mismatched to men, not because of some biological essence, but because the social order in which relationships are forged does not permit an easy equality of the sexes. In this sense, Heine's poetic products of the 1820s and the 1830s, taken together, can be seen as an implicit critique of the inequality of men and women.

In the 1830s Heine is also concerned with overcoming this inequality, and the ideological instrument he believed was best suited for this task was Saint-Simonism. Developed during the 1820s and 1830s by the disciples of Claude Henri de Rouvroy, Comte de Saint-Simon (1760–1825), the encompassing theory of social organization had become a powerful attraction for many liberal intellectuals during the Metternich Restoration. Like most of the early German enthusiasts for Saint-Simonism, Heine was less interested in the economic and the utopian-socialist dimensions of the doctrine than in the promise of liberation from an oppressive spiritualism and the emancipation of the flesh. Indeed, Heine's relationship to Saint-Simonism has been a matter of some dispute. While it is evident that he was fascinated by certain aspects of the doctrine and may have even come to Paris specifically to learn more about this movement, evidence in his letters, works, and personal conversations with friends and acquaintances demonstrates a more ambivalent attitude. Heine on occasion made rather derisive remarks about individuals and the movement as a whole, and in the most sustained piece of correspondence about Saint-Simonism, a letter written to Heine by Prosper Enfantin, commenting on *De l'Allemagne* (On Germany), the leader of the movement and chief apostle of the master criticizes Heine like an errant pupil who has strayed from the authentic path. In general, however, we observe from Heine's behaviour and writings that he deemed the followers of Saint-Simon the most advanced group in France, and he comments favorably on the movement in several published works, adopting at times key slogans and ideas from Saint-Simonist jargon. Perhaps most importantly he considered this group to be a political alternative to the Republicans, who themselves were an oppositional group, since the changes advocated by Saint-Simonists were more wide-ranging and dealt with much more than the political realm. For this very reason, however, they were perhaps less of a political force than the more focused Republicans, and the perception of Heine as a naive political thinker or even a frivolous dabbler in political matters that he neither understood nor took seriously enough stems to a certain extent from his predilection for the more philosophical and holistic notions of Saint-

Simonist doctrine. A close reading of Heine's texts, however, shows clearly that the influence of Saint-Simonism was more an exercise in confirmation of previously held views than a conversation to a new faith. The sensualism and pantheism that became hallmarks of Heine's ideological development during the 1830s were already obvious by the second half of the 1820s, and even the distinction between the ideal types of sensualist and spiritualist, the Hellene and the Nazarene, which structures Heine's book on the liberal republican writer Ludwig Börne, *Ludwig Börne: Eine Denkschrift* (Ludwig Börne: A Memorial, 1840), and functions as the climax and summation of his thought during his first decade in Paris, is clearly prefigured in numerous allusions in the *Reisebilder* (Travel Pictures, 1826–31).[9]

Heine's interest in Saint-Simonism, indeed, his attendance at regular meetings of the group and his friendship with men and women who likewise exhibited a predilection for the newly developed doctrine, must have brought him into proximity with thoughts on the emancipation of women. Although Saint-Simon himself does not develop a pronounced feminism in his writings, the equality of women is certainly suggested by him, and his disciples were thus not straying far from the master when they included it in their writings. The sixth session in the *Doctrine* of the year (25 February 1829), dealing with exploitation and property rights, clearly recognizes the subjugation of women and the need for emancipation:

> We have indicated the relations association establishes between the sexes as one of its most important aspects. This point will be the topic of a special discussion in which we shall show how woman, who at first was a slave, or at least in a condition bordering on slavery, was associated little by little with man, and acquired each day a greater influence in the social order, and how the causes which to this day have determined her subordination have been successively weakened and shall at last disappear and carry away with them that domination, tutelage, and perpetual minority which even now are imposed on women, and which would be incompatible with the social state of the future which we foresee.[10]

Heine's reaction to this part of the doctrine was similar to many members of the Young German group attracted to the French movement. Like the writers associated with the liberal intelligentsia during the 1830s, he understood the call for an equality of women as a social imperative, but more frequently expressed his views in terms of the emancipation of the flesh, the liberation of the hitherto repressed sensual aspects of both men and women, and the advocacy of free love. To a certain extent, the lesson Heine learned from his contact with the Saint-Simonists was not unlike the message George Sand adduced—and put into practice. Heine ignored for the most part the economic dimensions of this utopian socialist movement, focusing instead on social and philosophical implications. The poems in *Verschiedene* are thus largely consistent with Heine's ideological leanings at the time, and to a certain extent they supported a liberation for both sexes that was vaguely associated with feminist tendencies, and would probably have been recognized as such in the context of Paris in the 1830s. The courtesans whose names appear as the titles to the sections of this collection were not simply a reiteration of one side of the whore–Madonna tradition, but a provocation to bourgeois morality and simultaneously a call for a sensual life that would break with the oppressive spiritualism propagated by Christianity and prevailing morality. Seraphine VII, which presents the most open espousal of Heine's interest in Saint-Simonism, places the notions of sensualism and pantheism in the context of love unencumbered by societal sanction:

> Upon this rock we'll build a church,
> All suffering transcended—
> The church of the third Testament;
> The days of pain are ended.
>
> Annulled the great Antithesis
> That held us long deluded;
> The stupid torments of the flesh
> Are over now, concluded.
>
> Do you hear God on his dark sea?
> He speaks with thousand voices.
> And do you see how his sky overhead
> With a thousand candles rejoices?
>
> God dwells both in the heaven's light
> And ocean's dark abysses;
> God's spirit dwells in all that is—
> He dwells in our kisses. (DHA 2, 34; p. 332)

Heine's reference to a third testament has a long tradition in German letters, stretching back at least to Lessing's *Erziehung des Menschengeschlechts* (Education of the Human Race, 1780), and Heine himself had already made use of a similar idea in the *Harzreise* (Harz Journey, 1824), where he writes of the overcoming of Christianity with an emancipatory religion of the holy spirit. Here, however, the new religion is explicitly connected with the pleasures of the body, with sensual enjoyment, not simply on the part of the man, but in the relationship between man and woman. The pantheistic spirit that Heine conjures for us affirms a love in which sensuality is no longer deprecated as sin, but blessed as part of God's universe.

Heine as the street-wise poet of sensual pleasures is not simply the answer to Heine the poet of unrequited love, but rather his necessary complement. The two personae and the women with whom they consort represent two of the social possibilities in early nineteenth-century society. In some respects Heine's poetry of the 1820s and 1830s represents an endeavour to explore the alternatives that exist within the restrictions of his circumstances. In doing so, he often depicts women in roles that resemble the stereotypes of a misogynist literary tradition. It is easy and even tempting to associate the often clichéd women in the *Buch der Lieder* with the exalted and unattainable women that populate earlier verse, and to see in the courtesans of Paris in *Variae* the latest version of the lower-class, morally improper women of a more bawdy literary tradition. One can also bemoan the absence in Heine's prose texts of discussions directly related to women's rights and women's emancipation, despite his frequent and consistent advocacy of human rights and emancipation from the despotic regimes of nineteenth-century Europe. If we select the criterion that Straube assumes, namely that Heine should be cognizant of and validate the relatively sparsely distributed writings protesting the subordinate position of women in society, then he is deficient in both his knowledge and ideological tendency. We find no discussion of women's rights and women's emancipation in Heine's texts, and there is no evidence that he took an avid interest in these topics. In the context of the early nineteenth century, however, and the literary tradition in which and against which Heine composed his works, he displays a receptiveness to issues that were vital to women's concerns and to the equality of the sexes. He recognized and portrayed the lack of equality between men and women in at least two frequently encountered social settings and gives indications in his portrayals of a sensitivity to the straightjacket in which both men and women find themselves in their preordained roles.

His search for a solution to the central problem of his early verse led to the adoption of a sensualist doctrine that promised to liberate all human beings from the most oppressive ideological formations supported by the church and bourgeois morality. Heine may not be included as an early promoter of women's rights, and the women in his texts may not be exemplary for emancipation. But the dominant tendency in his writings resolutely opposes the very forces that maintained women in subjugation during the nineteenth century.

7

Mundus Muliebris

Baudelaire's World of Women

Rosemary Lloyd

I recently read a manuscript which, on the basis of a superficial and uncontextualized reading of 'Une charogne' (A Carcass) depicted the whole of Baudelaire's *Les Fleurs du Mal* (1857)[1] (The Flowers of Evil) not just as misogynistic, but as unworthy of any modern reader's attention. If I found this deeply worrying, my concern was not for Baudelaire's fate before the charges so belligerently levelled against him, but that feminist criticism itself is debased by the crudeness of such appraisals. It is not, of course, difficult to find evidence of misogyny in Baudelaire's writing, from his private diaries and letters through his criticism to his poetry. The virulence of the *boutades* in his diaries is undeniable. 'I have always been astonished that women are allowed to go into churches. What conversation can they have with God?' (OC 1, 693) and 'We love women in proportion to their difference from us. Loving intelligent women is the pleasure of a pederast' (OC 1, 653) are often quoted in this regard. Striking, too, is the uneasiness Baudelaire expresses when faced with women who write, and particularly his almost visceral dislike of the most successful of them: George Sand ('She is above all, and more than anything else, a *great fool*' (OC 1, 686)). More disturbing yet are the brusque injunctions to the woman who asks painful questions to be beautiful and hold her tongue, and above all poems such as 'À une Madone' (To a Madonna) 'Une Martyre' (A Martyr) and 'À celle qui est trop gaie' (To the woman who is too cheerful)[2] that apparently reflect longings to cause women physical or psychological injury.

Nevertheless, a reading of 'Une charogne' that presents it uniquely as an expression of disgust for the female body slides too swiftly over the multiplicity of other meanings embedded in this complex poem, which is also a cry of despair at human mortality and of fear faced with the power of desire, both male and female.[3] After all, as Baudelaire argued, *Les Fleurs du Mal* offers most importantly a representation of the agitation experienced by the soul in the grip of evil (OC 1, 195), a serious and deeply considered response to Milton and Dante, not a handbook on morality. A restrictive reading of any work backfires when forced into some critical grid or read too rapidly with the aim of making a particular point. The ironies, double-meanings, hidden implications and suggestive metaphors tear apart the very structure of such a grid, and destroy the wider argument they were called upon to support. What is more, to read any poem out of its broader historical and generic context is to amputate oneself from the multiple resonances it sets up, resonances that enrich a deeper comprehension not just of the poem, but of human experience. In particular, 'Une charogne' cannot adequately be read in isolation, not just cut off from Baudelaire's despair at being called 'the prince of carrion',[4] or from his anxiety that his 'repulsive ugliness' would repel women,[5] but also from the other poems in the 'Spleen et Idéal' section of *Les Fleurs du Mal* or such poems as 'Un voyage à Cythère' (A Voyage to Cythera) in which the poet urges himself to look on his own mortality and his own sexuality without disgust. Similarly, those poems revealing violent urges directed against women, while they cannot simply be overlooked (as has often been the case) or presented as harmless allegories, need to be set into the broader framework of the violence in the work as a whole.[6]

Equally, Baudelaire's particular chagrin and anger with George Sand demands an understanding of its personal resonance—his request that she promote an actress he supported was turned down (through no fault of George Sand's)—and the more intellectual context of what he saw as her rejection of the concept of hell, one of the under-girding premises of *Les Fleurs du Mal*.[7] The dagger thrusts in the intimate journals require a similar contextualisation, both within the framework of the genre (the private diary was used for venting frustration), of caricature (as practised in the contemporary press), and through cross-references within the diaries that add depth and texture to his comments. Thus, the remark about women and churches for instance needs to be considered in the light of the following apothegm: 'Of the

Church's femininity as the reason for its omnipotence' (OC 1, 650), a telling yoking together of power and the female, that is in close accord with contemporary arguments against female suffrage based on a purported fear that women would vote as their confessors advised them to do. And if the central character of *Les Fleurs du Mal* demands that his lover stop forcing him to confront unpleasant subjects, the poet himself has allowed her voice to be heard as she raises those very questions, without which, of course, the collection would lack much of its disturbing power.

All of the above is not of course to deny the misogyny in Baudelaire, but to seek an understanding of it that goes significantly further than mere accusations. As Ross Chambers has argued, the challenge is not just to perceive and reveal misogyny, but to find strategies for reading through and against it in ways that make the text yield up its many other possibilities.[8] To do so as I have proposed, we need to slow down, focus on areas that tend to be overlooked, sharpen our critical sensitivities, develop antennae responsive to a range of different stimuli.[9] Baudelaire, after all, has written poetry of great beauty and power: he showed how strikingly flexible and rich the apparently restrictive form of the sonnet could be; his prose poetry, while it did not inaugurate the genre, established parameters and set standards for it; his art and literary criticism raised questions of profound aesthetic importance. Moreover, his translations and adaptations of Edgar Allen Poe and Thomas de Quincey continue to astonish through their ability to convey the vibrancy of these writers' works, while his influence on international Modernism was far-reaching, to the extent that we cannot fully understand that vital movement unless we are familiar with Baudelaire.

The question is then this: how can feminist criticism better approach *Les Fleurs du Mal* and Baudelaire's other writings? What, to offer a slight alteration to Mary Ann Caws's scintillating 'What can a woman do for the late Henry James?', can a woman do for Baudelaire?[10]

First we need to establish Baudelaire's position in the historical, social, and artistic context. After the failure of the 1789 Revolution to honour its promises of equality for women, the growing misogyny of the age was given legal force in Napoleon's code of laws, while rapid changes in social conditions, especially in terms of a shift to the cities and to industrialisation, brought vast transformations in demographic patterns and in what both men and women came to expect from life. Women were legally debarred from high-paying professions as well as from many labouring jobs, and if for many women marriage offered the only hope of a career, the removal of the divorce law could transform it for the unlucky into penal servitude. Finally, male fear of female power was intensified by the burgeoning threat of syphilis, which was often, consciously or not, related to the deeply engrained sense of the association among women, sexual desire, and evil.[11]

Despite this radically altered intellectual and social landscape, and although Romanticism's sun had already begun to set, as Baudelaire himself reminds us in one of his sonnets, nineteenth-century French literary critics continued to uphold the standards and values of Classicism. Excellent Latin scholar though he was, Baudelaire brilliantly caricatures such rearguard conservatism in the striking opening to his *Notes nouvelles sur Edgar Poe* (New Notes about Edgar Poe): '*Literature of decadence!*—Empty words that we often hear falling, with the sonority of an emphatic yawn, from the mouths of those riddle-less Sphinxes that watch before the holy doors of Classical Aesthetics. Each time the irrefutable oracle reverberates you can state with certainty that what is at issue is a work that is more amusing than the *Iliade*' (OC 2, 319). Romanticism's dual depiction of woman as either saccharine angel or destructive demon was slowly being replaced by a more complex presentation of women and female desire, but Baudelaire (as he insisted in the notes prepared for the trial lawyer hired to defend *Les Fleurs du Mal* against accusations of offences to public morality) was convinced that, because the great poets had long since divided up 'the most flower-strewn provinces of the poetic demesne', all that was left for him to do was to 'extract the *beauty* from Evil' (OC 1, 181). This is to define himself against and outside the canon, and at the same time to throw that canon into question by the implicit suggestion that successfully confronting the enormous obstacles such a programme inevitably created brought into existence a far more powerful, far more modern form of literature. His refusal to respect the implicit notions of the canon is linked to the curiosity that made him able to respond for instance to the beauty of Chinese art well before most of his contemporaries and to do so in terms that in no way diminish the sense of strangeness it created. It remains for him 'a strange product, bizarre, its shape ungainly and its colour intense', as he suggests, adding in a remarkable and highly original twist to his sentence: 'and yet occasionally delicate enough to make you swoon' (OC 2, 76). For Baudelaire, aesthetic values that society held to be paramount were never more than starting points to be analysed, both in terms of literature and art, and in terms of female beauty.

This openness of mind not least to other aesthetic values and effects is also reflected in certain of Baudelaire's attitudes to women, albeit subverted, distorted and blinkered by nineteenth-century gender stereotypes and his own personal predicament and temperament. Baudelaire deliberately situates himself on the edge of the literary and social worlds, determined to carve out a niche for himself in terms of finding new material dealt with in new ways, in remodelling the sonnet and in expanding the possibilities of the prose poem as the expression of urban modernity. Thus, his vision of prose poetry as inspired by the crowd is at striking variance to Romanticism's image of poetry speaking for the crowd, while his verse poetry refuses the idealized image of woman promoted by both Romantic and bourgeois schools, stressing instead the inherent evil of both sexes. 'From the moment of their birth, men and women know that it is in evil that all pleasure lies' (OC 1, 652), he insists in his private diaries and reveals in his poetry.

Living in the increasingly materialistic world of Louis-Philippe and Napoleon III, Baudelaire was, in addition, intensely and increasingly aware of changes in value that emphasized physical comforts and conspicuous consumerism over intellectual and ethical concerns, a world which devalued pursuits of the mind in favour of the acquisitive displays of burgeoning capitalism. His fury at not achieving the recognition he was convinced he deserved, and that he would no doubt have spurned had it been offered, reflects his acute sense of a society dominated by philistine values, a domination he ironically acknowledges in the opening sections of his account of the *Salon* of 1846.

His emphasis, moreover, lies above all on his multivalent sense of the modern: as he himself argues throughout his *Salon* of 1846, the winds of modernity were blowing and demanded the attention of poets and painters, novelists and sculptors. It also demanded the attention of critics, as he urges in the study entitled *Le Peintre de la vie moderne* (The Painter of Modern Life), in which he specifically addresses the question of the canon by asserting that minor poets, that is those the canon designates as such, also have something to offer and that 'just because you so deeply love universal beauty, expressed by the classical poets and artists, you are no less wrong to neglect specific beauties, the beauty of the occasion and of customs' (OC 2, 682). Baudelaire's eagerness to explore such unknown territories was not limited to male-authored works, despite the distinct nervousness he felt at the very thought of women writing—the subtext here is so close to the surface as to be barely qualifiable as such—for his argument is that if women write they will take men as their subject matter, a prospect which filled him and many of his contemporaries with unease.

> Among the fairly numerous crowd of women who in our days have thrown themselves into literary work, there are very few whose works have not been, if not a desolation for their families, and even for their lovers (for the least discreet of men love discretion in the object of their love), at least stained with one of those masculine follies that assume in women the proportions of monstrosity. (OC 2, 147)

Part of the fear here is that pillow talk and prowess in bed might become public, although it must also be acknowledged that he is urging women to write as women, not to ape men. This is markedly different from Flaubert, who would insist (grotesquely) that Louise Colet should when she wrote: 'pull in, tighten the breasts of your heart, show it as muscle and not as a gland.'[12] Moreover, Baudelaire does point to the work of female artists in his *Salons* and he does, against his will but not entirely against his aesthetic judgement, enter into the poetic world of Marceline Desbordes-Valmore in a critical article that he chose to write rather than receiving as a commission, and that is all the more revealing because it is deeply ambivalent.[13] As a critic of contemporary literature he was, moreover, extraordinarily open to works that challenged the norms, while maintaining a toughly intellectual critical stance to everything he read. But he was of course shaped and moulded both by the atmosphere of his time and by his Catholic upbringing, by its bigotry and its belittling of women, by its virulent association of woman, evil, and humanity's fall from grace, and while he frequently moves outside the parameters of such thinking, he was not immune from it, as many of the comments jotted down in his private notebooks reveal.

Those notebooks, together with a range of attitudes conveyed in the verse and prose poems, have attracted the analyses of a variety of feminist critics, most of them writing in English. Tamara Bassim's exploration of women in Baudelaire's poetry offers a somewhat timid revision of the traditional male-centred 'Baudelaire chantre de la femme' (Baudelaire singer of woman) studies.[14] A much more aggressive reading of his exploitation of one of those women, Jeanne Duval, was propounded by Edward Ahearn and has been extended by Griselda Pollock in her exploration of the interface of art and literature focusing on Manet's portrait known as 'Baudelaire's Mistress'.[15] More adventurous feminist readings exposing the misogyny of Baudelaire's writing began in the mid-1980s with the work of Kerry Weinberg, Jean Anderson, Ross Chambers and the early 1990s by Peggy Kamuf.[16]

More recently, Elaine DalMolin has taken their work further to explore the notion of the cut within Baudelaire's representation of the female body.[17] Marie Maclean's luminous exploration of Baudelaire's textual strategies is rich in meditations on the feminine and the maternal. Several subsequent readings have provided provocative analyses of the theme of the maternal in the poet's life and work, notably those of Sima Godfrey and Margaret Miner.[18] Other critics such as Amy Ransom have explored the possibility of reading *Les Fleurs du Mal* as a woman, going against the grain of the programme apparently set out in the liminary poem to the (male) reader.[19] Among areas that have recently attracted considerable attention has been that of the apparent fetishism that has led Baudelaire, in several of his poems, notably 'La Chevelure' ('The Head of Hair') and 'À une passante' (To a woman passing by), to focus on only one or two aspects of the woman, her hair, her hand, her eye, for example. While this area is potentially rich, those working within it need, in my view, to pay sharper attention than they have done so far both to the constraints of the verse forms Baudelaire uses, and more importantly still to the long-established tradition of the *blason,* according to which precisely such aspects were the focus of a poetic listing of the beloved's charms. In other words, the role of tradition and convention, even for so unconventional a poet as Baudelaire, needs to be taken into consideration in order to assess to what degree this apparent dismembering can be attributed solely to personal psychological traits.[20] My own work in this area has looked at gender-definition in Baudelaire's creative writing, arguing that the poems, through their repeated invitation to plunge into the unknown, the multitudinous, the evanescent, seduce us into setting aside the gender-specific mask of the hypocrite reader, to live instead through that plethora of personae that mill about in his destabilizing and therefore liberating world.[21]

In order to suggest how a feminist approach might draw on this extremely useful ground work, I want to begin not with the more familiar area of *Les Fleurs du Mal,* nor yet the *Petits Poèmes en prose* (Short Prose Poems), but with one of Baudelaire's many contributions to aesthetic debate in art, literature, and music, his review of Wagner's *Tannhäuser,* a review that sets him sharply at odds with much of the conservative and chauvinist thinking of his time, where the German composer was derided in the press, mocked in caricatures and transformed into mindless clichés. Unlike many of his contemporaries, Baudelaire was overwhelmed by this music and by the vision Wagner was offering of the intensity of sexual passion, so much so that he offered him the ultimate accolade: 'it struck me', he confessed in terms very similar to those driving his recognition of kindred souls in Poe and De Quincey, 'that that music was *my own*' (C 1, 673). Baudelaire himself may gently mock such an attitude in Samuel Cramer, the protagonist of his novella *La Fanfarlo*, but it remains one of those vital keys to understanding his thinking, because what he is able to express in analytical terms about such works reflects directly on his own creative writing, for which he was unwilling or unable to write the explanatory notes that his publisher, Poulet-Malassis, urged him to provide. What he finds in *Tannhäuser*, as he puts it in his review of the work, in an analysis that begs to be read as primarily autobiographical, is 'the overflowing of an energetic nature, that pours into evil all the strength due to the cultivation of good; it is an unbridled love, immense, chaotic, raised to the heights of a counter-religion, of a satanic religion' (OC 2 796). This is clearly also an encapsulation of the central themes of *Les Fleurs du Mal* and indirectly it provides some essential keys to reading that work. In his letter to Wagner, a letter that so moved the composer that he came to Baudelaire's apartment to thank him in person (Baudelaire, of course, was not at home), the poet's response was expressed in terms of sexual passion, too: he claimed that in listening to Wagner's music: 'I often experienced a feeling of a pretty strange kind, which was the pleasure of understanding, of allowing myself to be penetrated, invaded, a truly sensual enjoyment that resembled the enjoyment you feel from going up into the air or in rolling on the sea' (C 1, 673). It is a sentence that sheds considerable light both on 'Élévation' and on the sonnet 'La Musique' from *Les Fleurs du Mal*, but what is remarkable and unmistakable about this confession is its explicitly sexual nature. *Pleasure* (*jouissance*), *enjoyment* (*volupté*), and *penetrated* (*pénétré*) are all erotically charged terms. While any one of them used on its own might be seen as mere metaphor or justifiable exaggeration, when grouped together as they are in this passage, they create an undeniably sexual context for Baudelaire's sense of aesthetic and intellectual pleasure. What is more, this is not (and cannot be) conveyed in traditional masculine terms of action and penetration but rather presents the writer himself as allowing this penetration and invasion to overwhelm him in what seems a more traditionally feminine response. Indeed, as Gretchen Schultz has argued, 'masculinity and submission are not mutually exclusive' in Baudelaire's writing.[22] If gender is always to some extent performative,[23] potential rather than given, and if Virginia Woolf urged writers to re-forge their gender in writing (becoming manly-womanly and womanly-manly), Baudelaire already seems fully aware of the complexity of gender identity and androgyny especially of the writer, both as seen through his or her writings and as experienced in everyday existence. If Baudelaire famously presented Emma Bovary as offering 'all the seductions of a virile soul in a charming female body' (OC 2, 81) in a sentence bristling with sexual innuendo, there is also a strong assertion of the pride he himself felt in allowing Wagner's music to penetrate him, a sense too of the erotic pleasure (*jouissance, volupté*) that doing so procured him. And his comparison—to the sensation of flying or rolling on the sea—is, to a post-Freudian reader, instantly interpretable in terms of dreams of sexual pleasure.

Music, however, while it may fill the poet with erotic pleasure and overwhelm him with a sense of submission, offers a quite different kind of stimulus from that of a woman. Nevertheless, it illuminates the pleasure he sought from love: most essentially, in Baudelaire's terms, Wagner's music provides an intellectual satisfaction, one that depends in large measure on the transformation of pleasure into knowledge ('transformer ma volupté en connaissance' (II 786) is the formula he provides in the Wagner essay), and one that always lies within the individual's control, even if to exercise that control he or she might have to leave the concert room. That combination of the intellectual and the voluntary is absent from the relationships with women depicted in Baudelaire's poetry, predicated as they are on a complex social context in which male and female roles were sharply delineated and in which the poet's own position was undeniably precarious, both personally and in terms of his function as poet. Desire, in these poems, is always irresistible and hence threatening, rising up within the individual as the tide rushes up over the rocks of the shore, plunging into the heart like a knife blade, leaving the individual helplessly exposed to the power of the other.

For Baudelaire's class and time, successful masculinity demanded both a suitable marriage and choice of a (professional) career that would support a family. Baudelaire had efficiently rejected such demands, both by his ostentatious and conspicuous consumption of his inheritance and by his determination to become a poet, a métier which, as Peter Gay reminds us in his masterly *Schnitzler's Century*, was seen as tantamount to telling lies for a living.[24] Even had he not taken such radical steps, contemporary education for women—a potent blend of the thinking of Rousseau, Napoleon, the church, and a patriarchy attempting to legitimize its own convictions—would have made it difficult for Baudelaire to meet women whose intelligence he could respect, even had he been capable of recognizing it.[25] The only women with whom Baudelaire could then come into contact were those with whom he could find no intellectual companionship. Baudelaire's chaotic personal life, especially his constant changes of residence, has left us only a fragmentary glimpse of his letter-writing habits, but there seems to have been no woman with whom he maintained anything like the sustained epistolary conversations that Flaubert had with for instance George Sand, while the venues he frequented—mainly cafés and brasseries—were not the kinds of places where he was likely to meet women capable of forming or challenging either his aesthetic or social notions. Towards the end of his life, in 1864, he did write to Judith Gautier, thanking her for her review of his translation of Poe's *Eureka* and including the following backhanded compliment: 'If I were not afraid of offending you by speaking ill of your sex, I would tell you that you have forced me to doubt those evil opinions I had forged concerning women in general' (C 2, 353). By then any salvaging of such blatant prejudice and misogyny was too late, as indeed his deployment of adynata from Classical rhetoric reveals.[26] In any case, Judith Gautier was not at that stage in a position to enter into an intellectual relationship with Baudelaire, although she was later to play an important role for Baudelaire's arch-rival Hugo and for his admired composer, Wagner.

What his Creole mistress, Jeanne Duval, had to teach Baudelaire was of a more intensely personal nature, vital for his awareness of himself and for his own capacity for self-abasement, or abjection, in Kristevan terms.[27] What he learned from Duval did of course challenge the accepted wisdom concerning women, as he makes clear in the untitled poem beginning: 'Je te donne ces vers' (I give you these lines) in which he addresses her in these terms: 'O shadow, barely present to the eye,/You lightly step, with a serene regard/On mortal fools who've judged you mean and hard' but to do that he has to enclose the powerful force she possesses within two images, one of her as a shadow leaving only an ephemeral trace, the other as a statue with eyes of jet (OC 1, 41; p. 81). What he recognizes in Jeanne and conveys in his poems is the danger she poses to stereotypical images of male superiority, a danger that can be conjured only by transforming her into shadow and sculpture.[28]

It is a danger that, in a typically Baudelairean ambivalence, he both fears and courts. This, after all, is the mind that recognises itself as both torturer and victim, the knife and the wound ('L'Héautontimoroumenos'), but Baudelaire knows that only such powerful women, among whom he also counts his mother, can bring out that vital duality so strongly. This is why, however much of a double he found in Edgar Allan Poe, Baudelaire implicitly rejects the American writer's vision of the etiolated and impotent woman, replacing her, in his poem 'L'Idéal', with the more energetic models of Shakespeare and Michelangelo (OC 1, 22).

If not directly caused by it, this situation exacerbated his complex relationship with his mother, as Sartre has so compellingly if so crudely analysed.[29] Baudelaire's dual need both to punish his mother and to attract her esteem is an embarrassingly constant element of his correspondence, which is pockmarked with letters that beg, wheedle, cajole, harass, threaten and whine. But his memories of his early childhood, especially the period between his father's death and his mother's remarriage, months he would come to construe in terms of an idyllic period spent in the house at Neuilly, with long tête-à-têtes in quiet rooms or tranquil gardens, leave their indelible stamp on his writing, and help him transform into knowledge another source of delight, the reading of De Quincey, in whose autobiographical *Confessions of an English Opium Eater* he found the seeds of a theory of childhood he was to generalize.

In an intense letter to his publisher Poulet-Malassis, who had raised a series of questions concerning his evocation, in his translation and adaptation of De Quincey, of the female influences over the child, Baudelaire explains both the expression *mundus muliebris* (the world of women) and his analysis of the subsequent nature of men who in childhood have been raised exclusively by women. 'The man who, from the outset, has been long bathed in the soft atmosphere of women, in the odour of a woman's hands, of her breast, of her lap, of her hair, of her floating clothes, [. . .] has contracted thereby a delicacy of the skin and a distinction of accent, a kind of androgyny, without which the most harsh and virile genius remains, where the perfection of art is concerned, an incomplete being' (OC 1, 499). Writing to Malassis, he asks: 'what is it that the child loves so passionately in his mother, his maid, his older sister? It is simply the being who nourishes him, combs his hair, washes him and rocks him? It is also her caress and the sensual pleasure she provides. For the child, this caress is expressed un-beknownst to the woman, by all her feminine graces' (C 2, 30). What we have here, then, is a detailed and dogged affirmation of the need for a creative genius to combine traditionally masculine with traditionally feminine elements, together with a rapid denial—that takes the nature of a habitual tic—of the woman's consciousness of the pleasure she creates. In this tic is encapsulated a long and tedious history of attempts to delineate the masculine as conscious intelligence, the feminine as spontaneous grace, one of those commonplaces that in other contexts Baudelaire would dig out with all the ruthless curiosity of a biologist exploring an ant nest (the metaphor is his own), but which here he slithers over in his anxiety to convince Malassis that he is right, that his *mundus muliebris* is not 'a mistake in his Latin' and decidedly not, far more importantly, a lapse in virility. What is interesting here is not just the overriding value Baudelaire places on being formed in childhood by women, but even more the fact that he knows perfectly well that women are far more intellectually cognizant not just of the charm they exert but of the work that goes into it, as his remarkable poem 'Confession' makes perfectly clear:

> Being a beauty is a hard affair,
> A banal business, vanity,
> The swoons of mad and frigid dancers, where
> The smiles are done mechanically. (OC 1, 46; p. 95)

But his mother's confession of that 'hard affair', her realization that she would have to remarry rapidly or sink into genteel poverty or worse after the death of her husband deprived her of the pension he had earned while alive, was something that of course the child Baudelaire, like the adult, could not accept.

It was adapting De Quincey's work that allowed Baudelaire to explore the importance of his early experiences in the world of women as an adult and as an artist retaining the androgyny such an upbringing promotes. Thus, introducing a lengthy quotation from De Quincey into his presentation, he prepares the ground with this statement: 'It is moreover good to allow readers to taste for themselves the author's penetrating and *feminine* style' (OC 1, 447; Baudelaire's emphasis). The blend of traditionally masculine and feminine traits within the great artist is something to which he returns in talking of 'a form of energy that is often found in the most feminine and sensitive of temperaments' (OC 1, 458). Elsewhere, moreover, he refers to this blend of the masculine and feminine in terms suggesting that it is universal and not just intrinsic to genius: 'the story of the double male and female element in a single soul' (OC 2, 604). And when, in his insertion in to the De Quincey text, he argues for a 'kind of androgyny' as a *sine qua non* in the great artist, he is making a claim to which he gives more poetic expression elsewhere, in the prose poem he dedicates to another musician he admires, the one in fact who did so much to make Wagner accessible to the French, Franz Liszt. It is in the poem entitled 'Le Thyrse' (The Thyrsus) that he depicts the artistic mind as uniting the two elements of the thyrsus: the stick around which coil in capricious meanders, as he puts it, the stems and the flowers. The stick, straight and firm, represents will power, while the flowers are fantasy wandering around the will, the feminine element executing its prestigious pirouettes around the masculine. There is something distinctly precious about all this, as if Baudelaire were slightly uncomfortable or hoped to make his dedicatee slightly uncomfortable with the image, which moreover he takes largely unchanged from De Quincey himself. But uncomfortable or not he let this metaphor for androgyny stand. The question for a feminist reader, indeed for any reader, is to know how to interpret this image, and whether it is possible to suggest that such a conceptualizing of genius mitigates misogyny, or whether what is depicted as feminine and masculine within the nature of any individual has as little connection to sexual or gender-based realities as grammatical gender. Reaching such an understanding would require extensive lexical studies of nineteenth-century French and European writing, studies that are beyond the scope of this essay but that could play an essential role in deepening our understanding of both Baudelaire and his age. Central to such an exploration, however, would be the concept of hysteria, a condition linked to women by etymology and tradition, but one that Baudelaire not only identifies in himself but uses with reference to both sexes in his prose poems. His interest in such questions, an interest that is not merely intellectual but also autobiographical, is made clear by a striking paragraph of his review of *Madame Bovary*:

> Hysteria! Why would this physiological mystery not form the stuff and basis of a work of literature, this mystery that the Academy of Medicine has not yet resolved, and that expresses itself in women through the sensation of a rising, asphyxiating ball (I am speaking here only of the main symptom) while in sensitive men it takes the form of all kinds of weaknesses and also by a tendency to commit all manner of excesses? (OC 2, 83)[30]

Gender, in Baudelaire's eyes, seems to be a fluid construct, linked only tangentially to physiological realities.

What both Baudelaire's verse and prose poetry offers is a complex portrait of that construct, refracted through his equally multifaceted temperament, one to whom women were all the more seductive and powerful in that they were at once intricately bound up with his own formation, as we have seen, and, *ex hypothesi*, irreducibly alien to him. His comment about love being predicated on difference may be couched in terms of defiance, but it reveals a gnawing fear that he who so loves the scent of women (C 2, 219) is dependent on the unknowable, and that his own formation by the *mundus muliebris* is both an essential part of his nature as poet and at the same time beyond his own ability fully to understand. If we look, for example, at one of his most exasperated outbursts, the untitled poem number XXV, this ambivalent attitude explodes, not just in the oxymorons of the closing line, but in the way in which the poet's mistress (like his mother as she is presented in 'Bénédiction') has been essential to shaping him as poet, however negative the experience may have been:

> Has this, then, never shrunk your heart with fear,
> When Nature, mighty in her secret plans,
> Makes use of you, o woman! queen of sins!
> – Of you, vile beast—to mould a genius
>
> O filthy grandeur! o sublime disgrace! (OC 1, 28; p. 55)

This is an early poem, inspired not by Jeanne Duval but by the prostitute Sara, from whom, it is usually agreed, he contracted syphilis. As a result, the moulding to which he refers, and for which he uses the verb 'pétrir', more precisely to knead into shape, as a baker kneads bread or a potter clay, is both physical and metaphorical, a combination frequent in Baudelaire. More importantly, what is at issue here is a failure of intelligence: the woman's failure to understand what the poem calls 'the law' of her beauty is offset by the man's failure to control those forces that will make him, as he puts it, a genius. Because it is so raw in its expression, a rawness the poet attempts to counteract by the closing conceits of the oxymorons, it is a poem that provides some insight into the joint concepts of melancholy and abjection that I would argue underlie much of Baudelaire's poetic depiction of the relationships between men and women.[31]

The mindlessness that the poet attributes to the female figure in this poem is associated with a particularly rich thematic in Baudelaire's writing, with its frequent accusation of the stupidity and blindness of those who surround him. Humanity, as the travellers in the closing poem to *Les Fleurs du Mal* insist, is 'mad now as it was in the past' (OC 1, 133). Awareness of evil, consciousness of abjection, acknowledgement of the overwhelming force of melancholia, these are the only possible solutions to what Baudelaire terms the eternal spectacle of sin. In many of his poems he finds sharp and bitter allegories for conveying this, allegories in which misogyny rubs shoulders with misanthropy. The prose poem 'La Femme Sauvage et la Petite-Maîtresse' (The Wild Woman and the Kept Woman) for instance sets out to portray men and women exactly as the travellers had found them to be the world over:

> Woman, vile slave, proud in stupidity,
> Tasteless and humourless in self-conceit;
> Man greedy tyrant, lustful, slovenly,
> Slave of the slave and sewer in the gutter. (OC 1, 132; p. 289)

In a fairground booth a pair of lovers see 'one of those animals generally called "my angel", that is a woman' with another monster, one who screams at the top of his voice, a stick clutched in his hand, that is, a husband (OC 1, 289). The narrator attempts to transform this vision into a lesson to be given to his constantly complaining mistress, drawing an intellectual conclusion that places him in a position of power over her, threatening to gobble her up if she does not accept its moral. The problem is that to do so he has to cast himself in the role of that other monster, the fairground husband: either way, whether he plays lapdog obedient to his mistress's demands or resorts to brutality to dominate her, she has won by forcing him into equally ignominious positions.

That same sense of the power and incomprehensibility of the Other who is woman is also central to the prose poem ironically titled 'Portraits de maîtresses' (Portraits of Mistresses). In a study which is also and perhaps above all a series of portraits of men, Baudelaire sets a conversation in a smoking room within a gambling den, a location steeped in resonances with other poems, verse and prose. In this 'male boudoir' as he terms it, each man tells the story of a woman who forces him to acknowledge his own impotence: one, because his mistress challenged the conventional division of labour between men and women, and who apparently also set social hierarchy at nought since he found her in *flagrante delicto* with his own valet; another because he was unable to give his mistress pleasure; a third, because her appetites were beyond his power to supply; and a fourth driven to murder his beloved because her perfection tortured him by revealing his own imperfection. Abjection is the dominant mode in each of these confessions, presented in terms of defiance that would end by sounding merely puerile were they not in the final case translated into expressions of violence.

Perhaps most striking of all to a feminist reading of Baudelaire is the sense of isolation his work conveys, of the ego locked into the prison house of self, even in the prose poems that specifically acknowledge their main source of influence as being that of the urban crowds. The poet is almost invariably the outsider looking on, observing the crowds or individuals within those crowds, but from a safe distance, or looking out from his sixth-floor window in search of a victim to assuage his depression or of profiles he can round out for stories that he knows are merely stories but that enable him to 'feel that I am and what I am' (OC 1, 339), that give him a sense of pride at having 'lived and suffered in others apart from myself' (ibid.). The poet may, as he asserts in the prose poem entitled 'Les Foules' (The Crowds), enjoy the incomparable privilege of being at will himself and other people, but the image he gives tells a rather different story: the poet, he argues, is like those wandering souls in search of a body (OC 1, 291). In other words, this image of the poetic imagination replicates the position of the narrator of 'Les Projets' in preferring to imagine other places rather than constrain his body to visit them: the wandering soul may change bodies but cannot encounter another mind. The only counter examples to this come in such dream stories as 'Le Joueur généreux' (The Generous Gambler) and the rare poems of ecstatic love, such as 'Le Balcon' (The Balcony) although even there we see only the lover's bliss, not any sense of shared bliss. If the feminine experience is shaped through networks and relationships rather than isolation, as many feminist theorists have argued, Baudelaire's poetry stands at the far edge of that isolated world of masculinity, the very embodiment of spleen. The sense of being 'a false chord in the divine symphony' (OC 1, 78) runs through *Les Fleurs du Mal* and dominates in more ironic and defiant mode *Les Petits Poëmes en prose.*

Forced through what he conceived of as his mother's rejection of him to seek out relationships that replicate that rejection (or that would at best place him again in a position of inferiority), Baudelaire reacts in his writing by railing against that situation, paradoxically affirming by doing so the power of women. Feminist readings of Baudelaire, rather than focusing on the surface aggression, can draw their own power from this awareness, and bring out his complex reactions to erotic love and to human mortality by delving more deeply into his intensely felt and intricately wrought verse and prose poetry.

8

Flaubert's Cautionary Tales and the Art of the Absolute

Mary Orr

Among the many *idées reçues* (received ideas) surrounding Flaubert's *œuvre* is his almost unrivalled art of the novel, the painful experience of finding the right words to express the stuff of humanity in well-wrought form. Endorsed by his voluminous *Correspondance*, his famous 'muscular' style is simply everything which leaky and unruly feminine outpouring is not.[1] Feminist critical responses to such aesthetic stipulations have then written Flaubert off as an unrepentant misogynist or sided with Louise Colet, George Sand, and Mlle Leroyer de Chantepie, his most famous interlocutrices, to affirm their courageous engagements with this prickly and reclusive wordsmith.[2] A different, but no less important feminist response has been to re-engage with Flaubert's works, to tease out his representations of women (and more recently un-masculine men) as more complex and critical of norms, whether envisaged from socio-critical or psychoanalytical frames of reference.[3] Little feminist work has been done, however, on the slippery nature of Flaubert's aesthetics, whether as an absolute of objectivity and scalpel precision, a masterpiece of impersonality through his no less famous development of the narrative technique of *style indirect libre* (free indirect style), or as the epitome of undecidability as lauded by deconstructive readings.[4] While objectivity, impersonality and undecidability encapsulate the art in Flaubert's narratives of showing rather than telling the reader what and how to think, each in various ways factors out gender considerations regarding narrative point of view, focalization and control, whether from within narrative sequences, or from an omnipresent narrator or other frame orchestrator. Clearly, feminist work to nuance or counter the tenets of Realism, Modernism or deconstruction offers a response to such critical appropriations of Flaubert, but does not necessarily offer any direction on how to rethink the particularities of his style, aesthetics or indeed ethics of writing. What this essay therefore proposes is to trial a reading of Flaubert's last works, the well-known *Trois Contes* (Three Tales) of 1876 and the unfinished novel of monstrous encyclopedism, *Bouvard et Pécuchet* (Bouvard and Pécuchet) of 1880, as sites to determine aesthetic criteria of a lifetime, and whether these mesh with those of his male contemporaries.[5] While such a modest proposal is not overtly feminist, feminist history and methodology (regardless of specific approach such as socio-critical, psychoanalytical etc.) are useful on at least two counts: they valorize investigation of the previously unwritten or over-written in the cultural narrative to address reasons for such omissions; and, by valuing alternative optics, may be reticent about simple categorizations.[6] By also examining the effects of dominant structures on those who are not dominant, feminist methodology foregrounds use of the official tongue, including questions of canonicity, by those working against its grain. By applying these feminist critical priorities for their investigative and unsettling powers to Flaubert's style, which critics of very different hues have discerned as disquieting, what has been off-limits about Flaubert's art will be of primary interest.[7] By also moving beyond feminist approaches focusing their main energies on 'representations of', whether women or men, I will argue for scrutiny of Flaubert's representations of the doubly human—doubles and double (even treble) endings are a hallmark of his works—as symptomatic of his aesthetics, an aesthetics which reconsiders the limits, limitations and boundaries of representational form as supremely ethical dimensions of a muscular art of re-presentation. For Flaubert specialists, this essay also undertakes an overtly feminist reappraisal of the last works on which, compared with *Madame Bovary* or *Salammbô*, there is a striking dearth of critical interest concerning gender, sexuality or power-relations.[8]

Flaubert's last works offer a peculiarly concerted insight into his aesthetic criteria honed and redeployed over a range of seemingly diverse novels, from *Madame Bovary* (1857) to *Salammbô* (1862), from *L'Éducation sentimentale* (Sentimental Eduation) (1869) to *La Tentation de Saint Antoine* (The Temptation of Saint Anthony) (1874, final version). The two texts for discussion here are often linked directly to earlier novels—the first tale of *Trois Contes*, *Un cœur simple* (A Simple Heart), is frequently compared with *Madame Bovary* for example—while *Bouvard et Pécuchet* is considered a diptych of *La Tentation*. Flaubertian motifs, angles of vision, use of over- or under-statement or 'le petit détail qui fait vrai' (the little detail which makes true), deployment of juxtaposition and inversion, repetitions with variations, alignment of seeming opposites all feature largely in the late works. Flaubert's equally (in)famous mode of concluding (perhaps the most problematic of *idées reçues* in Flaubert criticism)[9] had also found its level: the exact balance between pointed and open remark, a graft of particular and general statement converge in an open verdict.[10] The late works also crystallize the preoccupations of a late nineteenth-century French world in fictional form with regard to moral, social and philosophical values. The clear gender demarcations for society underwritten by the Code Napoléon of 1804, the certitudes of scientific and industrial progress, the position of France as an expanisionist, colonial power on the world stage have changed from 1830 via 1848 to 1870, and especially in the aftermath of France's defeat in the Franco-Prussian war, when Flaubert was completing his last texts under conditions of personal and financial difficulty. If his social critique had always found expression by a number of indirect aesthetic routes such as *style indirect libre* or by analogy in the integration of genres such as fictional reportage of contemporary history (*L'Éducation sentimentale*), ancient historical epic (*Salammbô*), or reworkings of familiar stories from the *Golden Legend* or the Bible in *La Légende de Saint Julian l'Hospitalier* (*The Legend of Saint Julien the Hospitalier*) and *Hérodias* respectively in *Trois Contes*, moral and social considerations are more explicitly expressed in the last works by the genre choices of the *conte* or mock utopia to explore encyclopedism.[11]

The modest proposal of this essay is that Flaubert's last works exemplify a questioning of extremes, their representation and the value judgements associated with them by pressing on the limits of the genre of the novel and the moral tale from formal (aesthetic) and moral (ethical) standpoints. How these inter-related elements function as markers of the limits or deviation from moral or formal 'norms' of nineteenth-century French canonical novel or short-story writing will be elucidated by means of a reconsideration of Flaubert's engagement with the three classic ends or absolutes of high art. The first is expression of the Beautiful, often inscribed in writing by the vehicle of the beautiful, inspirational female protagonist. Her sacrifice by the work's end to anonymity and sublimation in the 'happy-ever-after' of perfect marriage idealizes her as representation of fulfilment within the patriarchal fold. Beautiful deaths usually of maidens or youths in their prime, which cheat nature and the mortal coil because these protagonists never grow old and ugly, is a related absolute of art as depiction of the Good. 'Reward' for aspiration to higher values or ideals elides moral and aesthetic representation of higher ends. Sublimation is not a living death in the happy thereafter of marriage, but in the hereafter of idealized morality. Endings also pinpoint a third absolute of art, representation of the True, ascertainable in the logical, moral and aesthetic qualities of the *dénouement* and import of the final words. Exploration of these three limit situations in Flaubert's last works—marriage, tragic death and the moral impact of the concluding sentences—will test the canonical status of Flaubert's art, but with a feminist spin, to determine whether it exemplifies an art of muscularity.

If *Madame Bovary* is above all Flaubert's novel of marriages (Charles experiences two by the first of the three parts), and *Salammbô* the exploration of marriage as an arrangement to forge political alliances, *Trois Contes* combines his treatment in both works of exorbitant female sexuality (and the punishments meted out for it) with a more cynical set of tales questioning the myth of marriage on either affective or socio-economic grounds. In *Un cœur simple* Félicité's employer, Madame Aubain, is a widow, eventually double-crossed by the scheming M. Bourais, whose philandering, dressed up in his role as 'financial advisor', is targeted specifically at wealthy widows. Félicité's 'love' of the ironically named Théodore is also unrequited as he rejects her to wed a wealthier older match, while the description of Madame Aubain's daughter, Virginie, dressed as a 'bride of Christ' for her first communion, further attacks the double standard of marriage as institutionalized prostitution to the State under the guise of the moral authority of the Church. She dies too young to experience anything but the empty shell of state and church ritual, but in her premature death escapes all circumstance which could change her virginal name, or that of her literary antecedent in Bernardin de Saint-Pierre's *Paul et Virginie.* In *La Légende de Saint Julien l'Hospitalier*, the anti-marriage litany is no less overt. Although Julien's parents enjoy all its 'happy-ever-after' attributes in the earliest descriptions of their harmonious château, their fate is to die by the hand of their exemplary progeny Julien, and in *his* marriage bed, thanks to the hospitality of his stereotypical, good and beautiful wife, given as a reward to Julien by her father with the fairy tale pre-requisite of half a kingdom. After this double patri-matricide, which puts to death his own marriage and the marriage myth designed to 'domesticate' male bloodlust at the same time, Julien casts himself out of a marital Eden and into the chaos of unbridled Nature. Similarly in *Hérodias*, Flaubert does nothing more than copy the already critical and problematic account of the eponymous heroine's marriage as recorded in the Bible in both Mark 6 and Luke 3. As a heady brew of incest, active manipulation of political power not affective union, and political control by means of the sexuality of both Hérode her husband and Salomé her daughter, Hérodias is shown as a cynical advocate of marriage for its social power. It is Flaubert's version which underscores her particular vendetta on John the Baptist for pointing out her crimes of incest, not of religious persecution. Hérodias is among few wives in Flaubert's *œuvre* who live the length of their narration, but as perhaps more than an anti-model of virtue or epitome of the wicked step-spouse of the traditional fairy tale. Only marriage to the king could permit her unrivalled power within the world of her times. If marriage is increasingly portrayed for its convenience for the scheming of both sexes, and for intelligent, powerful, sexy and persistent women in particular so that it becomes an institutional trap for weaker men,[12] Flaubert's *Bouvard et Pécuchet* delights in portraying this in doubled form. The gullible and sexually naïve Pécuchet, victim of Mélie's advances (and syphilis) fares no better or worse than his more worldly-wise widower friend, Bouvard, who is the target of Madame Bordin's marriage schemes to catch a comparatively wealthy husband. In his intertextual makeovers of marriage in the idealistic worlds of legend or scripture, and of the Realist tale and novel describing the marketplace of nineteenth-century matches of convenience, Flaubert unrelentingly portrays the institution as dangerously open to abuse, and therefore to be avoided at all costs.

Or so a feminist reading of a certain sort might conclude, in order to nail Flaubert's misogyny, cynicism or fear of phallic mothers. My alternative feminist reading for the limits of limit situations is rather different. As a cornerstone of social relations, marriage and its representation is too crucial a vehicle to jettison or discount because it conflates moral, aesthetic and gender considerations so neatly. Flaubert therefore threads changes to the accepted marriage script into each of his last works, but precisely to create a disquieting set of moral and aesthetic repercussions.[13] On closer inspection, the *Trois Contes* do more than mock the institution of marriage, its conventions and gendered subdivisions of roles and attitudes. They challenge the structural conventions of tales, especially cautionary ones, where marriage for the beautiful, the good and the true is the sign of reward, whereas the ugly, the bad and the false are punished by denial of this supreme state. By situating the household context of *Un cœur simple* within respectable widowhood and a bond of fealty with a spinster servant of a different social class but similar marital status, such situations of social limitation, but enduring values, contrast with the abortive 'love' relationship (illustrated by Théodore) or trading arrangement masquerading as marriage (Bornais). The female outsiders to the model (widows and orphan servants), whose sexuality is thus supposedly non-existent, are therefore principally on view, which then troubles any easy correlation between person and virtue, or marriage as reward (or even punishment). Similarly, the placing of Julien's ending of two marriages simultaneously in *La Légende de Saint Julien l'Hospitalier* in the second of the three parts, when he murders his parents, clears the way for the no less shocking union at the end of part three. Here the mysterious leper and Julien enact a variation of the 'fatal attraction' plot and subsequent consummation in 'marriage', the whole presented as a same-sex transfiguration.[14] But Flaubert goes further in *Hérodias*. The acme of human power may be overtly expressed in the fateful cocktail of male, youthful and mature female sexualities embodied in the famous dance of Salomé at Hérode's birthday feast. Underpinning it throughout the story, however, is the sway and control of the unchallenged rule of Hérode and Hérodias as a lethal marriage partnership. It is this absolutist power which is stopped dead, literally, by the appearance of John's severed head since Hérodias's reaction thereafter is never seen, only reported, while concentration on the day after the night before in the closing pages firmly eliminates Hérode from the text. Moreover, as now wordless speaker of experience beyond the plot of human history, whether in terms of some greater fulfilment than marriage in a world to come (from the viewpoint of belief), or of greater horror and chaos in the here and now (from the viewpoint of shocked disbelief at human cruelty and power), the severed head of John the Baptist annuls the sexual contract as apotheosis, perhaps especially in its institutionally recognized highest form, marriage of rulers. As a further twist to such institutional unassailability, *Bouvard et Pécuchet* completely inverts the centrality of the marriage plot especially as reward or culmination of events. On the very first page of the novel, he sets his two aging bachelor-widower copyists on a collision course of 'love at first sight', fatal attraction and complete compatibility turned up to thirty-three degrees. This parody of the quest for 'Mr Right' is followed by the burlesque 'happy-ever-after' the two eponymous protagonists create in Les Chavignolles, which is like

Rousseau's Clarens in *La Nouvelle Héloïse*, but without its Julie. In equally anti-Rousseauesque fashion, Nature then turns nasty on Bouvard and Pécuchet, bringing not mellow fruitfulness to their mutual endeavours, but decay and destruction. Even the fruit of their educational labours, their ward Victorine, is seduced and raped under their very roof. Alternative, same-sex modes of cohabitation to marriage therefore hold sway in Flaubert's last works as much for his unlikely older male as older female characters, in order to challenge the ideal and ethics of marriage as earthly reward or goal for good citizenship and the cornerstone of family values. Flaubert's formal destabilization and rewriting of the marriage plot thus questions the central position of the institution of marriage (in both religious and secular form) to social, sexual and fictional norms. It is perhaps the union of unlikely bed-fellows and aesthetic forms which Flaubert's last works most overtly portray to caution against the invidious myth of marriage as social panacea, end in itself, or end of the novel.

If marriage is never the goal or ending of Flaubert's works, are their endings reserved for moral speculation or, as deconstructive criticism would have it, are they the ultimate locus of undecideability? *Madame Bovary* famously unleashed public outcry because its eponymous heroine was not perceived as sufficiently 'punished' in the novel for her adulteries,[15] while all the feisty protagonists in *Salammbô* are sacrificed in one way or the other to the might of Carthage by the final scene.[16] Such overplay (and literal overkill) cannot be 'undecideable'. Rather, if provocation of righteous moral indignation on the reader's part is the objective, Flaubert's corpus is particularly noteworthy. After the tragic deaths of both Emma and Charles Bovary, Homais's reward at the end of *Madame Bovary* with the légion d'honneur offers a striking example. In aesthetic terms, the endings of Flaubert's works prior to those under consideration here complicate neat formal, let alone moral, conclusions by being doubled. In *Trois Contes*, there is an immediate triplication of endings where it then does not necessarily follow that the ending of the final story crystallizes all three. It is manifold death, however, that is singled out at the end of all three tales as the ultimate limit experience and, significantly for feminist readings, is no respecter of gender.[17] Whether of servant, master or prophet, death provokes scandalized moral and aesthetic response in *Trois Contes* for the un-beautiful (Félicité), the un-good (Julien) and the un-true to worldly value systems (John the Baptist) are 'rewarded' with it. Moreover, it is death magnified in unrelentingly gruesome final circumstances that seemingly 'sanctifies' and distinguishes each figure from common humanity, its common, or indeed fictional, lot. Regardless of the agony of death by consumption or the sacrilegious preposterousness of Félicité's final vision of Loulou her parrot as the Holy Spirit in *Un cœur simple*, it is this last exorbitant claim and moment that elevate her beyond mediocrity. Whether Julien is worthy by worldly or divine standards of justice for elevation after a life of killing of the innocents and subsequent repentance in the form of self-abnegation and service, it is the ultimate act of dispossession of his very body in the embrace of the untouchable that warrants his final ascension. In *Hérodias*, Flaubert adheres to every detail of the beheading of John the Baptist in Mark 6, except on one count which increases its horror. Whereas the Biblical executioner executes his orders and the prophet at a single stroke (verse 27), Flaubert's Mannaeï requires two attempts, despite the macabre humour of a detailed account of his impressive and impeccable credentials as executioner supreme. The reason for the unprecedented failure to deliver is a digression of pure fiction. At the first attempt, Mannaeï encounters an executioner even greater than himself, the 'Great Angel of the Samaritans, everywhere covered with eyes and brandishing a huge sword, all red and serrated like a flame' (OC 198), which only heightens the enormity of the second, final, act.[18]

To heap such sadistic delay and cruelty onto the horror of John's imprisonment and meld it with supernatural intervention is not however a heady brew reserved only for the final tale. *Trois Contes* is a catalogue of near-death experiences in confined circumstances with providential outlets for each protagonist. In *Un cœur simple*, Félicité narrowly escapes being savaged by the bull and also saves Mme Aubain's children from a similar fate (although Virginie fails to cheat death twice).[19] When the animals seek revenge for Julien's savage and wanton killings of their kind by encircling and harassing him at the turning point of the tale, they allow him to escape into a worse fate, the killing of his parents (although Julien has narrowly avoided killing his mother with an arrow prior to his departure as a crusader against the infidel). These 'narrow escapes' then only heighten the horrific and very final ends of all three tales and their protagonists. Each tale's doubled and troubled death accumulates into a catalogue of disquieting deaths by the end of the collection, thus defying reference to any neat moral or aesthetic frames of judgment, let alone feminist critique based on the sex, context or generic parameters of the death. Are the sublimely grotesque deaths of all three figures in the *Trois Contes* 'prophetic' of a return to essential *human* values, to the value of life however mediocre or extraordinary outside the barbarisms of institutional religion, law or government? Or is Flaubert challenging where ultimate priorities and values, moral and aesthetic, lie?

Although the novel was unfinished, deaths of central protagonists are surprisingly absent in *Bouvard et Pécuchet*. As Flaubert's last work, and in the light of the horrors of *Trois Contes*, this strange fact, and the equally striking absence of the Flaubertian hallmark descriptions of decaying corpses or bodily mutilation perhaps shed light on the unresolved questions just posed. I have argued elsewhere that it is the unexpected love interest of *Bouvard et Pécuchet* that confounds its pseudo-scientific experiment or its parody of encyclopedic ventures which abort at every turn.[20] The death interest of the work equally confounds the Enlightenment tenets which are the source of the novel's monstrous double-take in terms of its contents but also its form. The death interest is arguably the means by which the generic tenets of the novel itself are called into question. Paradoxically, it is uninvited death that is the main trigger of new energy and life throughout, while invited death redirects the work in unforeseen directions. At the outset for example, it is the unexpected death of Bouvard's 'uncle' that releases an inheritance which allows the protagonists to retire to Les Chavignolles and begin the novel, their new life of experiment together. While their efforts in a number of disciplines confound any 'normal' process of generation or propagation of species, the rot, mould and decay that result from their experiments are more than a humorous debunking of scientific method.[21] It is these failures, not successes, which cause Bouvard and Pécuchet to embark on new endeavours. Indeed, the slow decline of their fortunes on every level is counterbalanced by the new and even more outrageous and grandiose projects outside their competence, whether the education (à la Rousseau's *Émile*) of two wards, or the envisaged productions (which Flaubert never finished) of an anti-Enlightenment *Encyclopédie, Le Dictionnaire des Idées reçues* (Dictionary of Received Ideas) or a new *Praise of Folly, Le Sottisier* (collection of howlers), as 'companion' volumes to this novel. The key moment, which sets in train the first of these regenerating thrusts of the novel, and regenerating in several senses, is the little-discussed scene of the two protagonists' invitation of death, their suicide attempt on Christmas night, and the 'divine intervention' which aborts their double, male *Liebestod*.[22] Its ingredients are interestingly black comic variations of the sadistic delay, horror, supernatural intervention and death so graphically combined in the case of John the Baptist discussed above. In *Bouvard et Pécuchet*, instead of religious persecution and imprisonment, the protagonists' suicide is envisaged as their only means to escape their despair and disappointment (horror) at not finding in books absolute truth and certainty. The thought that 'intervenes' to stop them realistically in their pseudo-romantic tracks is providential in quite worldly, not spiritual, terms. Unlike Bouvard's 'uncle', they have not made a will ('testament' in French, and a secular variant of the Old and New Testaments of the Bible), and as only children, orphans and bachelors, they have therefore no heirs along any of the recognized lines of inheritance stipulated in the Code Napoléon. That it 'so happens' it is Christmas Night, and the commemoration of the arrival of the Christ Child, is only part of the literary joke. The decision to adopt children is their practical solution to the conundrum of being intestate, providing the vital force that gives them new life, direction and a new project. As the whole episode is however built on surrogacy of models, so too is Bouvard's and Pécuchet's method of procuring their offspring. Eschewing the all-too-dangerous natural route of recourse to women of childbearing age, they opt for a male version of the 'Virgin Birth', adoption of 'instant' ready-formed children in their own image: Victor and Victorine are sibling orphans like themselves in a male and female mini-version. This 'contra-natural', as well as sacrilegious, method of reproduction (and they remain throughout the work supremely copyists) not only foregrounds their 'natural' same-sex sexual preferences. The gender implications of the roles each plays within the relationship are highlighted. In Victor and Victorine their wards, the outcome of Bouvard's and Pécuchet's Christmas Night crisis of knowledge allows a further joke on the part of their creator. In spite of educating both children outside gendered models and norms, both Victor and Victorine 'go by the book' by reverting to gender stereotype and essentialized male and female behaviour, as well as general unruliness, which counters the blueprint of the innocent child à la Rousseau at the same time. Like the near-death experiences in *Trois Contes,* Bouvard's and Pécuchet's defiance of death on Christmas Night is also a prelude to further disaster not of their own making, but is in this case revivifying. If the novel has been read as a critique or parody of the positivist dream of progress and of science as the panacea of all ills including victory over illness and mortality, this scene does more than pierce the pretensions of promethean humanism in the doubly farcical forms of Bouvard and Pécuchet. It epitomizes the site of progressing even the most self-conscious of novel forms and on several counts. Because the Christmas Night episode represents experience outside the scientific manual and puts to death the eponymous protagonists' old puppet- or clone-like selves, it allows some individuality to emerge in what are Flaubert's most bloodless creations, not least by launching their educational and surrogate parental personae. Clearly for the contents of the novel, the unfinished trail of disaster that ensues, including Victorine's rape, enlarges the scope of possible failure of new ventures. The episode also disrupts the organizational structure and pattern of the novel thus far: Bouvard's and Pécuchet's programmatic bungling through the human sciences bifurcates to include parallel patterning in the adventures of Victor and Victorine. By thus bringing the novel form itself to the brink of its own self-destruction by sheer force of knowledge and picaresque overload, the Christmas Night scene unlocks new formal heights and possibilities beyond either the 'encyclopedic novel' of Balzac's *Comédie Humaine* or Zola's *Rougon-Macquart* series, or the anti-novel in the vein of *Don Quixote* or *Tristram Shandy*.

Such stage-managed work on limit experiences as incorporated in the pivotal moments (near deaths) *as well as* the endings or *dénouements* of Flaubert's last works reveals an art of death (and death of old generic conventions) as the beginning of vibrantly renewed art when based on seemingly sterile or conventional forms. *Bouvard et Pécuchet* sheds light retrospectively on the aesthetic importance of the near deaths in *Trois Contes*, while the moral implications of the final ends of the latter make of Flaubert's unfinished novel a cautionary tale of gargantuan proportions (like the inedible monster melons Bouvard and Pécuchet grow in the text). Birthing the monstrous, however, is not of unequivocally female provenance or connected to female sexuality in either *Trois Contes* or *Bouvard et Pécuchet*. Rather, the monstrous is birthed when the doors are closed to any value system or canon of knowledge save a self-reflecting, self-serving and self-congratulatory one. Complex moral-aesthetic shifts in the last works are triggered by the acts of characters who appal for their abuses of power, wanton cruelty and violence, or experiment. By reworking the heady mix of the marriage plot and death sentence together (perhaps most overtly in the ending of *Hérodias*) as sublime site of absolute human horror, a truth in Flaubert's art is now uncovered: there is no necessarily just or unjust reward thanks to man's inhumanity to man.

If the gender of death is clearly unimportant for Flaubert, the endings of *Trois Contes* for many critics (including feminist) nevertheless invite important questions about the ultimate artistic or other end they then serve. In terms of Flaubert's ethics, the moralizing tone yet high amoral ground of the final words in *Trois Contes* pose additional problems for feminist readings since the alleged objectivity of the narrative voice of the conclusions smacks of an ironic, supercilious, observer who, if not on the side of patriarchy, does not side with its victims either. Do the endings then exemplify Flaubert's misanthropic (rather than misogynistic) sadism, or ultimately endorse his aesthetic muscularity, that is a virtuosity or even moral superiority, to remake in his image the models of grand Passion, Tragedy, or the most canonical text of all, Scripture? Or is Flaubert's treatment in *Trois Contes* and *Bouvard et Pécuchet* of limit states, including final statements and the limits of genre, tacitly formalizing the sentiment that the form and moral import of these ideal models are outmoded, uselessly idealistic in a post-revolutionary France defeated in the Franco-Prussian war?

When viewed through the optic of *Bouvard et Pécuchet*, which lacks final words, virtuosity of formal experiment as an end in itself is none the less overtly debunked by Flaubert, both in the burlesque account of the over-ambitious bungling of his copyist protagonists to follow generic prescriptions in any discipline including creative writing, and by taking them beyond the script. Following the letter of the Law exactly (copying) kills the spirit of individuality, yet creation as total freedom from models, especially for belated copyists, is equally impossible. Death put to old clichés, stereotypes, models, or generic conventions such as the *Liebestod* as demonstrated in the Christmas Night episode above, however, is the beginning not only of new life for the protagonists, but also for the generic and formal possibilities of the novel. When pressed into a new order or to carefully managed limits, what appears stereotypical, hackneyed and second-hand (including formulae for endings and 'the moral of the story') paradoxically releases startlingly vibrant individualization and innovation. By applying these aesthetic lessons from *Bouvard et Pécuchet* to *Trois Contes*, it is the combination of protagonist stereotypes—the faithful servant, the fearless Knight, the prophet unwelcome in his own land—near or final deaths as exemplary of limit situations, and of final words challenging and unseating moral or aesthetic platitudes that make these tales so alienating and familiar, revolting and compelling. The ultimate end is then to shock even the most informed or sensitive of readers from moral and aesthetic complacency since what Flaubert implies about his age and art still holds. All suffer from 'la bêtise humaine' (human stupidity) until our clichés (responses, moral judgements etc.) are put to death and Death is put to clichés in artful combination so as to revivify an appropriate moral and aesthetic sense for our times.

Instead of indifference or undecidability in the final lines and words of the *Trois Contes*, the end of each story makes tangible this shock-shift as movement beyond the script (whether vertically in the case of *Un cœur simple* and *La Légende de Saint Julien l'Hospitalier* or horizontally in the case of *Hériodias*), and arguably also beyond the representational framing devices of the stained glass window or the Biblical intertext of the two final tales. Transcendence of the expected, pithy, final moral rejoinder central to the classic tale is also delivered variously as a final shocking *coup*. In each of the *Trois Contes,* a deft and unexpected switch of tone constitutes the final single breath of the text analogous to Félicité's final gasp in *Un cœur simple.* Here, la Simonne's unreliable witness account of Félicité's last death throes is grafted into a medically knowledgeable viewpoint of the latter's afflictions, not to gender the 'unreliable' female and reliable male viewpoints, but to set up the final exorbitant use of the verb of personal opinion and religious belief, 'croire': 'and, when she exhaled for the final time, she thought she saw ['elle crut voir'], in the parting heavens, an enormous parrot, soaring above her head' (OC 177).[23] No final assessment of her death as just, unjust, timely or provident can be made in this statement by rational analysis of character, preceding events or generic form. What is made possible instead is a richly comical, empathetic, personal and imaginative other version. In *La Légende de Saint Julien l'Hospitalier*, the tone also shifts dramatically in the closing final sentence, which is also separated visually by a blank line. The third-person voice of pseudo-chronicle from somewhere alongside Julien's final transfiguration is abruptly earthed by the matter-of-fact voiceover in the first person, which particularizes and resets the fantastic in a different light in 'real' time and space through the image of a representation in a stained-glass window:

> The roof flew off, the firmament opened; and Julien ascended into the wide, blue space, face to face with our Saviour Jesus, who was bearing him heavenwards.
>
> And so by and large the story goes of Saint Julien the Hospitalier, as told in a stained glass window in a church in my country. (OC 187)

In *Hérodias*, similarly, the revised version of the standard account of the beheading of John the Baptist shifts to a place outside the authority and momentous religious significance of the Bible account, debunked less in the use of the aramaic names for familiar figures (such as

Ioakananann for John) than in the coda of pure fiction. As with the fictional digression concerning Mannaeï to focus attention elsewhere on the supernatural, here the elsewhere is the natural. The issue is one of the most practical and banal of human concerns, and one which also poses the chief problem at the core of crime writing. What does one do with the body, or even a bit of it, after a murder? The final line (which is also a final mini-paragraph) is a masterstroke of bathos and post-gallows humour: 'Because it was very heavy, they carried the head in turn ['alternativement']' (OC 199). In its other sense of 'alternatively', 'alternativement' exemplifies Flaubert's art of rewriting differently for his times even the most sacrosanct of forms (the Bible) and literary conventions such as those of tragedy, where death takes the final curtain.

The disquieting moral of the *Trois Contes* as a collection is that the absolute of death or its more affable face, marriage, are not in themselves the *dénouement*, end or acme of human expression. It is only by going beyond both marriage and death, as is seen structurally in Flaubert's writing of his tales in their crucial final sentences which plot the after of the aftermath, that raw (in)humanity is discovered. The impossibly weighty bearing away of the prophet's voiceless head at the end of *Hérodias* says almost more than the fulfilment of John's prophetic words in a time to come. The final line of extenuating circumstance is a moment to ponder and contemplate the full horror (weight) of human inhumanity regardless of sex or gender, to require readers to acknowledge the effects of a single life and epoch-changing human acts. The only moral response to such hubris is compassion for such folly latent in everyone, and for the value of human frailty.

As subversions of models and unclassifiable as Realist or Romantic, Flaubert's last prose narratives demonstrably run the gauntlet of offence to canonical forms (the *conte*, the novel) as well as offence to public morality, for which his *Madame Bovary* was condemned. Close feminist rereading of the limits of the limit situations in *Trois Contes* and *Bouvard et Pécuchet* as expression of Flaubert's aesthetics judged by art's three classic absolutes has shown that the last works cannot be judged as misogynistic in style or moral. Neither can the seeming narrative aloofness and impersonality of his endings be labelled masculinist at worst and arrogantly male at best, or if gender-free, undecidable. Because Flaubert punctures the tenets of a male high aesthetics (virtuosity, formal experiment, imitation of models) as part of 'la bêtise humaine' in *Bouvard et Pécuchet* by turning draughtsmen-copyists into mock-artists (albeit in the hands of a more able practitioner), his muscular art is no synonym of 'art for art's sake'. Likewise, aesthetic dogmas about the ends of art being the good, the beautiful and the true, or the tale as idealized exemplum complete with final moral, have been severely tried by Flaubert's aesthetics of death in *Trois Contes.* It is precisely through feminist perspectives that Flaubert's own challenge to the muscular style he himself lauds can be identified as that which Flaubert also presses to the limit. Perhaps it was through railing against the style, subjects, and aesthetic expression of his particularly tenacious female interlocutrice, Louise Colet, and his constant epistolary engagement with Mlle Leroyer de Chantepie and especially George Sand, to whom he dedicated *Un cœur simple*, about art's ends and means, that Flaubert was forced and enabled to separate clichéd, canonical high art from an art wrestling to articulate the sublime in human folly. If a feminist rereading of Flaubert's last works thus unpicks virile aesthetic muscularity from the *muscular* flexing of form in Flaubert's *œuvre* as putting death to cliché, tired form and platitudes including aesthetic ones, then two related areas of investigation for feminist work reopen. Flaubert's many positive representations of women and un-masculine men can first be explored more deeply with regard to the 'leaky' aspects of these figurations present within his own muscular style. Second, Flaubert's concatenation of death and the limits of form challenges the classic absolutes of art with an art of the absolute. It is the dual force of the word—the absolute frees but also completes, as the endings of *Trois Contes* so graphically depict—that a feminist reading looking for incomplete accounts can help to unravel. Against the absolutism of art's perfection or purity (whether forms, models or aesthetic expression), a feminist approach to Flaubert's muscular aesthetics reveals a more radical sense of untying rules from conditions. The corollary of this line of investigation is the question of Flaubert's canonicity and place within the canon of the nineteenth-century male novelists such as Stendhal, Balzac, and Zola. By testing the limits of the clichés and formulae of marriage and death in the *conte* and novel, and revivifying both to move the parameters of these genres to new limits, Flaubert's non-conformity with his contemporaries is striking. By reinvesting in new versions of older story traditions in his return to the cycle of tales in *Trois Contes*, or to the highly digressive quest narrative in *Bouvard et Pécuchet*, Flaubert's feat is to reveal the old clichés of marriage and death as still central to the modern novel of his canonical male contemporaries. It is then not unsurprising if Flaubert's most enduring and memorable creations remain *imaginary* female protagonists (Emma Bovary, Salammbô and Félicité) or that his most tenacious interlocutors on his style are his interlocutrices. It is their individuality, personality, and separation from the herd that should also inspire feminist critics to beware the trap of deadly clichés.

9

Manly Men and Womanly Women

Aesthetics and Gender in Fontane's *Effi Briest* and *Der Stechlin*

Patricia Howe

In the first chapter of *Effi Briest* (Effi Briest) Effi tells her girlfriends about the man who was once in love with her mother:

> 'I've seen him too, Mamma's old friend, over in Schwantikow. He's a Landrat, and very handsome and manly.'
> 'That's the main thing,' said Hertha.
> 'Of course it's the main thing, "women should be womanly, men should be manly"—that's one of Papa's favourite sayings, as you know.' (NFA 7, 173–74, p. 11)[1]

Paternal wisdom deceives Effi in one respect, for in Wilhelmine society womanliness does not precede manliness but follows it; women are seen as deviating from and dependent on men. If one adds to this Fontane's avowed preference for 'Magdalenas' rather than 'Genovevas', for transgressing, suffering, but ultimately submissive women, and his scant sympathy for his progressive heroines, one might expect these divisions to prevail in his work. Indeed feminist critics (and the first writer of an extended piece of academic criticism was a woman) tend to want more rebellion and less acquiescence.[2] But *Effi Briest* and *Der Stechlin* (The Stechlin) suggest that gender is a mutable concept, susceptible to change as the discourses that construct it are threatened by their own contradictions and by the passage of time. Feminist criticism often focuses on divisions between classes and genders, but I shall suggest that by reading these texts inclusively, if occasionally against the grain, and by noting the exchanges that take place between the aesthetic and the moral centres and margins of the text, we can see how the conventional model of gender is unsettled. In this way the configuration of womanhood in Fontane's novels contributes to a movement away from classical aesthetics towards modernism.

Every age has a temporary canon, a 'repertoire of active genres', but in Germany the novel's bid for canonicity is retarded by critics who see its lack of aesthetic regulation and its ability to model a world that resembles the 'real' one as potentially subversive.[3] But with the rise of the middle classes after 1848 and the unification of Germany in 1871 the novel's capacity for interaction with life makes it the ideal form for capturing the complex, contemporary world. The problem of its lack of aesthetic regulation is taken up in the 1850s by Friedrich Spielhagen, an admirer of Schiller's political views, who is stung by his hero's description of the novelist as the poet's half-brother. Drawing on the aesthetics of Schiller, Wilhelm von Humboldt and Friedrich Theodor Vischer, Spielhagen tries to redeem the novel from its apparent formlessness by bringing it into line retrospectively with classical aesthetics.[4] From the novel's ability to create pictures, which seems to him to invite comparison with the superior, plastic arts, he establishes normative criteria of objectivity, totality and representation. Objectivity requires the author to withdraw behind the action, avoiding narratorial intrusion which promotes formlessness. Totality approximates to the unity and completeness of the plastic arts, counteracting the Romantics' blurring of prose and poetry and their taste for fragments. When completeness proves impossible totality comes to mean integrating all elements into the relationship between narrator and hero, in practice making the hero the author/narrator's mouthpiece. Representation stresses mimesis and ultimately asserts the priority of the 'real' world over the fictional one.

After 1871 'the real world' means, above all, the 'manly cause' of unification and empire, which prompts a re-interpretation of past and present, and of the writer's role. The Romantic prophet, the cultured mediator of the *Vor-März* becomes an authority with the obligation to make the novel mirror the real world. This often means that fidelity to a moral, social or political intention is as powerful a reality as circumstantial authenticity.[5] The borders between serious and popular novels grow hazy, the middle classes read voluminous historical novels, and Wilhelm II suggests that art should sustain the common people after a hard day's work by reminding them of 'the ideals', but it should not show their misery to be greater than it is.[6] This prohibition reflects German scepticism about Naturalism and Zola's experimental method. Fontane's generation are wary of the apparent pessimism of this method, of its links with social democracy and of its immorality; Fontane suggests that its inherent determinism is unbelievable. Above all, Zola's experiments seem incompatible with the German novel's traditional focus on the intellectual, spiritual formation of an individual, usually but not inevitably male.[7]

The tension between serving a cause and showing a complex, modern world shapes the novel's conventions. The former promotes monolingualism, single perspective, closed form. The narrator must use a linguistic register commensurate with his authority and public responsibilities.[8] The writer who disregards the stylizations imposed by ideology reduces the chances of publication in journals that insist to varying degrees on moral wholesomeness and political conformity. Pluralism, polyphonic discourse and open form, which we now associate with Fontane and in a different way with women's writing, can only be muted, tentative techniques of resistance. Women writers and eponymous heroines are discouraged except in moralising, popular literature. Spielhagen advises George Eliot that *Middlemarch* would not be 'so barbaric (in the aesthetic sense)' if she had followed his prescription to base novels on action, but then she is 'a woman, an Englishwoman and without real classical and philosophical training'.[9]

It is superfluous to say that authority is masculine. It is informed by 'a military ethos [. . .] and a self-conscious masculinity that viewed women as weak, sub-ordinate creatures', and by 'a fear that German virtue was threatened by enemies without and within, the latter including homosexuals and women'.[10] But even without property rights, independent legal status or much formal education, and assigned to the domestic domain, women know that they can participate vicariously in the public sphere and benefit from the 'manly project' through their husbands, fathers or other legal guardians, but *only* through them. This is reflected in the way womanhood is constructed. The ideal German woman is not Coventry Patmore's 'angel in the house' but the 'woman whom the world talks about least', that is, she whose vicarious participation in public matters is so discreet that she *appears* to inhabit a totally private sphere.[11]

Disclaiming the Prussian obsession with rank and with being at the centre of things, Fontane treats the canon as a dressing-up box rather than as an icon.[12] His views about literature are pragmatic and strategic, reflecting both a temperament that recoils from the dangerous silliness of extremes and his dependence on publication. He rejects a hierarchy of talent for the more liberal view that all sorts of new writers can broaden the novel's range.[13] He is sceptical about Spielhagen's theories: he is capricious about narratorial intrusion, and stresses the lack of action in his own novels, but happily places the novel's pursuit of verisimilitude close to that of the plastic arts, especially contemporary art. Like all authors destined to become canonical, he wrestles with the 'anxiety of influence'.[14] This may inform his critical view of the artificial dialogue of Goethe's *Hermann and Dorothea* (1797), the text taken by Spielhagen to bridge the gap between classical epics and modern fiction, and his resistance to Spielhagen's comparison of *Effi Briest* with *Die Wahlverwandtschaften* (1809) (Elective Affinities). But Goethe's and Schiller's dramatic heroines offer a resource that counters the centrality of male heroes in the German novel. The 'great precursors' enable him to create networks of reference through which his own works can be read and can enter a tradition, but the canonical legacy also interacts with current debates about nature and civilization with which his journalism keeps him abreast.

Insofar as these debates concern womanhood and womanliness they are still governed by the idea of 'Bestimmung', which may be translated as 'destiny' but also implies regulation and purpose. Woman's natural purpose is seen as marriage and children, a view of nature that begins in biology but serves the ends of political unity and economic efficiency, and so demands the involvement of both body and mind, or in the language of the time, body and soul.[15] The emphasis on nature in entries on women's education, legal position and marriage in Brockhaus's *Konversationslexikon* for 1894 disguises the extent to which woman's so-called destiny is the product of conventional socialization. The female soul is moulded by internalizing external constraints and values, some of which are shared with men, such as fear of disgrace and ridicule, desire for orderliness and diligence, and an ethic of achievement. But while all women must be regulated into decency and respectability, it is class that determines the extent to which infidelity, illegitimate children or paid employment are tolerated (Panke-Kochinke, p. 1). This is all a long way from nature and destiny, and suggests that what is meant here by nature may simply be a set of conventions, invoked positively by the author and negatively by feminist critics who see it as the projection of male fantasies of sexuality, weakness, or inferiority. But Fontane's critical reviews, for example, of a performance of Gretchen's role in *Faust* in December 1877, where he discusses the elements of 'natural naturalness' and 'manufactured naturalness', suggest that he knows nature to be a slippery concept (*Causerien über Theater*, NFA 22/1, 626–29). Perhaps the best we can do here in considering the part nature plays in the construction of womanliness is to bear in mind its shifting meanings and the sleight of hand that makes them synonymous.

Some of the discrepancies and gaps inherent in the contemporary view of womanhood emerge in Fontane's attitude to the women in his private and professional life. His preference for suffering, submissive heroines is at odds with his practical need for steadfast, capable and determined women, able to cope with his artistic need for solitude and freedom.[16] Satirical mockery marks his representation of strong women in fiction, perhaps reflecting his unwilling dependence on the rejected category of healing and nurturing Genovevas. But these fictional figures relate only tenuously to the complex relationships with his wife, his daughter, his sister and the female friends in whom he confided and who supplied him with society gossip, material for his novels and insights into woman's predicament.[17] His most problematic real-life relationship is with his daughter, Martha, who is closest to him and openly jealous of her mother; Regina Dieterle argues that his narrative treatment of father-daughter relationships and his obsession with girls on the brink of womanhood originates in this relationship.[18] But he disguises real life sources fastidiously and dreads *Effi Briest* falling into the hands of its 'heroine', despite his efforts to disguise her story.[19] In fact women readers were eager to claim his stories as their own, but this kind of popularity is a mixed blessing because it also invites comparison between his heroines and those of popular novelists like Eugenia Marlitt or with the so-called 'Berlin' novel, which he rejects vigorously. Yet he is encouraged when women show serious recognition of his talent and, in turn, acknowledges talent in women.

Despite Fontane's general preference for the small accidental population of late realist novels *Effi Briest* refers to over eighty different female figures. All feed into Effi's attempts to establish a coherent sense of self and a habitable world within the discourses on education, marriage, health, social and political allegiance that shape womanhood in this society As Effi pursues an identity and a role these discourses are articulated in choruses of approval and disapproval, claims and counterclaims on her mind. She compares herself consciously and is compared with other women, including her mother, her girlfriends, older and younger, married and unmarried women, professional women, and even—though she resists this comparison—with her servants. This confronts her with a succession of identities that describe the parameters of womanhood. In the early part of the novel a series of imaginary and imagined personae create the illusion of freedom and choice: her mother describes her as 'daughter of the air' and bare-back rider (NFA 7, 172, p. 10); in her friends' imagination she becomes the Cinderella-like *Das Käthchen von Heilbronn* of Kleist's play; in her own she is Cinderella awakening as a princess, a fantasy that confuses her with Sleeping Beauty; she identifies with a series of romantic literary heroines: the faithful wife, Ella, in Ernst Wichert's romantic comedy *Ein Schritt vom Wege* (One False Step), the old lady saved from danger in Brentano's poem 'Die Gottesmauer' (God's Wall), the unfaithful queen in Heine's 'Spanische Atriden' (Spanish Atridae). Contradictory though they are, and therefore unhelpful as models, these poetic roles have a clarity and sense of being sanctioned that the restless Effi lacks. They are already redeemed as art. Whether they redeem the dismal determinism of her socialization is less clear, because Fontane introduces them in dialogues, letters and reflection, which makes them unstable. None the less Effi's imaginary identities, and the labels and roles imposed on her suggest the struggle for possession of a vacant soul, and this may explain why, in comparisons with more driven heroines like Anna Karenina or Emma Bovary, she seems insipid. Effi hopes for salvation, and her story has been read through and against Christian iconography, but it is also a secular morality, an attempt to negotiate a path to womanhood through a landscape peopled with other female figures proclaiming moral and social alternatives and echoing with received ideas.[20]

Effi is socialized by a chorus of voices whose ideas about womanhood are distorted and already old-fashioned. Her chief educators are her parents and the local pastor, in accordance with aristocratic Protestant practice, hence the final discussion about responsibility implicates the pastor's poor discipline. Her typically meagre formal education does not enable her to defend herself against coercion into the role of submissive wife or lover. Her husband sneers at her ignorance and her lover exploits it. She can be seduced by Heine's poetry because she does not know that it is being misquoted to that end. Nor do the traditional accomplishments of aristocratic girls—painting, playing the piano, reading approved literature—provide an emotional resource while Innstetten pursues his career or a living after her divorce. This inadequate education cannot mitigate the effects of a childhood that is extended by her parents, her husband and even her lover beyond accepted limits. At fourteen the Protestant daughter is confirmed and effectively becomes marriageable, yet Effi is repeatedly referred to as a child and the text confirms her infantilization literally by not letting her speak for herself at crucial moments, such as her engagement, her marriage, her divorce. She ultimately denies the similarity between herself at fourteen and the coquettish Cora Ring, but to Sidonie von Grasenabb it is palpable. It is a sign of the changing times that Effi and Cora may arrive at social exclusion by different routes, Effi as an unfaithful wife, while Cora, in Sidonie's words, 'will go to America and become a millionairess or a Methodist preacher; which ever it is she's a lost woman' (NFA 7, 305; p. 118).

The purpose of Effi's upbringing is marriage, where, again, she inherits old-fashioned ideas. Her father enjoins her and her bridegroom to embrace their respective roles in the image, found in Campe's 'Väterlicher Rath für meine Tochter' (Fatherly advice to my daughter) (1789) of a plant entwining itself with a strong support. Briest is, like Campe, a benevolent father teaching his only daughter how to approach her female destiny and to understand that men and marriage are far from perfect, but by the 1880s, when *Effi Briest* is set, the image has trickled down to popular novels, and is already treated satirically in the opening paragraph of Anthony Trollope's *Rachel Ray* (1863); there it becomes the failing of the desperately dependent woman who, with 'tendrils creeping along the ground', 'will swear conjugal obedience sometimes to her cook, sometimes to her grandchild, sometimes to her lawyer. Any standing corner, post, or stump, strong enough to bear her weight will suffice.'[21] Although the poetic image embarrasses Effi's mother, it is she who enforces the contradictory idea of twisting her daughter into shape for what is supposed to be her natural destiny.

Novelistic patterns and social expectations also inform society's discourse on marriage and hence Effi's aspirations. To the newly-engaged Effi, Innstetten's aristocratic birth, promising career and good looks qualify him as 'the right one' (NFA 7, 182; p. 18), although her comment that anyone answering this description would be acceptable shows that it is not a personal wish-list, but a traditional recipe. Her sister-under the skin is Mary Wortle in Trollope's *Dr. Wortle's School* (1880), who cannot see any reason why she could not love the young Lord Carstairs: 'It would be very nice, she thought, to love him. He was sweet-tempered, bright, and thoroughly good-humoured; and then his position in the world was very high. Not for a moment did she tell herself that she would love him.'[22] Reader, she marries him.

A chorus of approving comments traces Effi's progress from the fantasy identities of girlhood to briefly successful wife, offering a sort of continuous assessment; she is 'such a young wife (NFA 7, 271; p. 92), an 'enchanting little wife' (NFA 7, 293; p. 110), 'an angel' (NFA 7, 325; p. 135) and 'the most delightful wife in town' (NFA 7, 360; p. 165). Ironically she survives life in the remote, isolated town of Kessin, where she cannot choose her home, run her household, appoint her own staff or look after her child, only to lose the rewards of Innstetten's promotion, which give her a domestic role as Annie's mother and a social one as his wife. Divorce, degradation and banishment follow, proving that success, like choice, is an illusion.

Success dissolves in the collective 'we women' (NFA 7, 221; p. 49), a notion introduced to Effi by her mother which becomes a counterpoint to the chorus of approval. Phrases like 'we women must be cautious' (NFA 7, 191; p. 26), 'we women are not as bad as that' (NFA 7, 221; p. 49), 'wives and mothers' (NFA 7, 268; p. 89), 'we wives' (NFA 7, 325; p. 135), create a ghostly forum in which Effi tries to measure her ability to feel guilt against that of other women, and concludes that 'I don't feel that, or not properly, or not enough [. . .]. If all women are like this, then it's terrible, and if they're not, and I hope they aren't, then things don't look good for me' (NFA 7, 359; p. 164).

Innstetten echoes Effi's private reflections when he confides in Wüllersdorf, and so again opens the gap between the self and society's expectations:

> I am from this moment on, and there's no going back on it, the object of your sympathy—not in itself a pleasant thought—and you will weigh every word you hear me exchange with my wife, whether you intend to or not, and if my wife were to talk about infidelity, or sit in judgment, as wives do, on what other women get up to, I wouldn't know where to look. (NFA 7, 375; p. 178)

Both Effi and Innstetten fear disgrace and ridicule or exclusion, but cannot stop themselves from provoking them. They show more integrity, but a weaker sense of self-preservation than those in their society who treat infidelity as a practical problem rather than as an existential crisis. But this crisis is not just a matter of psychology, but of the aesthetics of the text. Fontane sharpens the plight of his central characters by making them singular. Both are only children, they have one child, and Innstetten has no living relatives except some distant cousins and nothing that connects him to his parents but a name and a roll-top desk. Moreover, Effi is surrounded on the one hand by women who combine the severest propriety with self-indulgence and on the other by women whose humanity co-exists with disregard for social norms, but not by other young, aristocratic wives and mothers, who might provide a comparable reflection of her own situation. There are young girls, eligible young women, older women who know how to manage their husbands, single women who fend for themselves—always with some loss of dignity or reputation—but there is none whose choices so clearly reflect the constraints of the social, political system at a moment when these are changing. Effi's family connection with Prussia's rise stretches from the battle of Königgrätz in which her ancestor participated to her daughter's birth on its anniversary. Innstetten's service in the army, study of law and attachment to Bismarck's staff make him a shining contributor to the 'manly project'. This union of the personal and the political raises the stakes in their marriage. But Effi's hankering for 'das Aparte' ('something out of the ordinary', NFA 7, 185; p. 21) aligns her with the alien Other, the foreigner, who is by definition outside both the new Germany and rearguard attempts to maintain the old Prussia.[23] Hence her choices are not private but exemplary: the validation of all the other ways of being a woman in this society depends on them.

Interdependent moral choices belong to morality plays, but modern moralities ask about the cognitive processes involved in choosing right and wrong, rather than assuming that these are given, and this is what Effi's reflections on her predicament suggest. Her questions counteract the temptation to excuse her transgressions, her infidelity, her knowing abandonment of her child, because it is easy to justify these in terms of social constraints or to blame her husband's coldness or her mother's match-making. Ultimately even, perhaps especially, a feminist reading has to accept that she knowingly transgresses. Otherwise it dismisses her anxieties, her fantasies and disappointments, and, above all, what she thinks and feels about her failure compared with what she is expected to feel. The gap, which she consciously acknowledges, is the locus of her difference from other women and of potential change in the idea of womanliness. It is the turning-point in the transformation of her early fear of Innstetten, because he has principles and she has none, into her final condemnation of him as a man without real love.

Against the network of discourses that enforce a rigid concept of gender, Fontane sets another that blurs it. The limits of gender and generation are unsettled by affective preferences, by familial relationships and by illnesses. The process begins with Effi's boyish appearance and behaviour; she wears a sailor's smock, and imagines herself as a cabin boy and a midshipman, or a young lieutenant wanting to marry her mother. Clearly Effi's path to womanhood starts a long way off, but scarcely has she travelled it when Innstetten falls prey to the kind of hysterical, nervous illness attributed to women. In this society illness is gendered and testifies to moral or psychological weakness—we are not far from Freud's view that the hysterical body is a symbolic body. Women suffer from hysteria, men from neurasthenia. Hysteria is considered unmanly and un-German—after Sedan it is attributed to the French—whereas fighting a duel is seen as a test of strong nerves. However, when men are found to suffer from 'railway spine', a condition in which physical shock has the same symptoms as psychic shock, nervous illness is accepted as a male condition.[24] Like other female maladies, hysteria threatens to dissolve the unitary body in tears, in fainting fits and daydreams; health regimes, therefore, insist on woman's need for containment with precisely prescribed exercise programmes, supervised diets and cures, such as Effi undertakes. When Innstetten discovers the letters from Crampas he cannot contain himself and gives way to the nervous temperament indicated earlier by his liking for Wagner, whose music famously prompted hysterical crises among women. Innstetten's most profound crisis comes when he returns to Berlin by train after killing his rival. The 'unmanning' of Innstetten may support the recent suggestion that a 'queer' reading of *Effi Briest* could show 'all the interactions between the three men [Innstetten, Wüllersdorf, Crampas] as an effort to disguise, contain and mediate (through the figure of Effi) their desire for each other'.[25] It might be a counterpart to the struggle for Effi's soul, but it might also leave Effi as no more than a possession and a cipher. As an empty vessel or a soul to be claimed she is much more than this.

The most extreme form of generational confusion is quasi-incestuous; Effi's choice in a text that is not richly populated with wealthy young men in want of a wife, seems to be between remaining her father's daughter and marrying a man who might have been her father. In her heart she chooses her real father, returning to his house for holidays without her husband, being summoned from banishment by him, being buried in his garden. Contrary to the notion that fathers are always uncertain, Effi's one sure identity is being Briest's daughter; the name 'Effi von Innstetten' is presented throughout the text as alien or inappropriate. Ultimately she authorizes her own story, reflecting on it, interpreting it, and with her decision to be called Effi Briest on her grave finalizing her identity in union with the novel.

As the aesthetic focus who is banished to the moral and social margins of her society, Effi denies the naive aesthetic of fairy tale underpinning many nineteenth-century novels, whereby the good and attractive triumph. But Fontane does not reject this benevolent model in favour of Flaubertian *impassibilité*; he displaces the moral centre to the periphery, connecting it with the aesthetic centre by means of sympathy. The narrative perspective and narratorial intrusions in *Effi Briest* testify to this sympathy, as do the kindly interventions of characters like Gieshübler, the hunchbacked apothecary; of Rummschüttel, the doctor, who tacitly supports Effi's reluctance to return to Kessin and later asks her parents to take her back; of her father, who finally defies society by accepting her; and especially of Roswitha, originally her child's nurse, who cares for Effi after her divorce. Even Innstetten and Wüllersdorf acknowledge Roswitha's superiority: Wüllersdorf 's comment that 'she's a cut above us' (NFA 7, 419; p. 215) acknowledges that morality does not depend on class or gender.[26] It anticipates the idea of a masculine morality which involves obeying the rules and a feminine morality which involves caring for people and things (Panke-Kochinke, p. 159). The last encounter between Effi and her mother is a struggle between a feminine and a masculine morality, with Effi condemning Innstetten's inability to love, and her mother telling Effi she brought her troubles on herself by disobeying the rules. As this shows, Fontane does not endow his characters with moral attitudes along gender lines: both male *and* female figures nurture, care for, love and heal Effi, and she is condemned by both male *and* female guardians of the moral conventions enshrined in the alliance of Lutheran church, Prussian state and army. In the end morality is not even peculiar to species: the unconditional loyalty of Effi's faithful Newfoundlander, Rollo, who seems set to lie on her grave for ever, suggests that, ultimately, manly men and womanly women may be less important than dogged dogs. Ten years later, nurse and dog are conflated in the Newfoundlander Nana in J.M. Barrie's *Peter Pan* (1904).

Effi Briest undermines the contained, finished, 'masculine' text that emerges from Spielhagen's aesthetics of the novel, and, as Jeffrey Schneider (p. 278) argues, exposes masculine authority as unstable and incapable of creating a habitable world. Instead of Spielhagen's male hero, a mouthpiece for author, narrator or society, and a plot generated by action, there is a female figure, who remains the aesthetic centre while failing to meet the moral, social, political and legal claims and counterclaims imposed on her. The narrator's sympathy for her defies Spielhagen's demand for objectivity, while containment—implicit in his idea of 'totality'—proves impossible. Thematically and formally the novel leaves gaps, questions and ambiguities, ending with gestures of closure rather than resolution.[27]

Like *Effi Briest, Der Stechlin* asks how we deal with the claims and burdens of the past, determine what is fittest to survive and construct a viable, humane future, not least for women—all issues that are germane to the subject of canonicity and feminism. *Der Stechlin* questions the concept of womanliness more overtly than *Effi Briest*, extending the range of female figures while foregrounding an idea rather than an individual. Both opening and closing chapters emphasize the priority of the idea by summoning up the multiple entities that share the name of Stechlin—a place, a lake, a castle, and a family, the patriarchal hero, Dubslav von Stechlin and the novel itself. Further, the debate between a valued past and a viable future becomes a universal, not a private or parochial one because the Stechlins enjoy a symbiotic link with the world beyond their secluded, provincial existence. Lake Stechlin, generally silent and calm, shows its links with the outside world by responding to eruptions elsewhere by throwing up a water-spout; or at really historic moments, like the Lisbon earthquake, 'instead of the water-spout, a red rooster comes up and crows loudly so it can be heard all over the countryside' (NFA 7/I, 5).[28]

Although society in *Der Stechlin* is still dominated by men, women's growing influence is more consciously debated than in *Effi Briest*. Pastor Lorenz asserts that 'in the end women decide everything' (NFA 7/I, 254), but the novel does not demonstrate this conclusively and female figures are closer to representative modes of womanhood than to unique personalities, an effect enhanced by the fact that, if one includes references to saints, biblical figures, queens, and background figures, the novel has a huge accidental female population. Women are measured by their commitment to the past and potential contribution to the future through children, legacies, or promises, but none of these comes to fruition before the end of the novel. In the first section women are absent, functional figures—dead or hypothetical wives, or potential dinner guests. Unlike his father, Dubslav rejects serial marriages, which encourage this unparticularized view of women, leaving his son, Woldemar to ensure the survival of the Stechlins and to replenish their fortunes.[29] As Dubslav's health declines and Woldemar chooses a bride and a career, the random, functional image of women becomes selective and focuses on representative modes of being female.

Contemporary models of womanliness combine with the legacies of history and mythology. Three generations and ways of being a woman are represented by Adelheid von Stechlin, Dubslav's spinster sister,

Armgard, whom Woldemar eventually marries, and Agnes, who may possibly be Dubslav's child. The glories of Prussia and empire mean nothing to the rigidly puritanical, class-conscious and reactionary Adelheid von Stechlin, who belongs to an older, more exclusive, local aristocracy that believes its survival to be paramount. The celibate, childless *Stiftsdame* contributes to the future by promising to leave Woldemar her fortune if he marries a Lutheran wife from the Mark Brandenburg. In the event Woldemar's bride, Armgard von Barby, comes from the wealthy, urbane European aristocracy, but impresses by her quiet preference for country life and the charitable, conservative role of Biedermeier lady. This picture of cosy domesticity is briefly unsettled by the indeterminacy surrounding Woldemar's choice of Armgard rather than her sister; his proposal is a gap in the text, represented by Armgard's dim feeling that she might almost be engaged. Yet she rises to the challenge of marriage, which defeats her more extravert sister, and may still fulfil the hope Woldemar places in her 'The future lies with *you*, then' (NFA 7/I, 360). This future is more obviously presaged in Agnes, the small, illegitimate daughter of a prostitute and granddaughter of the local witch, whom Dubslav takes into his house to keep him company in his final illness. She becomes a focus for diverse charitable impulses and political views, chiefly for Adelheid's fear of a socialist future, for the reactionary benevolence of princess Ermyntrud Katzler who tries to take her into the orphanage she is opening, and for Armgard's more liberal suggestion that she and Woldemar should adopt her. But the final word on her future is that of Krippelstapel, the teacher, who suggests that the better, if more hazardous way, would be to let her make something of herself.

The novel questions female identity more thoroughly, and more probingly through Armgard's sister, Melusine, in whom the 'new woman' co-exists problematically with a mythological figure. Melusine disrupts received ideas of womanliness both as a divorced, aristocratic woman with no real role in society and as one of the elusive, seductive, ultimately untamed Melusine figures who float through Fontane's work, sisters to the Undines of Fouqué, Droste-Hülshoff, or later, Bachmann.[30] Compared with Effi Briest's longing for salvation, Melusine's restlessness makes her an unhoused soul. She threatens regulated German womanhood, calling traditional views into question. While the legendary figure may be read as a protest against the narrowness of woman's role, as a symbol of artistic freedom and imagination, it is difficult to see her as politically radical, because the legend is constrained by the metonymic discourse of realism. The legendary elements may point beyond prevailing views of womanhood, and the implication is that they point forward to a broader vision, but they are also inseparable from a figure who in realistic terms is an anachronism. The references to England, where Melusine has lived, to which Woldemar is sent, and where ideas about the new woman are said to originate, do not make her a modern figure since she leads the dependent life of feudal womanhood. In her conversations with the Christian Democrat Lorenz she is eager to listen to democratic ideas, but shies away from their practical implications for her own class. Neither the legendary nor the realistic Melusine can find or create a habitable world for herself or for anyone else.

Many readers see Melusine through the sympathetic gaze of indulgent older men, of her father, Dubslav von Stechlin, Pastor Lorenz, and, not least, the narrator. But recent critics read her increasingly against the grain of narratorial sympathy as frigid, hysterical, narcissistic, unproductive. Edda Ziegler links Melusine figures, as Effi is linked, with 'das Aparte' and its connotations of the alien, the erotic, but ultimately uncommitted and childish.[31] Melusine's pact with the equally uncommitted Pastor Lorenz may be inspired by genuine political insight or by a craving for excitement. Lorenz undermines his promise to Dubslav not to interfere if his heir reverts to the ways of the past by adding 'I won't be the one guiding him. That's taken care of. The times will have their say, and beside the times, the new household, the pale young wife and perhaps the beautiful Melusine, too' (NFA 7/I, 344). Perhaps Dubslav should hear a warning in this, for Melusine believes that 'We should love everything old, as far as it has a claim to be loved, but we should really live for the new' (NFA 7/I, 251). Yet Melusine's history casts doubt on her words, and her discussions with Lorenz disguise the fact that neither of them will be active in bringing about change; at most they will bless the enterprise and applaud from the sidelines.

Melusine, for all her restlessness, does not develop. She has returned to her old life in her father's house after an episode in a railway tunnel on her honeymoon, which persuaded her that marriage would be misery. The usual explanations, namely that Melusine's husband claims his conjugal rights too eagerly or not at all, are immaterial; what matters is that she rejects the 'paradise' of marriage evoked by her husband's name, Ghiberti, the name of the sculptor who made the 'paradise doors' of the Baptistry in Florence. The gap diverts readers from Melusine's personality to the man and the institution that she rejects. The absurd suggestion near the end of the novel that Woldemar's friend, Czako, would improve his chances of marrying her if he Italianized his name, shows that her unchanging personality is the deciding factor.

The lives of women of other classes suggest that, in the absence of a modern concept of womanliness, Melusine and her aristocratic sisters are only acting imagined roles. Armgard models herself on female saints and queens. Ermyntrud Katzler, the princess married to a forester, lurches uncertainly to and fro across the social divide as she embraces motherhood and charity. Equally confused about their roles are the parvenue Frau Gundermann, who has not learned to deal with children or servants, and Riekchen Schickedanz, the Barbys' landlady, whose unexpected wealth, in the form of two lottery wins left by her husband, destroys her sense of where she belongs and makes her think she is a princess in a fairy tale. Their lives appear frivolous beside those of poor country women like Agnes's grandmother, of her mother, the prostitute in Berlin, or of Hedwig, the servant, but they reflect, albeit less urgently, uncertainty about how to survive as women. The only answers are regressive or circular: Melusine returns to her father; Armgard retreats to the country; as most of Ermyntrud Katzler's daughters die in infancy, she decides to open an orphanage, but there is no way of knowing whether the image of a mother of lost children taking in the children of lost mothers promises wholeness or threatens destruction. Hedwig leaves successive employers because they pester her and refuse to provide her with a proper place to sleep (the two problems are really one, a combination of lust and parsimony), until she finally becomes Armgard's maid, a step which combines personal improvement with reinforcing social divisions.

Both the uneasy shifts between classes and the blurring of gender are treated satirically: Adelheid, who herself slaughters geese, condemns smoking as a masculine habit; Dubslav imagines his new daughter-in-law giving a ball after his death at which the guests will include a male pianist whose long hair sweeps the keys, and a short-haired female translator of so-called adultery plays. The confusion of classes and of genders contributes to a sense that the future of the Stechlins and of women will be alien and incomprehensible to their forebears, while the satirical tone may disguise regret that this is so. Like Thomas Mann's *Buddenbrooks* (1901), *Der Stechlin* ends with a female voice hoping for a future that preserves the best of the past, but the novel offers no confirmation that the hope will be fulfilled. The ambiguity of the last words underlines the unresolved issues of the text, which are kept at bay, until his death, by the central, unifying, conciliatory presence of Dubslav.

If the canon is, as Bloom suggests, what is worth re-reading, then Fontane enters it by ignoring Spielhagen's limited aesthetics in favour of a more ambiguous, open form which becomes a legacy to later writers in re-readings, new interpretations and original works.[32] As he moves away from depicting a central female figure who falls victim to conflicting claims, to a group representing a debate which the text itself does not resolve, he shows women's lives to be constructed increasingly by contradictory and unstable discourses. Implicitly he questions Friedrich Theodor Vischer's view that the family hearth is the point from which the German novel should see the world.[33] He shows it instead to be an unstable refuge. In so doing he participates in the shift in sensibility that in the early twentieth century will undermine home and family in *Buddenbrooks,* expose the 'unhomely' in Freud's 'Über das Unheimliche' (1912) ('The Uncanny') and leave family and community vulnerable to an authoritarian ethic in Heinrich Mann's *Der Untertan* (1918) (The Man of Straw).[34]

I wish to thank the British Academy for a grant to enable me to visit the Theodor Fontane Archive in Potsdam in April 2003 to prepare this essay, and the staff of the Archive for their generous assistance during my visit.

10

Bodies in Crisis

Zola, Gender, and the Dilemmas of History

Jann Matlock

In memory of Naomi Schor

The satirical magazine *La Silhouette* ended the year 1889 with its 'predictions' for the following year, including a caricature showing Émile Zola 'admitted into the French Academy and forced to collaborate on its famous dictionary' (Figure 1).[1] By foretelling Zola's election to the literary institute alongside events as unlikely as a Martian landing, the caricaturist Moloch joined Paris press attacks on the novelist's campaign for consecration among the 'immortals' of letters. Unsurprisingly, on 1 May 1890, in what the left-leaning *Gil Blas* called 'L'Élection Zola',[2] the best-selling novelist came up empty-handed in a vote that pitted the practitioner of a genre frequently spurned by the Academy against several conservative literati including anti-Naturalist Ferdinand Brunetière, editor of the powerful *Revue des deux mondes*.[3] This election was distinctive for the way it called into question the very notions of Frenchness supposedly upheld by the Academy: 'Once again', wrote journalist Maurice Talmeyr, 'the Academy door is barred to an author who has achieved glory.'[4] When the balloting resumed in November, Zola again met rejection after attaining only the smallest show of support. In the next years, his name would reappear in eighteen more Academy elections, but he won only increasing ridicule. Like Balzac before him, Zola would make the shortlist but never be

M. Emile Zola sera reçu académicien, et forcé de collaborer au fameux dictionnaire, ce qui remplira de joie ses ennemis.

1. Moloch, from 'Predictions for 1890', *La Silhouette*, 29 December 1889. Photo: Bibliothèque nationale de France, Paris.

welcomed among those designated as the posterity of the French literary tradition.

Zola's fortune as outsider would not change until over a half century after his death in 1902, but when he at last became 'canonized', he gained a status as representative of the best of French literature and of the best French aesthetic modernity. In a 1960s study, he was named the author best known to young people with a secondary degree.[5] In France, doctoral dissertations regularly appeared on his work from the 1950s, quickly followed by his novels' appearance among the volumes of the Pléiade and as a subject for the *baccalauréat* in 1978.[6] The Bibliothèque Nationale commemorated the centennial of his death in 2002 with a huge exhibit and an international conference.[7] No one visiting this celebration of Zola's work would have guessed that only a few decades earlier, the caretakers of Frenchness would have mocked him, scorned him, and even—during the Dreyfus Affair—censored and jailed him, rather than imagine that his voice provided a model for their language, literature, or values.

Given Zola's meteoric rise in the canon of nineteenth-century French literature, one should not be surprised that an industry of academic writing has burgeoned around his work.[8] Despite—or perhaps because of—Zola's long, troubled relationship with the literary establishment, much of that criticism embraces the most traditional paradigms for the human sciences. Paradigms of genius poetics and author intentionality, bolstered in part by 'genetic criticism',[9] recur beside formalist literary analyses. Interdisciplinary research like that currently embraced in other disciplines remains marginalized among Zola studies, though it has much transformed work relating to other periods of French literature, and even concerning other nineteenth-century French authors. The 1970s and 1980s nevertheless trumpeted heady moments of change in Zola studies. Thought-provoking analyses of the power relations of gender, class, and race in Zola's works emerged through the path-breaking work of Naomi Schor, Charles Bernheimer, David Bell, Peter Brooks, Janet Beizer, and Dorothy Kelly.[10] Few sustained studies emerged, however, in the following decades to continue the work of this extraordinary scholarship, to respond to the challenges of gender and queer theory.[11] Zola studies have remained strangely mired in models of genius, myth, and rhetoric. With the rare exceptions in the work of Dorothy Kelly and Sharon Marcus, feminist studies of Zola have fared particularly badly since the 1990s.[12] Despite good intentions, the *Cahiers naturalistes* volume on 'Figures du féminin' (Female Figures) turned primarily to stylistic issues relating to 'images of women' and took its tropes so literally as to render women mostly metaphoric. More peculiar still is a work that seems to parody the preoccupation with the corporeal evinced by gender studies: Sylvie Collot's *Lieux du désir* catalogues body parts in Zola's fictions in relation to his mythic (again), thematic (again), and formal stylistic (again) preoccupations.[13] More puzzling is that although French, American, and British historians have, since the 1970s, radically transformed explorations of nineteenth-century society, such explorations have barely touched the Zola enterprise despite their preoccupation with a central aspect of the Zola novel, the body. Recalling the extraordinary contributions of Naomi Schor, who revolutionized nineteenth-century French studies in the interests of feminist theory, this article calls for a shift toward interdisciplinary research that rejects the frontiers traditionally assigned to the literary and that depends on historical research to understand the worlds of the novel. To do this, I turn to the extensive debates that surrounded Zola's seventeenth novel of the *Rougon-Macquart* series, *La Bête humaine*, which appeared in serial form between November 1889 and March 1890.[14] As my analysis of the debates about society and the novel at the time of Zola's first Academy campaign will demonstrate, even the novelist's champions were daunted by the stories of bodies that his work made its principal thematics. They set out, for better or for worse, to unravel Zola's reputation from the scandals of the flesh that late nineteenth-century critics had made their clarion calls. I want to look, therefore, at what those scandals entailed. This essay seeks to use the tools of historical analysis and the questions of feminist theory to put the scandals back into Zola's fictions.

A Scandal of bodies

In December 1889 the *Écho de Paris* interviewed Zola about his Academy campaign. 'You've come because of the famous poster, right?' Zola interrupted journalist Jules Huret on the threshold with an allusion to an image that the press roundly perceived as procuring much 'curiosity' for the novel that had just begun to appear in serial form.[15] As soon as the poster began covering the walls of Paris, proclaimed one journalist, '*La Bête humaine* already had its own history.'[16] Being able to see the 'highly colourful' picture meant that 'passers-by' would already have an idea what this novel invited them to witness, wrote Paul d'Armon, evoking not only a story of vision but anxieties about what such vision implies: 'The plot of *La Bête humaine* is thus made from a horrible tragedy [. . .] [T]hat's the first thing one is forced to see, and it violates those who look.' According to this critic, Zola's novel not only attacks his protagonists but also those very 'passers-by' who are caught up by the sensationalism of the poster and recycled into participants in the novel's crimes: 'It is not enough for the author to kill all the protagonists of his drama, he wants other victims by the cartload: random victims, even those just walking by, uninterested or anonymous.'[17] The novelistic 'history' imagined here conflates several processes relating to the novel's workings: committing crimes (represented in the novel), reading about crimes (reading the novel), and being assaulted criminally (act that the poster would achieve on behalf of the novelist and in advance of the novel's own assaults). Although this approving review imagines the poster as a useful preparation for the

2. Poster for Zola's *La Bête humaine*, Autumn 1889, colour lithograph, 145 x 100 cm. Henri Céard Collection, Musée Carnavalet, Paris. Photo: Photothèque des Musées de la Ville de Paris.

novel's brilliant assaults, Zola's detractors easily found fodder for their own attacks in the images plastering Parisian walls.

Zola protested that he did not see why a novelist should be responsible for the advertisements for his work.[18] In fact, Zola told Huret that he had nothing to do with the advertising campaign besides having indicated to his editor possible episodes for 'a poster's subject: a husband who wants to kill his wife and an assassination.' While his friends alleged that the poster destroyed his candidacy for the Academy, massacring with one visual assault on the city of Paris his chances of becoming a representative of French letters, he remained blasé: 'It's not very artistic', he remarked, 'its biggest fault, in my eyes, was not being by Chéret.'[19] Oddly enough, both Zola and several journalists expressed confusion over what exactly the two people in the image are doing. 'What's wrong?' asks Zola, 'A husband who, after a good lunch, wants to possess his wife, doesn't that happen every day in real life?' Yet Zola also claims to Huret to have thought, upon seeing the poster in the street for the first time, that the image depicted two people fighting: 'Good, there's the husband who wants to kill his wife.' His confusion surfaces again when he tells Huret he saw a knife![20]

Zola's confusion may well result from the fact that there were, in fact, two posters that advertised *La Bête humaine*. One, a life-size colour lithograph measuring about five feet high and three feet wide, shows a man pushing a struggling woman onto a bed (Figure 2). The second, in black, white, and red, is about a ninth the size of the first and shows a man brutally beating a woman (Figure 3).[21] It is hard to know whether the smaller poster, which used as its illustration the cover image from the first instalment of the feuilleton run, replaced the larger one after the press outcry or whether both posters continued to be used for the duration of the novel's four-month serialization in *La Vie populaire*.[22] We can be certain from Zola's discussion with Huret that both posters appeared in November 1889 and that the novelist saw both of them, even if he has a strange way of conflating them when arguing against accusations of obscenity that seem initially to have touched only the larger poster. That the press expressed so much outrage about the colour poster, which depicted the moment in the novel's first chapter where Roubaud tries to force his wife to have sex with him, does not derive from the coercion that makes Roubaud's act in the novel verge on an attempted rape (in fact one newspaper remarked that the only thing wrong with the poster was that it did not declare explicitly that the man was the woman's husband!).[23] Rather, the colour poster's scandal seems to have erupted from the way the image projects a 'foreseeable'

3. Poster for Zola's *La Bête humaine*, Autumn 1889, colour lithograph, 41.20 x 30.30 cm. Henri Céard Collection, Musée Carnavalet, Paris. Photo: Photothèque des Musées de la Ville de Paris.

sexual act just beyond the frame of the represented scene. That both posters were ultimately equated by critics as functioning in a way that violated the vision (if not also the innocence) of passers-by, says much about how late-nineteenth-century moralists understood the relationship between scandal, sexuality, and physical brutality.

The more violent of the two posters is particularly instructive in this context. That poster evokes the novel's early scene where Roubaud beats an admission out of his wife Séverine that her foster father, railway director Président Grandmorin, had sex with her when she was sixteen: 'Confess that you slept with him!' Roubaud repeatedly shouts.[24] The image focuses on the scene's feverish movement through the fork flying across the room in the foreground. The poster thus encourages viewers to imagine the fork landing alongside the overturned chairs, just as it projects our vision into two other future events —the hand striking and the train disappearing beyond the window frame. Ingeniously, the illustration here plunges the novel's potential reader into the middle of a drama where the motors of narration stimulate interest in what will happen next, what happened in the past, and what these characters say about those events. The poster particularly compels viewers to imagine what will follow this beating. In the novel, in fact, this violence results in Séverine's confession of past sexual encounters (inspiring, in turn, Roubaud's plot to kill Grandmorin). But even there, the text leaves the actual content to the reader's imagination, substituting the narrator's euphemistic paraphrase for Séverine's actual words. In this way, the novel replaces the woman's version of abuse with Roubaud's obsessions: 'he suffered all the more from these details [. . .] forever conjur[ing] up the abominable image' (*BH* 71). Both publicity posters likewise stand in for the novel, urging their audiences to imagine the next scene, but, paradoxically, both posters are also available to read into other plots than those of the novel they advertised.

Zola's 'confusion' about the posters rehearses that rhetorical troping and, most significantly, underlines the way the subject of this novel turned into a scandal of bodies. Like the nineteenth-century novel in general and specifically the genres associated with Realism, Zola's fiction revolved around the body. Zola's work turns especially on the ways that bodily transmission predisposed individuals to criminality and illness, madness and alcoholism, genius or lust. While previous *Rougon-Macquart* novels explored fleshly obsessions in terms, for example, of adultery and prostitution, *La Bête humaine* was projected as the book about criminal urges.[25] From the story of the jealous deputy stationmaster Roubaud and his battered wife Séverine, whom he will coerce into a hack murder plot against the molesting railway bureaucrat, the novel turns to the mad express-driver Jacques Lantier who discovers the couple's secret and uses it, first to seduce Séverine and ultimately to harass her—until his indelible savage compulsions drive him to her murder. Nearly every character in the novel has a secret and the text ultimately represents several crimes from Grandmorin's murder of Louisette to Misard's poisoning of Phasie to Flore's slaughter of a trainful of voyagers. Though it revolves around a criminal investigation, this novel makes little attempt at avenging victims or bringing perpetrators to justice. Instead, like other Zola works representing fragile social systems, *La Bête humaine* exploits an omniscient narrator who ironizes about the collapse of investigative justice, thus providing an alternative history of a world nearly contemporary (1869–70) with the one into which the novel was published.

As the battles over the posters suggest, the novel enacted, at every level of its deployment and reception, a radical confusion about how narratives account for what one sees bodies doing. '*La Bête humaine* already had its own history', wrote the critic about how a poster could enunciate *a story* that these images would imprint indelibly on whatever the novel might tell. But with that story, the novel also already had its relation to history. For even if the poster images seem to shirk the novel's relation to the 'real' social world—a world clouded by both images' sensationalistic rhetoric of sex and crime—the interaction between a violating man and a violated woman cannot but raise questions about what spectators in fin-de-siècle France are being invited here to watch, and what histories are at stake for those who do.

Observing Naturalists

Realism is a theory of looking, I have argued, and all the more so because the language of Realism was invented—not by the novelists but by their critics—to marginalize a certain kind of novel. Realism named the way literature was turned, by conservative critics, into a locus of anxiety. Its derogatory terms legitimized censorship—not only of texts but of the kinds of bodies they represented.[26] One is inclined to ask if Zola's brand of Realism—which he formulated as Naturalism and explicitly grafted onto literary texts associated with the theorization of the 'real'[27]—is also a theory of vision, and if so, what kind of theory, and in relation to what kind of spectators, what kind of spectacles, and what kind of optics?

Zola articulates a project for Naturalism in a series of texts whose writing spanned the *Rougon-Macquart* novels. 'Le Roman expérimental' (The Experimental Novel, 1880) has often been read as Zola's blueprint for his monumental project. His enemies saw this essay as mapping the theory behind the dangerous Naturalism he embraced; his friends applauded it for launching the novel into the spaces of science, positivism, and even truth. As Dorothy Kelly has shown, the science of Zola's Naturalist project is a gendered one, and the 'virility' he repeatedly associated with the new novel's scientific results is a mad masculinity. Peculiarly obsessed with differentiating itself from the girl business of the sentimental novel tradition, Zola's Naturalism is dead set on inventing a language that would let this scientific approach to the novel mask those aspects of the realist novel that supposedly gave it cachet among women.[28] Zola's theory, it seemed, would extract the novel from the pathological wax museum and the morgue—spaces of pure display where what was shown was not likely to change[29]—and plunge it into the positivism of the laboratory, where experiments on people as well as substances might enact metamorphoses. Zola's twenty-novel series was billed from the outset as a *history*—the *Natural and Social History of a Family under the Second Empire.* Astonishingly, his adversaries refused to imagine that this history reflected any aspect of their social world.[30]

Zola's opponents saw no possibility of a history so recent. This was especially the case for those most opposed to a literature that would interrogate the politics of their notions of Frenchness. Whether they were monarchist, Napoleonic, Catholic, or Protestant, these critics resolutely concurred that those who were not white, male, Christian, and bourgeois should not expect literature to suit their interests. Contemporary critics had shockingly limited notions of the possibilities for cultural texts, as Alain Pagès has shown through his research on the 1885 reactions to *Germinal.*[31] While Balzac's 1840s critics raged that detail obscured moral messages in novels like *La Cousine Bette*, and Flaubert's 1857 censors ranted about looking through the eyes of an adulterous wife, Zola's critics complained that there were certain subjects they did not want to study. Jonathan Crary's attempt to delineate 'an observing subject who was both a product of and at the same time constitutive of modernity in the nineteenth century' is instructive for thinking about the resistance to the novelistic spectatorship called Naturalism. Whereas Realism was theorized by the opposition to a certain kind of novelistic engagement with the world, Naturalism emerged through the promotion, by the literary actors, of new theories for studying the world, what Zola explicitly evokes as a combination 'of an observer and an experimenter' (*RE* 7). Crary has argued that the transformative moment for disciplining vision in the nineteenth century is the relocation, in the first decades of the century, of subjective vision in the human body. Observation is thus defined by

Crary as the process through which a spectator is 'embedded in a system of conventions and limitations.' The observer 'conforms [his] action, complies with, as in observing rules, codes, regulations, and practices'; he is an '*effect* of [. . .] discursive, social, technological, and institutional relations'.[32] The kind of study that antagonized Zola's critics played out just these kinds of effects while reflecting on what purposes such observation served. Naturalism was a theory of looking that promoted a new active spectatorship with a power to change the subjects under its glass. For Zola's critics, the danger seemed that such study might enforce their compliance in observing social change.

A remarkable tactic used by the press for attacking Zola consisted in taking absolutely literally the theoretical programme of *Le Roman expérimental.* This occurred in one extraordinary incident during the Academy campaign, as a caricatural excursion into Zola-lambasting culminated in censorship. It happens that none of Zola's *Rougon-Macquart* novels was censored (though they made the Vatican's 'index')—a lucky break for the novelist whose more daring works appeared after the liberalization of censorship laws in the late 1870s.[33] What *was* censored in 1890 in France was an *image* of Zola. The image in question, by Louis Legrand, labelled 'Le Naturalisme' (Figure 4), appeared just as the Academy battle was heating up, on 30 March 1890 in the satirical left-leaning caricature journal *Le Courrier français.*[34] Juxtaposed with Legrand's 'Le Romantisme',[35] the censored 'Naturalisme' showed a man (recognizably Zola), his camera set up to photograph a nude woman whose backside he is examining through a magnifying glass. 'Le Naturalisme's' woman is not naked, testifying to another contemporary battle over the erotics of partial nudity:[36] like other figures censored in this same paper, she wears stockings, a hat, and a boa—the gear of showgirls in dancehalls (and brothels), and, in turn, of Zola's own novelistic prostitute Nana.[37] The Zola up for censorship here, therefore, is the one who speculates on women at the fringes of society. It is the one precisely who seems to trouble those reflecting on the Academy election: in the words of a later caricature in *Le Courrier français*, there were 'Two Zolas', one of whom would claim, '—I'm the one who did *The Dream*! and that pig over there did *Nana*!'[38] Although Legrand's 'Naturalisme' did not flatter Zola any more than had dozens of other caricatures ridiculing the novelist,[39] it also did not seem to provoke censorship. The lithograph neither exposed much flesh nor particularly challenged decorum with regard to political representation of the body. In fact, one wonders if this caricature was censored not for what it showed but for what it exposed, the hypocrisy

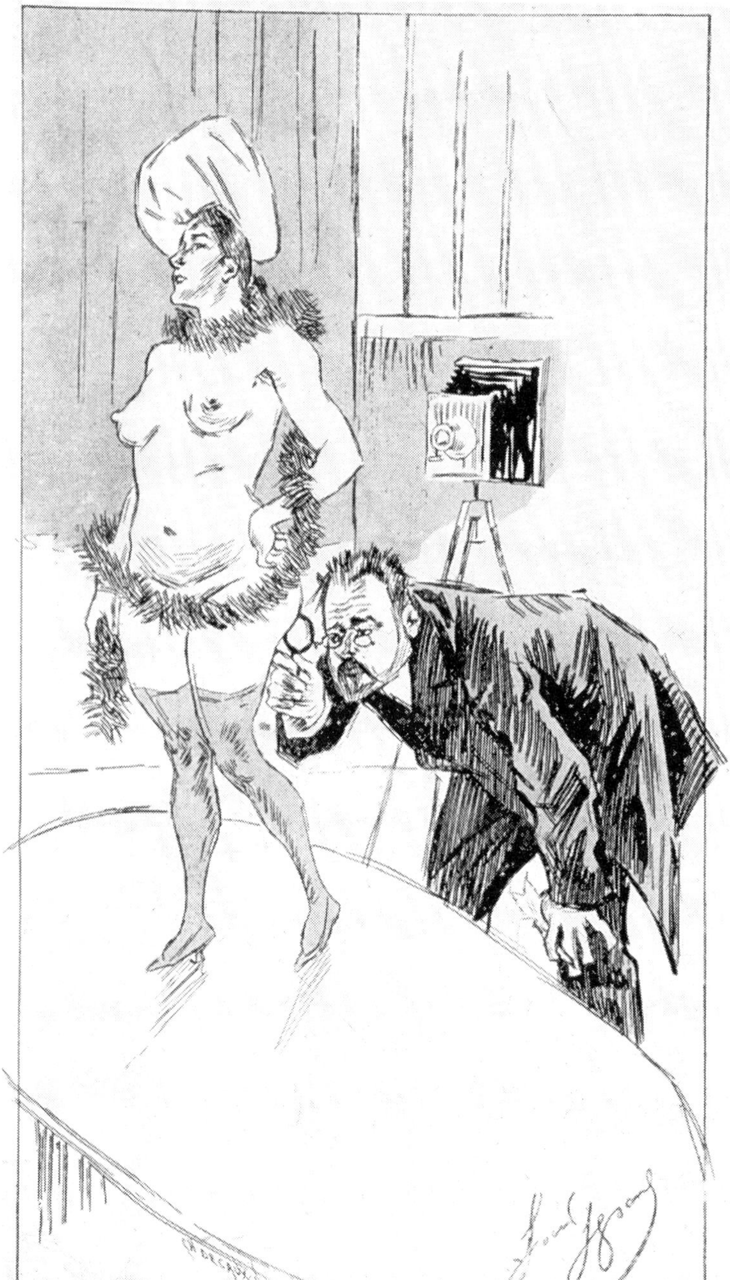

4. Louis Legrand, 'Naturalism', *Le Courrier français*, 30 March 1890.
Photo: Harvard University Libraries.

of a certain kind of observation. If one did not know the title or recognize the man with the magnifying glass, it would be easy to mistake the caricature for a mockery of the obsessions of government censors and press moralists, who fervently studied bodies while pretending to police them. Zola's most vituperative critics constructed an image of the novelist that made him the one hypocritically fixated on the body's exposures. Legrand's caricature may have made Zola out to be an obsessive, but it did so while also evoking the hypocrisy inherent in the image used by the right-wing press to undermine Zola's candidacy for the Academy. A look at the rhetoric of those attacks should help us better to understand how the press characterized the observations of Naturalism.

A good deal of the criticism banked by *La Bête humaine* in 1889–90 revolved, concretely, around the status of Zola's *study* of criminality. Even those who praised the novel voluminously concentrated on how its author approached his subjects: 'Zola draws on the people to make studies that he labels novels.'[40] Although *Le Figaro*'s Jules Lemaître remained ambivalent about the values Zola gave his characters, he praised the novelist's approach: 'Zola observes and translates [human feelings] when they are practically reduced to instincts and sensations. That's his sovereign realm.'[41] Long-time enemy Armand de Pontmartin rehearsed in one last review his complaint that Zola's form of observation betrayed the essential: 'Mr Zola, who has made such a hubbub with his notorious human documents, neglects completely the true human document, the analysis of characters, passions, and feelings, the study of the countless phenomena of the invisible world.'[42]

Although reviewers weigh what kind of observation Zola achieves, even those who do not like the novel no longer fulminate here—as they had over Balzac, Flaubert, or the first *Rougon-Macquart* novels—about a kind of observation that shows too much. Instead, one witnesses a repeated concern with the relationship of his 'scientific' studies to real life: 'Despite Zola's well-known love for documents, can't those sceptical of his work nevertheless contend that he has willingly given flesh to pure imaginings?' asks one commentator about the way Zola's novel represents criminal insanity.[43] *Le Figaro*'s 'Caliban' wonders if Zola plans to rewrite the entire Penal Code by attempting to demonstrate that criminals have no responsibility whatsoever for their crimes.[44] The novel's advocates rely on the elaborate discourse of positivistic science that has repeatedly accompanied Zola's justification of his work: 'We know that Mr Émile Zola sees in the novel a means of scientific investigation and flatters himself for leaving nothing either to chance or to convention.'[45] Such critics nevertheless struggle to explain how they defend the morality of the work and what the implications may be for its representation of criminality: remarking that the novel's most heinous criminals are soundly punished, Zola's advocates seem to breathe a collective sigh of relief that they can champion his science without needing to uphold a doctrine of insanity that might release a mad murderer from criminal responsibility.

Zola's novelistic philosophy proved a heavy burden for those promoting the scientific project of his work, in part because the novel broached highly volatile contemporary debates about criminality. Several well-known cases haunted the novel, transporting into the critical reception the manifold anxieties channelled through late-nineteenth-century crime. Two railway assassinations (of President Poinsot in 1860 and Prefect Barrême in 1886) and a murder where a woman served as bait for her husband to kill her lover (Feynarou in 1882) were seen by critic Lepelletier as 'furnish[ing] Zola with tragic documents for his plot.'[46] In spring 1890, perhaps in an attempt to substitute his scientific persona for that of the sensationalist who, as a result of the poster, had opened the eyes of France to the dirty underbelly of a marriage, the novelist launched a publicity campaign to promote his documentation of the railways, as evidenced by the full-page cover of the popular weekly *L'Illustration*.[47] But he has also continued to broadcast his relationship to crimes he studied for this work—and even to comment on newly discovered murders as though his novelistic observation has professionalized his understanding of criminality. Although he insists that he has 'no responsibility' for influencing the acts of a man who has tried to kill his children after reading *La Bête humaine*, Zola nevertheless abides by his connection to the criminal: 'I am well aware that this poor man has given me publicity, and I thank him very much for it.'[48] Zola was not above exploiting crime to market his novel—at least if we are to believe interviews published in 1890 about a case that his novel could practically have invented.

Crime pays

In August 1889 a trunk containing the remains of a bailiff named Augustin Gouffé was found abandoned near the railway tracks in Millery, near Lyons, where it had been shipped by train from Paris. An attractive young woman named Gabrielle Bompard and her lover Michel Eyraud were soon suspected of killing Gouffé in July 1889 before leaving the country. Bompard returned to France that December on the arm of a new boyfriend (whom she had refused to lure into her old lover's trap), turned herself in, and testified that Eyraud had coerced her into criminality. Multiple versions of the crime story proliferated as *La Bête humaine* was appearing in serial form. The same newspapers, abuzz over the Naturalist's new novel and his Academy campaign, also fixated on the mystery of the trunk. Others mulled the modernity of criminals who shipped their victims on the newest steam locomotives: 'What distinguishes our civilization is that we use for murders the procedures of science and modern industry. After we kill people, we like to make them travel, altogether or partly.'[49]

This case focused public attention in the years 1889–91 on issues that dovetailed remarkably with Zola's novelistic project: criminal responsibility, the role of heredity in determining a propensity to criminality, men's coercion of women and women's capacity to be coerced—in this case, through hypnotism—and gender differences in criminal behaviour.[50] Had Eyraud masterminded the crime without Bompard guessing his murderous designs, as she contended, simply using her as bait in a blackmail plot that ended accidentally in Gouffé's demise? Had he coerced his lover's participation in his scheme through hypnotism, as her advocates claimed during the trial, or had she been in on the murder plans from the outset? The fact that the case was frequently labelled with only *Bompard's* name tells a story further reflected in press depictions of her as an especially fascinating—and treacherous—subject for study.[51] Shortly after her first testimony and before Eyraud's capture, *L'Illustration* represented her anthropometric observation at the Police Prefecture (Figure 5).[52] Although the woman in this engraving is fully clothed, she is not less under investigation than the feather-boaed floozy of Legrand's caricature.

That the press sought Zola's comments on this case is hardly surprising. Just as the *Courrier français* ridiculed both Zola *and* his critics by depicting his observation of a woman similar to his literary subjects, the popular press elicited Zola's participation in the Eyraud-Bompard investigation as much to expose his interests as to interrogate his observations. Zola shows an awareness of these dangers, in his first remarks on the case in January 1890 in *La Lanterne*, by sidestepping aspects of the crime associated with his literary concerns.[53] He there concentrates on his moral outrage at the way Eyraud's family has denounced him, a bizarre emphasis given Bompard's testimony that same week about a crime that seemed to have leapt from the pages of Zola's current serial.[54] Another interviewer soon managed to extract

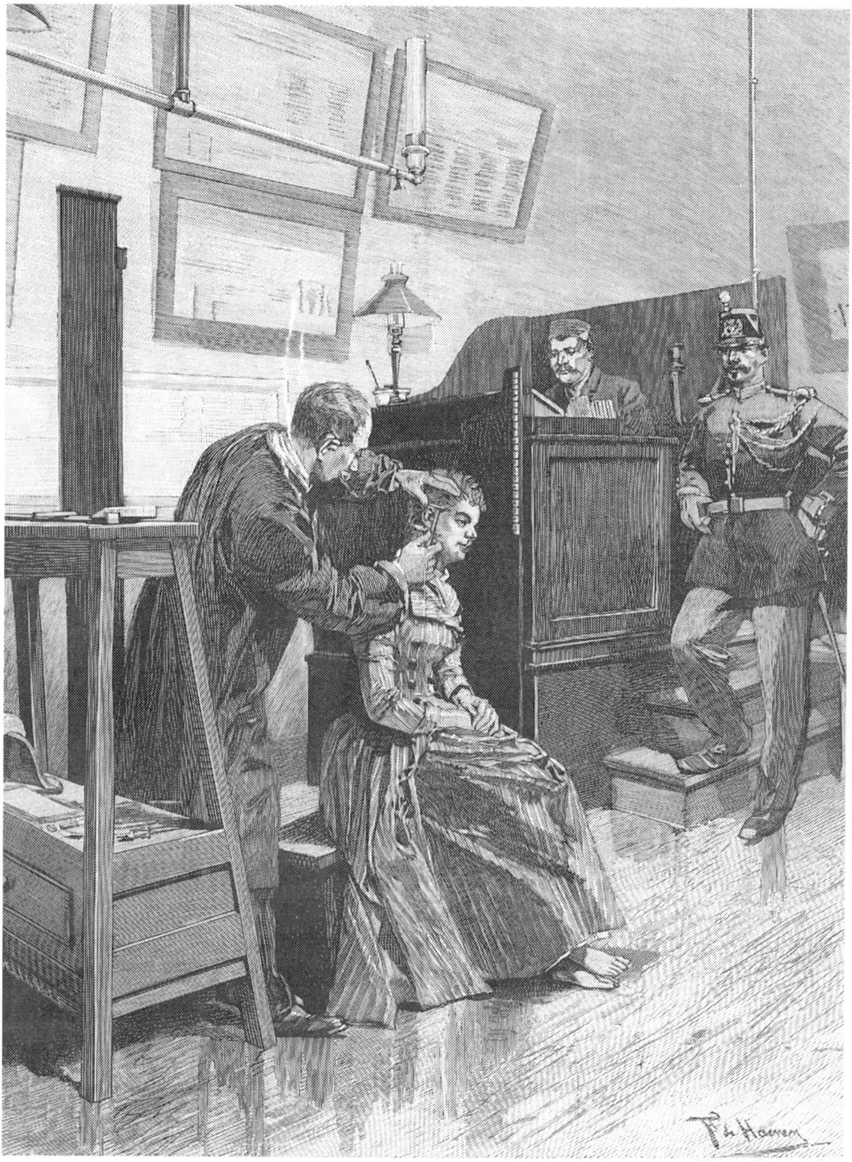

5. F. de Haenen, 'The Gouffé Affair: The Anthropometric service taking Gabrielle Bompard's measurements'. Lithograph, *L'Illustration*, 1 February 1890. Photo: L'Illustration International, Paris.

more detailed views from the novelist about the crime. At stake was Bompard's conduct, from her participation in the crime to her confession that 'sold out' her lover. Zola does not shy from offering medico-legal opinions about the case—even though his knowledge derived exclusively from newspaper reports! Pronouncing Bompard guilty ('she killed, or else she helped kill'), Zola narrates his version of the crime—'She [. . .] knew the violence of her lover's character. She had everything to fear. She dared it all'—then concludes that she was not coerced.[55] Zola offers such testimony not only on the basis, as one interviewer notes, of his long experience in analysing humanity,[56] but with the support of the studies offered in his current novel. He uses the interview to advertise for the understanding of female psychology offered by *La Bête humaine*. Readers are invited to seek there 'analogies it presents with the adventure of Gabrielle Bompard and Eyraud'. Zola suggests, in fact, that his literary expertise could explain not only Bompard's psychology but that of other women, criminal or otherwise:

> Women are all that way! All of them! Whatever their social situation, their education, or their character [. . .] [they forget] the man they loved the day before and the evidence of affection they received from him. A man has more consideration. He continues to pity the one he once loved but no longer loves. The woman does not know such delicacy and treats the man she no longer cares about as if he were a stranger or an enemy.

Women's inferior sense of loyalty, declares Zola, explains why one should never take a female accomplice: 'Two men can have a cadaver between them; a man and a woman never can.'[57]

Bompard, according to Zola, is the worst kind of criminal. She knew exactly what she was getting into, she enjoyed the ride, and now, remorseless, she was trying to have her cake and eat it too, to switch lovers and manipulate the public. The novelist provides a shocking armchair psychologization of Bompard, transforming her into a character like those in his fictions. Indeed, Zola seems to have more patience with the murderous female accomplice in his own novel than with Bompard, whom he later characterized as 'a passionate hysteric, sick and degenerate'.[58] From her case he projects not just another literary work, but a feigned insight into half of humanity: 'What a lovely novel if we could interrogate Gabrielle! But she wouldn't tell the truth. Women can't ever tell the exact truth about things. They lie to everyone: to judges, to their lovers, to their maidservants, to themselves.'[59]

Did Zola really give this interview? It is hard to know for sure, though it seems all the more likely since a similar interview appeared in the small right-leaning *L'Estafette*, just after Eyraud and Bompard were pronounced guilty.[60] What I think more relevant is that a mainstream newspaper of *Le Figaro*'s importance could engage Zola as a mouthpiece for such misogynous views without anyone protesting.[61] Given the newspaper's visibility among the Parisian elite, one suspects that Zola used this interview to promote his scientific expertise as useful in realms far beyond literature. Was this related to his Academy campaign? It must have seemed to advance that cause or else he would have demanded apologies, as he had when *Le Journal des débats* decried the poster's 'offence to public decency'.[62] Zola was well aware that his novel's subject made him vulnerable to accusations of abetting crime, as demonstrated by his protest in March 1890 that 'my Séverine did not create the "case" of Gabrielle Bompard'.[63] His *Le Figaro* interview answered the worst accusations lodged against his novel by promoting that very fiction as a key to understanding real crimes. He seemed to be claiming that the insights that made him a good novelist lent him the competence of the best medico-legal experts. If he could offer convincing observations on such a significant case, he surely deserved to become, as his champions proclaimed, a member of France's most powerful body of letters.

Zola's interviews about the Bompard case underline the gendered construction of the 'scientific' process of Naturalism. Like the late-nineteenth-century scientists he aspires to imitate, Zola conceived of scientific research as 'the virility of the true'.[64] The dangers of women whom he challenged with such masculine virtue have multiplied beyond those of the tearful female novel-readers who gave a bad name to Romanticism:[65] what is at stake for the 'naturalist' observer are the very real crimes that women were imagined to perpetrate when they flout the restrictions on their desires, movements, and aspirations. Naturalism is also gendered because it made no attempt to investigate the misogynous assumptions about women's nature on which nineteenth-century social theory—medicine, psychiatry, criminology—and ultimately social policy depended. At the very foundation of Naturalism's central research project on degeneration and heredity we find, obsessively recurring, a fantasy of women's primal taintedness. Tante Dide is the source of the stains on the Rougon-Macquart family tree, not by a coincidence of gender, but because in the terms of nineteenth-century science no woman could have been untainted: marked by their difference, women are all always already criminal and crazy, ready for barter in the maddest schemes of the experimental novelist, ripe for exposure to every experiment that seeks social 'truths'. Zola's opinions on the Bompard case remind us how much his literary enterprise depends on a kind of investigation of bodies that obtains strict gender difference through normative grids.

Zola's work had more success with criminologists than with the Academy. In 1892 renowned criminologist Cesare Lombroso dedicated an article to Zola's novel, declaring it a near-perfect demonstration of his theories.[66] Zola's criminological expertise soon found other champions: two major criminologists of the fin de siècle cited Zola from *Le Figaro* to explain female criminality.[67] Future criminologists would be invited to glean from the great novelist these titbits of misogyny, now detached from their original context, branding all women fickle, prone to squealing against their accomplices, inherently untruthful, and indelicate in their approach to crime.

Novel investigations

The 'discourse of crime', Michelle Perrot has argued, 'translates the obsessions of a society'.[68] The novel participates in that discourse not just by reflecting the obsessions but by enacting the process of normalization inherent to policing practices: the novel does not just police its characters but it invites its readers into a process of self-policing.[69] Fiction about crime works similarly to crime reporting in the press and in the legal system, elaborating an account of the details that a crime investigation makes visible, representing the criminal so that, ostensibly, he or she can be known. As Judith Walkowitz has demonstrated, the interchangeability of different kinds of discourses about crime only further underlines the complexity of the obsessions such discourse always fails fully to contain.[70] The stories told, whether through newspaper speculations or in police files, have so much in common with novelistic versions of crimes that one is often hard-pressed to determine which are more far-fetched. As critics and criminologists noted in 1890, Zola's crime novel put theories of biological positivism in the limelight and popularized widespread stereotypes about normative gender difference in society as well as crime.

Zola's *Bête humaine* makes all its male characters criminal, but it also makes them all potential investigators of crime. In this respect, the novel's trumpeted role in the process of naturalist (scientific) observation dovetails with the roles it assigns its characters. The reader is invited to follow the narrator into the criminal mind of one after another character whose reasons for turning to crime give an illusion of a complete survey of case-types: molester Grandmorin has killed young Louisette; Misard poisons his wife to get hold of her thousand francs; Roubaud kills his wife's violator out of jealousy; Cabuche killed a man purportedly in self-defence; Pecqueux's alcoholic binge leads to a brawl that claims his own life and many more; Jacques Lantier represents the mad assassin, modelled on Jack the Ripper according to a very French conception of criminal degeneration. Figured as unable to control his urges and unable to be stopped either by the law or by any criminal investigation, Lantier, as critic D'Armon points out, serves as an 'impenetrable mystery'.[71] The novel exploits the paradox of his crimes, suggesting he needs punishment, but letting him escape it by a 'nature' that one critic complained was too 'literary', and another proclaimed dangerous for civilization.[72] Lantier is the character least equipped to observe the law because the novel strips him of his responsibility, creating in him an atavistic figure who carries in his bloodstream a hereditary hunger for revenge against women (*BH* 99). Despite his flaws, Lantier becomes the novel's double for the naturalistic investigator because he is the one, improbably, who is allowed both to see the premeditated crime *and* to reinterpret that crime when it is told to him by his lover, Séverine.

The novel thematizes observation through, on the one hand, a criminal investigation, and on the other hand, through the actual spectatorial activities of its characters. Lantier happens on the Grandmorin murder by peeking in train windows, but he is not the only character in *La Bête humaine* who engages in spying. Indeed, Cabuche, described as a kind of classic fetishist (who carries off the clothing of the woman he covets to such an extent that he is blamed for her murder), is caught peeping by other characters.[73] Certain female characters likewise have propensities for spying. Flore has witnessed activity between Séverine and Grandmorin in the past (*BH* 301) and now watches from her strange perches in the forest, hoping to reveal Séverine and Jacques to the police (*BH* 300–01). Madame Lebleu is said to have died because she can no longer spy on her neighbours (*BH* 355). At the end of the novel, during the criminal investigation, Jacques excites the ladies so much they cannot take their eyes off him (*BH* 371).

Not surprisingly, for a novel concerned so significantly with investigation, this one spends a great deal of time telling us exactly how characters watch one another—and much of that watching could be characterized as voyeuristic. Like Nana in *L'Assommoir*, who is caught by the narrator peeping on others' sexual activities, and Octave Mouret in *Pot-Bouille*, who will ultimately be given Zola's figure by caricaturists and critics hell-bent on constructing the novelist as an exposer of what should remain hidden,[74] the characters of *La Bête humaine* seem to be repeatedly positioned as stealing others' privacy. But there is more to that voyeurism in this novel than just stolen looks.

This is a novel that turns on the problem not just of *investigating* crime but of *witnessing* crime—and that turns, likewise, on a mystery quite different from that of Lantier's murderous urges. *La Bête humaine* does not operate in the least bit like a traditional detective novel since it neither points in the direction of assorted wrong criminals nor does it in the end procure 'truth' by locating the 'right' criminal.[75] All this novel's criminals are the 'right one', but one of them has left a piece of writing that might testify to more than just the crime. The novel makes a central mystery of what has happened to the letter Séverine is forced by her husband to write to Grandmorin. By the end of the novel, we will learn that the letter has been burned by another spy, Grandmorin's childhood friend. Camy-Lamotte has every interest in protecting his friend from scandal, even in death, for such a cover-up also protects the corrupt state that is, in the novel's timeframe, about to explode into war. Although Séverine is likewise long dead when Camy-Lamotte burns her letter, the novel's resolution of the mystery of her writing reminds us that the true stories of criminal events survive only by chance, perhaps by word of mouth, as did the 'truth' about Louisette's murder by Grandmorin, or perhaps not at all, for at the end of this book the only person who seems to know the truth of what has happened to Séverine is the corrupt statesman who destroys the evidence.

Since its first chapter the novel has posed the question of what happens to the woman who has written, of whether the letter will reveal, ultimately, the coercion of her victimization, and of what can be made—narratively and thematically—of her testimony. The novel has at the same time repeatedly coupled this potential testimonial document with its own investigations into what the characters see in and through one another. The confessions exacted by this novel have no purpose except to demonstrate the inherent guilt of the characters. No one will be allowed to testify. No testimony is ever permitted to occur. This is a novel that has, from the outset, explored the question of whether any witnessing can endure. At the conclusion to the novel, after the investigation into Séverine's murder metamorphoses into absurdity, one can have little reason for faith in official history. Can we imagine that the novel does a better job of witnessing history than the investigations it thematizes?

In his writing about the Naturalist project, Zola claimed that the novel is a privileged space for observing, and especially for witnessing the occurrences of the private world and the familial sphere—since, after all, his twenty-volume series is a history of a family. Zola can best promote the necessity of a novelistic substitute for official history by imagining that surviving documents will not tell stories we would want to know. He must project scandals in which crucial documents are destroyed and corrupt officials leave behind only lies.

But not all official stories need be corrupt, scandal-ridden, and unreliable for testimony about the past. In the state archives today, the case files of the Bompard investigation permit historians to understand the misogyny through which female criminality was constructed in late nineteenth-century France. In the Bibliothèque Nationale in 2003, the journalistic 'archives' of press obsessions from 1889–90 could let me construct the story in these pages. Through considering what could make a novelistic truth, I have been able to question the aesthetics through which the French of the fin de siècle were able to imagine great literary authors. I have been able to consider how the account of Zola's first attempt at immortality in the French Academy casts him as a scapegoat of a biased, narrow-minded literary establishment that had not yet adjusted to the goals of a democratic state.

Because so little seemed to remain to enable them to reconstruct women's stories about their private lives, feminist scholars in the 1970s and 1980s turned to literature for testimony about those lives, about the conditions through which women were, far too often in previous centuries, silenced. But the archives do not just contain accounts of cover-ups and silencing, of voyeuristic revelling in the victimization of women and of perverse exposures of their ostensible mendacity. Literature relays accounts of bodies in crisis, but we can only understand those crises by depending on the archives to tell us what those histories can mean. The bodies in crisis in *La Bête humaine* complicate the uses to which Zola's work has been put, just as they raise questions about the ways novels like this one could function in their own time. The scandalous bodies evoked in and through this novel in 1889 and still today, continue to elicit speculation, will go on for a long time relaying their scandals. Gender, class, and race mark the space of stories that novels evoke as scandalous, but only interdisciplinary historical research can enable us to see what may have been in the real letters that determined the fates of women whom literature, like science, marked as cases deserving investigation.

The values of the literary canon today continue, with our complicity, to be constructed on notions that are not so far from those that enabled the French Academy to marginalize Émile Zola. Those values are also based on notions of gender difference and class difference that made it impossible even for Zola himself to conceive that a woman like his character Séverine deserved anything other than to be disbelieved, ridiculed for her fickleness, and denied her rights of due process under the law. Like some of Zola's critics in 1890, one is inclined to find the views on female criminality, as espoused in his novels and in his interviews, questionable indeed. As a feminist theorist, I see my work as contributing to an understanding of what values grounded both Frenchness and such misogyny in late nineteenth-century France. What will need to have changed for women's sphere to be made not just of feckless feminine figures and hapless desires, but of history? What will it take to keep these new letters we write from being burned?[76]

11

Karl Rossmann, or the Boy who Wouldn't Grow Up

The Flight from Manhood in Kafka's *Der Verschollene*

Elizabeth Boa

In European culture of the early twentieth century America symbolized both future and origins. In the vanguard of modernity yet less alienated from the wilderness than Europe, the New World promised liberation from class oppression, emancipation from patriarchal repression, while the melting pot would dissolve ethnic enmities to restore pristine human nature or give birth to a new humanity. Although Max Brod suggests that the ending was to be optimistic, Kafka's unfinished first novel, *Der Verschollene* (The Man who Disappeared), subverts the utopian vision of America as once and future Eden.[1] Seventeen-year-old Karl Rossmann, having been seduced by a maidservant who had a child by him, is dispatched by his parents to the New World, but fails to grow up into all-American manhood. For although he travels forwards physically, at each challenge he regresses psychologically. The successive retreats can be seen in the context of changing gender discourse under the impact of modernity. Modern man throws off the shackles of the patriarchal order only to unleash naked competition between men and the sex war between men and women. The New Woman as emergent female subject drives the modernizing project forwards but threatens male dominance, whereas Woman as fleshy object of distracting lust retards Man on his Odyssey to transform the world. Faced with such challenges Karl Rossmann flees and is no closer to manhood at the end than the beginning.

Although explicitly feminist approaches have not figured largely in Kafka criticism, the representation of sexuality has attracted much attention. Walter Sokel associates Kafka's troubled relation with his father and his failure to marry with Oedipal plots, seeing female figures as marginal to the hero's quest to confront power face to face.[2] Larysa Mykyta, by contrast, offers a more radical reading of the disruptive force of female sexuality.[3] Deleuze and Guattari also detect a pervasive eroticism infusing social engagement in Kafka's novels, seeing women as connectors who draw the heroes on, although fortunately 'they nonetheless operate within a territory beyond which they will not pursue you'.[4] Underlying this account are the myths of Faust drawn on by the Eternal Feminine, embodied sequentially in actual women, or Odysseus sailing on past the Sirens to further encounters. But no Penelope awaits in this Odyssey. For as Elias Canetti notes, Kafka felt marriage to be incompatible with literature, hence the writer's guilt which Detlev Kremer also analyses in a witty study of the deflection of sexual desire into the desire to write.[5] Another critical strand examines sexual themes in a Jewish context. Ritchie Robertson relates Kafka's revulsion of sexuality to aspects of Jewish tradition and to Otto Weininger's *Geschlecht und Charakter* (Sex and Character) of 1903, which sold widely through into the 1930s.[6] Weininger claimed that all human beings have a mix of masculine and feminine traits but countered the consequent implication that individuals might cross the line by reasserting an absolute difference between men who have 'character' and can transcend nature and Woman as 'the Sex', sunk in undifferentiated fleshly existence. His tract mixed misogyny with anti-semitism in excoriating the Jews as an effeminate race. Weininger is an often cited intertext: for Sander Gilman in relating images of the male body in Kafka's work to anti-semitic discourse; for Rainer Stach who sees the female figures as ego-less creatures submerged in their bodies yet as erotic connectors to power; for Mark Anderson who, more positively, sees Kafka as transforming Weininger's stereotypes of women and Jews by depicting them from the inside; for Dagmar Lorenz who also emphasizes differences from Weininger, arguing that Kafka de-essentializes gender and turns masculinity and femininity into positions within power relations rather than qualities inhering in men and women.[7] Weininger too destabilized sexual difference but tried to recuperate an ideal of ascetic manhood with homoerotic undertones. Frank Möbus detects a mix of homoeroticism and sexual disgust in some of Kafka's stories.[8] Drawing on Julia Kristeva's concept of the abject, meaning the disgusting or unclean which resists cultural integration, Anne Fuchs sees Kafka as translating signs of difference in racist discourse into gender difference, so shifting the site of abjection from the male Jew to woman.[9] For Winfried Menninghaus disgust is the key to Kafka's deceptive aesthetic which shows forth yet conceals the obscene and where disgust masks desire.[10]

My own study combined several of these tendencies in exploring how the interplay of gender, class and racial discourse generated anxieties which Kafka expresses in striking body images yet also masks by mixing different signifying systems—realism, fantasy, myth, allegory—so leaving the reader unsure of how to read the signs.[11] Following a similar approach, I will argue here that the vision of modernity in *Der Verschollene* displays a repeated pattern reminiscent of the master/slave dialectic in Hegel's *Phenomenology of Spirit*.[12] In modern, competitive society, birth no longer determines status and established ethnic hegemonies are threatened as subject peoples claim nationhood and empires crumble. (Empire here designates not overseas colonies, but the Habsburg or Ottoman contiguous lands, where neighbour is set against neighbour.) This is the moment of the struggle between self and other to enforce recognition and so stabilize identity. But Kafka's novel tracks a boy's flight both from dominant manhood and from subjection. Without an adult subject position, whether as master or slave, Karl Rossmann is trapped in childishness, though his choice of 'Negro' as nickname in the Theatre suggests which side he would take if forced to choose. Hegel's dialectic is highly abstract. In Kafka's novel, the struggle for recognition is played out across multiple dimensions of identity: family upbringing and personal history, gender and sexuality, nationality, class, race, institutional status, and those incalculable gaps between person and persona which leave space for self-performance, as the Theatre fragment makes explicit. In this mobile world, who I am and may become, even who I was, is up for grabs, entailing constant struggle with others.

Feminism explores the two-way traffic in the distribution and exercise of power between the sexual field and social relations at large. In exploring the battles for mastery Leopold von Sacher-Masoch's novella, *Venus im Pelz* (Venus in Furs, 1869) offers interesting comparison with Kafka.[13] Often adduced in commentaries on 'Die Verwandling' (The Metamorphosis), it is also echoed in *Der Verschollene*.[14] *Venus im Pelz* offers a performative account of sexuality with the imagined audience always present, whether as the performers watching themselves or as third parties. A gestural language enacts power relations which infiltrate and shape desire. Like *Der Verschollene, Venus im Pelz* too begins with an encounter with the statue of a goddess. Man is the desiring subject, so the statue of Venus explains, and woman the object. Yet any clever woman can turn a man into her slave and plaything, for although the man will sober up if the woman abandons herself, the crueller she shows herself, the more his passion and with it her power will grow. The dreaming narrator's manservant then shakes him awake. He had fallen asleep while reading Hegel. We are not told which bit, but it seems a fair guess that it was the Master/Slave dialectic. The protagonist, Severin, twice mistakes the statue of Venus for Wanda, the real woman, suggesting that the woman too may be shaped by Pygmalionesque projections. For the man sets the masochistic agenda, calling himself Gregor in his role as slave, the name Kafka will give the insect-man in 'Die Verwandlung'. And whether Wanda is really cruel or just playing the masquerade is hard to determine as she switches between the personae of dominatrix and loving woman. The performative model could suggest that one is not born a man or a woman but learns roles which would change were power relations to change. Yet performance, however transgressive, may merely ritually reinscribe roles and re-stoke the same desires. Whether Kafka's novel unsettles the model of dominance and subjection is one question for a feminist critic. And if so, then is it through deconstructing polarized gender qualities or by gesturing towards changing social relations?

In Kafka's fictional worlds, the mythic intrudes incongruously into the real and the symbolic arrives embodied in hyper-realistic detail. The angel of justice in *Der Proceß* (The Trial) is a fat man in a uniform travelling between the worlds of a bank and a bedroom. The feminist reader must therefore look not only at realist representation of social power, but at how myth and metaphor infiltrate and shape desires and fears. *Der Verschollene* is almost Kafkaesque, but does not quite achieve the mesmerizing unity of tone yet doubleness of vision as real and imaginary inextricably intertwine. Here hybrid mixing of genres is shown forth. But many moments do generate the characteristic hesitation between naturalistic, metaphoric, iconographic, or fetishistic readings of textual detail. The telling details tell different things depending on the choice of genre to privilege, as the reader also oscillates between the hero's naïve view and the knowing gaze of a covert narrator which fetishizes the innocent detail. To start with genre, then: Kafka's first novel is a travel narrative. His working title, *Der*

Verschollene, centres the hero, a modern Simplicissimus, in an echo of the picaresque. *Amerika* by contrast, Max Brod's title for the posthumous first edition, centres the New World and the utopian quest. But several episodes track misprision and injustice, the themes of melodrama, and individual episodes gesture towards further genres and traditions. The opening chapter is Dickensian in manner, realism heightened by the melodramatic imagination: larger-than-life figures, a looming sense of injustice, the shadow of nightmare shot through with comedy. Still umbilically bound to the past, Karl gets stuck in the ship's bowels as in a birth canal between the Old World and the New, until his magical rescue by a good uncle—fairy tale is a further ingredient. But we hear too of ship's machinery, electric wiring and skyscrapers. We are in transit from old to new, and from nineteenth-century Realism to New Objectivity. The luridly lit-up Statue of Liberty in the opening sentence meshes with the birth metaphor to strengthen utopian (or dystopian) symbolism within the hybrid mix. The second episode is pervaded by the semiotics of modernity: skyscrapers, city streets, electric trams, telegraphs, telephones, and a large modern shower installation. Circulation, whether of traffic, money, English as lingua franca, or modern plumbing, finds emblematic expression in an American desk with an amazing rotating mechanism. But no sooner has he arrived in the city than Karl is whisked off into a gothic romance in an eerie country house where he meets in Klara a threatening amalgam of dollar princess, bossy New Woman, and vamp. Yet by the midnight hour, the hero is expelled from romance—or is it nightmare?—into a road movie and the vamp makes way for the buddy. Karl has now forfeited his uncle's wealth, but the American Dream is not just about money, it is also about youth and new frontiers. Karl Rossmann is no easy rider, however, more a Charlie Chaplin with his umbrella, second-best suit, family photo, and suitcase. And in the next episode Karl flees from bullying buddies under the motherly wing of the Head Cook in the Occidental Hotel, finding a job as lift boy and a sisterly friend in Therese, a Chaplinesque sweet heroine with a Dickensian past as daughter of an immigrant deserted mother. The hotel is the scene of a rat-race among young men and of oedipally inflected melodrama, with Karl as victim of the Head Waiter and the ogreish Head Porter. Yet again Karl escapes, only to land, after a farcical pursuit by keystone cops, in Brunelda's musty, dusty, shadowy lair. This episode anticipates expressionist chiaroscuro or film noir, but heavily laced with farce, and repeats the pattern of engulfment followed by escape, this time through the birth canal of the underground tube, which deposits Karl in a recruiting fair for the Theatre of Oklahoma. A last fragment shows our hero on the train with jolly Giacomo, young men going West.

Mixed genres go along with mixed signifying systems. The opening sentence places Karl between the maidservant who seduced him and the Statue of Liberty. The real woman belongs to the European past, the statue is iconic of the New World future and casts a symbolic shadow forwards towards later instantiations. The boy has escaped the threat to his freedom posed by the woman but must now face up to the statue. Ominously wielding a sword not a torch, the statue may promise liberty, but may threaten retribution since the boy-victim is also the guilty deserter, fleeing paternal duty and betraying a loving woman. European literature abounds in stories about the double morality: the short-lived lure of maidservants; sexual and class injustice towards loving women and deserted mothers. Gretchen's act of infanticide, then her death, which free Faust to move on, are replaced here by a textual infanticide: Karl is the eponymous 'Verschollene', but the infant back in Europe disappears entirely except for a phrase in the first sentence. In transit towards late modernity, these old stories should no doubt be left behind in the name of freedom. But this goddess of liberty wields the sword of justice. To appease her and in displaced atonement to a poor maidservant Karl champions justice for the poor stoker in his protest against a Rumanian being set in authority over a German on a German ship. If Karl's boyish boldness promises well for a manly future, less promising is a countervailing regression back down into the ship's belly, into literal cabined and cribbed confinement in the stoker's cabin and his bed. 'Getting into bed with the stoker'—the equivalent idiom is 'unter einer Decke stecken'—is a literalized metaphor for making common cause. But Karl's support for a German fighting to keep old imperial privileges as other nations win new rights suggests little understanding of the American melting pot. Moreover justice loses out to wealth, for Karl does not follow the poor stoker's case through but goes off with his rich uncle. Alternatively, 'getting into bed with the stoker' suggests infantile regression: rejected by his own father for becoming a father, Karl childishly shelters with a surrogate father. But for some readers an obscene shadow falls across the stoker's bed, silhouetting the kind of thing sailors get up to with cabin boys, so calling cynically into question the hero's innocence and with it the discourse of justice. Mixing of genres, of signifying systems, of an innocent and a knowing gaze make the details hard to read.

Even harder to read is getting into bed with the maidservant as filtered through memory distorted by repression: Karl recalls the maidservant only under the pressure, we are told, of a past being pushed ever further away. Karl again plays the innocent. The stereotypical gestures of an older man seducing a girl are reversed: here an older woman put her hand disgustingly between the boy's legs and rubbed her stomach against him. But this is not enough to do the trick. The male member, absent in this account, must have played some part in the maid's pregnancy. As the woman rubbed against him, Karl felt as though she were a part of him, a formulation suggesting that *she* is the missing organ. Karl's retreat from male dominance began, then, in his first sexual encounter in which he casts himself as the plaything of a dominatrix or phallic mother. The reversal of active male and passive female echoes the masochistic scenario. But the maidservant failed as dominatrix, for she had neither social nor sexual power over a boy whom she loved too well and who could not be enslaved through a passion he did not feel. This was a gruesome coupling of the equally castrated. Karl's journey to America is, then, a flight from the male role in both its paternal and sexual aspects. But the shadow falling across the stoker's bed falls also across the maidservant's: can the one woman have been so abusive yet so caring; can Karl have been quite so innocent?

The hero of *Venus im Pelz* often speaks of female nature, but at the end concludes out of the blue that it is how man trains her up that dooms woman to be either man's slave or his despot; only when she enjoys the same rights can woman become man's companion. This is in keeping with Hegel's drama of self-identity forged in struggle: the master/slave moment is but a phase on the path towards full self-consciousness through mutual recognition. In Klara, Karl meets a girl closer to his own age and more apt than a servant to be an equal companion. Her name, almost an anagram of his own, suggests a female other self. The encounter is framed, however, within an opaque set of relationships among men jockeying for power: Karl's uncle, and two business acquaintances, Klara's father Pollunder and Green, a bachelor in his prime. Karl has come to Pollunder's house in a first disobedience of his uncle, who will duly expel him from the paradise of his wealth. As the evening wears on, Klara gradually becomes sexualized, first through her wish that Karl stay, which sets her against his uncle, then through her red lips which Karl notices as like her father's, then through Green, who obviously desires her, which for the first time causes Karl to see her as attractive. The desirable woman is thus constructed through the gaze as token in male competition or bonding. Klara's charisma as a rich man's daughter, admired by powerful men, lends her too a lively, unrestrained (p. 43; 'unbändig', p. 69) gaze.[15] Yet she remains marginal to male society and Karl only reluctantly leaves the men with their cigars and foaming glasses to follow her. The moment takes the form in his imagination of a struggle for mastery. Because Green pays no attention, withholds recognition, Karl imagines that Green is imagining that the essential social relationship between them will eventually be established through the victory or the destruction of one or other of them. Such psychic mirroring follows the Hegelian scenario. After this imaginary struggle, the real tussle with Klara follows Sacher-Masoch's scenario. When Karl insists on inspecting his own room before visiting hers, Klara almost pushes him out the window, then when he tumbles safely back into the room, to his amazement picks him up bodily, threatening to push him out in earnest. In a wrestling match with erotic undertones Klara sneakily gets the upper hand. Yet if he had only learned ju-jitsu he might have given her a thrashing (p. 47). 'Durchprügeln' (p. 73) is the verb; 'Prügel' (cudgel) is slang for erect penis. Klara threatens to box Karl's ears, to strike left and right till his cheeks swell (p. 47). The noun is 'Backen' (p. 74) which, with the prefix 'Hinter-' means buttocks. The *double-entendre* is a narrator's obscene wink to a reader who knows about spanking. Following this encounter, Karl tries to leave, but is delayed by various machinations till past midnight, when he creeps off in the night. Thus Karl flees again, this time from engagement in male–male struggles for mastery and from single combat in the sex war. The goddess with sword foreshadows the sexually liberated New Woman and her ju-jitsu. The vamp and oriental wrestling will have a long cinematic afterlife, motifs grotesquely combined here. Sporty Klara's steely body (p. 46; 'vom Sport gestählten Körper', p. 72) also anticipates that icon of modernity, the metallic machine-woman in Lang's *Metropolis* (1927); a more appealing cousin is the gutsy eponymous oyster-princess in Lubitsch's comedy, *Die Austernprinzessin* (1919).

Single combat in the bedroom might suggest an encounter of equals in a war of the sexes unleashed by women's emancipation. But Klara's attraction is still socially generated through the male gaze in a more public part of the house. The electrically lit dining room offers a bright yet threatening field of imagined conflict, but elsewhere flickering torches or candlelight in labyrinthine corridors and shadowy bedrooms signify psychic turbulence in a house where old forms of power are assuming new guise and where male battles for mastery mix ambiguously with emergent female power as the goddess dons a human form still half-shaped by the male imagination. Before turning to Brunelda as another avatar of the goddess, I want to look at encounters offering competing versions of masculinity: between the boy and surrogate fathers and with young men who oscillate between being buddies or bullies. Traces of Karl's upbringing and naive sense of justice offer a rule-governed, but constantly disrupted arena. For justice never prevails. Karl instinctively chooses hard work as the path to manhood. From the mid-nineteenth century onwards, the character-forming value of work was a prime ingredient in Germanic manhood, a national stereotype set off in racist discourse against 'polnische Wirtschaft' (Polish conditions). But the surrogate fathers withhold recognition and the young men compete unfairly. The ascending and descending hotel lifts comically signal a snakes-and-ladders existence in a mechanical metaphor like Chaplin pinioned to clock hands in *Modern Times*. After first encounters with the wealthy, Karl meets on the road the abject poor and wandering displaced. Robinson claims to be Irish, the equivalent of Polish in British racist discourse. Drunkenness even unto vomiting bears out the stereotype, though his name, echoing Defoe's hero, looks quintessentially English. Kafka's Robinson is no proto-capitalist, however, but a lumpen anti-Crusoe, who turns up in the hotel as the threatening other not just to Karl's ambitions, but to the whole modernizing project of the Protestant work ethic. The shower installation could be set against vomit as emblems of modernity and its abject. Grown men ruthlessly drive the project forwards. Young men join in the rat race or chaotically disrupt the hero's honest efforts. As for the Head Waiter or Head Porter, they are 'letzte Männer', uniform-wearers like the hotel porter in Murnau's film, *Der letzte Mann* (The Last Man, 1924). They point up a contradiction within modernity between a liberal ideology of individual rights and free competition yet subjection to systems and hierarchy in the name of order and efficiency.

Thus a sequence of men show forth dominant or competitive masculinity, from the stoker as exemplar of the subordinate other to unruly Robinson as sand in the machinery of power. Karl himself seems a nice little chap, if somewhat prissy, and one would not wish him to turn into any of these types. Better he remain like Peter Pan, 'the Boy who wouldn't grow up'.[16] But can Karl survive in this cut-throat world? He does get help from women, but a woman precipitated the first flight and the first American encounter is with a threatening goddess, later incarnated in Klara. If Klara's modern body is slimmed down compared with Sacher-Masoch's Wanda, in Brunelda luscious curves have swollen into a mountain of flesh. Just as a collective male gaze generates Klara's attraction, so Brunelda's revolting yet fascinating lure is produced through a trio of servitors. In *Venus im Pelz*, a second or third man confirms the performative aspect of the masochistic scenario directed by a man and projected for male eyes: an artist is invited to paint a portrait of Wanda in the bathroom holding a whip, her foot resting on a kneeling Gregor; later Gregor plays Peeping Tom as Wanda whips the painter; then in an overtly homoerotic twist Gregor is whipped to Wanda's orders by a young man, beautiful as the Apollo Belvedere, wearing high black boots and tight, white leather trousers. In *Der Proceß* the Byronic cavalry officer is replaced by a bit of marine rough in the whipper who wears a black leather vest open to the waist and has a sailor's wild, fresh face; the man being whipped is fat and the watcher is Josef K. In fat Brunelda's domain, Karl and Robinson are the watchers, or rather listeners from behind a screen to splashings and plashings, as Brunelda bathes in company with Delamarche, slapping the water with her fist. The *double-entendre*—literally a double-hearing by two listeners—arouses suspicion in the reader if not in Karl that Brunelda may be slapping more than the water. Although Brunelda bathes, her habitat is anything but pure. The bathing scene leads into a visit to a kitchen full of dirty dishes with disgusting remnants of food such as skin on boiled milk that Kristeva writes of in her essay on the abject (*Powers of Horror*, pp. 2–3). Brunelda's rooms are heaped with grubby clothes, curtains and blankets; the dining-table drawer is full of old powder puffs, locks of hair, nameless bits and pieces stuck together. Under the sofa, the floor is covered with balls of fluff mixed with women's hair. Like Robinson's vomit, such bodily waste signifies something monstrously disordered and disgusting, the disgust perhaps masking desire for the billowing flesh of ageing whores as Menninghaus (pp. 351–52) suggests, or for the pre-Oedipal maternal body as Kristeva (chapter 3) would have it.

Crosscutting the fetishistic detail in a pornographic subtext is allegorical meaning in a political subtext. Karl tries to escape down into the street to a scene of democratic electioneering. But the populist mood is not reassuring. Because of the crush the candidate's bearer could not move at will: there was no possibility of turning, or advancing, or retreating; the crowd was in chaotic flux. Up in the flat, Karl too cannot move at will: he is imprisoned on the balcony by a gargantuan madame who forces him to look through opera glasses which stop him seeing anything. She holds his head so cushioned on her breast that he could move it neither sideways nor back. The juxtaposed images of engulfment create a disturbing equivalence between the press of the crowd and the weight of female flesh, between the irrational mass and the woman's neurotic moodiness. Like

Sacher-Masoch's Wanda, Brunelda is subject to rapid mood switches. Like a monster baby, she is wheeled out in an invalid buggy. And splashing like a baby, she has to be sponged down and dried off. The father in 'Das Urteil' ('The Judgement') and Gregor Samsa in his first post-transformation phase are also uncannily like babies, who clearly belong with other monsters in Kafka's bestiarium. Yet as a girl Brunelda, the liveliest of her companions, had swum in the Colorado River. If Brunelda is an embodiment of America, then she has long since ceased to be a spirit of the wilderness—laughing water, Mini Haha—and has become an irrational force of subjection, sleaze, and neurosis. If this is Woman, who would want to be a Man? If this is America, perhaps Europe has the edge. Or perhaps this America is a mirror of Europe, a premonition of the failure of liberal emancipation and an irrational politics of the masses.

If steely-willed, violent Klara and hysterical, unreasoning Brunelda are the statue come to life, they do not bode well for the future. The theatre episode makes a comical plea through stereotypes to get rid of stereotypes: little girls are not all angels, nor little boys devils. But the message remains abstract with no practical pointers forwards. I conclude, then, that Kafka's travel narrative runs counter to modern faith in human perfectibility. Eruptions of the abject will always disrupt the perfection of rational order. Kristeva gives a psychoanalytic explanation of the powers of horror inhabiting the abject, which she sees as flowing from the necessary break with yet primal desire for the maternal body (*Powers of Horror*, ch. 3). A more historical view might suggest that the horror of unsanitized bodies may be an outcome of the modernizing project, of *Körperkultur* (body culture) and the cult of hygiene, order, and efficiency.[17] Rabelais's Gargantua, in Bakhtin's account, humanizes the world by ingesting it and shitting without shame, but whereas Gargantua recommends goose feathers as *torche-cul*, we now have shower installations and hide our body odours with the perfume Brunelda so shrilly demands.[18] Those balls of stuff under sofas become horrible because vacuum cleaners have created an ideal of sterile cleanliness. If we have moved on from the Renaissance body as measure of all things to anal retention and cold showers, there is no way back either to Romantic primitivism. Yet *Der Verschollene* keeps open more hope than some of Kafka's later work of serial escape, if not of final arrival. Karl may be running like the mouse in 'Kleine Fabel' (Little Fable) towards a choice between trap and cat, but at least he keeps going. *Venus im Pelz* draws the moral that he who lets himself be whipped deserves to be whipped. Compared with Georg Bendemann in

'Das Urteil' or Gregor Samsa in 'Die Verwandlung', Karl does not knuckle under, in that respect being more like K. in *Das Schloß* than Josef K. in *Der Proceß*.

But the core dystopian feature remains the choice which modern competitive society seems to offer between dominance and subjection. Evading that choice leaves Karl trapped in childishness and often in company with women. But such alliances cannot last. For women collude in sustaining the power of dominant males from which their sub-dominant maternal or sexual power still flows. The Head Cook anticipates Gardena in *Das Schloß*, powerful in the village but ultimately in thrall to Klamm, as the Cook is here to the Head Waiter. Karl could for a spell play surrogate son to the Cook. But as soon as sexuality comes into it, as happened with the maidservant back home, the boy feels challenged to become a Man; even sisterly Therese looks as if she might make demands on Karl that he grow up. (Grete Samsa too gets fed up with being a sister and as object of desire draws Gregor into mortal danger.) If even such benign, domestic women pose a threat, how much worse the two exemplars of sexual women. A comic caricature of sexually liberated woman, doubly refracted through an innocent yet knowing gaze, Klara scarcely offers hope for equal companionship. A wrestling match suggests not culture becoming feminized, but woman becoming like man in a parody of equal-rights feminism. In *Das Schloß* K.'s comic dream of men wrestling is also parodistic, mocking the strain of homoerotic utopianism in the youth movements of the times.[19] It may be, then, as Lorenz ('Kafka and gender') suggests, that Kafka shows masculine and feminine traits aligning with power relations rather than inhering in men and women. The anti-feminism in the portrait of domineering Klara follows less from misogyny than from a primary horror of dominance. Even so, the female reader might resist and root for Klara, feeling that women need for a while to become more pushy, as we may also sympathize with Grete Samsa or with Amalia's radical denial of the phallic summons in *Das Schloß*.

To a certain extent, then, Kafka aligns masculinity and femininity, or childishness, with the distribution of social power, so de-essentializing traditional gender attributions. He also conveys a sense of historically changing relations between men and women. And even if the changes are not all welcome, there is no return to patriarchal tradition, for mastery, in whatever guise, and the concomitant subjection of the other, are the problem. If, as Gail Hart has argued, Goethe's Eternal Feminine and Sacher-Masoch's dominatrix are feminized projections of Faustian man, then Kafka's Karl is an anti-Faust.[20] Not drawn on by but fleeing the goddess and her avatars, just as he flees the surrogate fathers, Karl refuses engagement in the power game. As icons of modernity, then, the Statue of Liberty and the figures of Klara and Brunelda convey socio-political rather than socio-sexual meaning. Yet the interfusing of mythic icons and human figures draws rhetorically upon misogynistic tradition in order to mock or provoke disgust at abuse of power as even more ugly and humiliating when perpetrated by women. Thus the misogyny is re-inscribed as a by-product. Brunelda is a more disturbing image than Klara, not in muscular likeness to a man but in the fleshy excess of her difference, though both women are, in the discourse of popular misogyny, ball-breakers. Brunelda's taste in clothes and furnishings may point towards the oldest profession, but in other respects she is a modern figure. Doubly independent as professional woman and divorcee, Brunelda subjects the young vagrants financially as well as psychologically. (New Women such as Fräulein Bürstner in *Der Proceß* or the schoolmistress Gisa in *Das Schloß* become less horrific in Kafka's later work.) If Brunelda's earning power is modern, her physicality caricatures gender typology since antiquity, which set woman as material nature ('das Stoffliche') over against engendering spirit ('Geist'). Yet neurotic Brunelda is a distinctly modern version of this equation of women with their bodies. The German Romantics rejected the spirit/body dualism in favour of the whole human being ('der ganze Mensch'), but all too often the ideal of unalienated wholeness served merely to pathologize deviations from the same old norms.[21] Modernization was held to endanger women especially: too much social emancipation, too much cultural ambition or sexual freedom, would virilize woman (viz. Klara) or make her neurotic. Brunelda is a hysterical neurotic, alienated from her body and yet engulfed by it. Bodily symptoms signal deviation from proper manliness too: Robinson slobbers over sweets stuck disgustingly together into a ball; Gregor Samsa in his initial plump, slimy phase gorges on rotten remains, though he will dry up and flatten out. But Brunelda does not thin down. A horror emanating from the anorexic imagination, a travesty of the Rabelaisian body, Brunelda provokes shrinking disgust of female flesh. That disgust may disguise lust, as Menninghaus suggests, may amuse, but will scarcely enthuse the feminist reader looking to move past the reduction, or in this case expansion, of women to their bodies (see Menninghaus pp. 351–52).

Yet there may be another way of seeing Brunelda, and Karl too, as the first of Kafka's performance artistes.[22] Brunelda's name and profession most obviously recall Brünnhilde, another larger-than-life goddess. The male audience watching Wagner's Brünnhilde hold opera glasses at the ready to peer at her enormous bosom when the breast-plate finally comes off. 'That is not a man!' (Das ist kein Mann!), the hero helpfully sings at the end of *Siegfried*. In immobilizing Karl's head in her bosom and reversing the direction of vision, Brunelda takes spectacular revenge on a puny exemplar of the male world, reducing him virtually to a puppet. Cartoon-like, the moment parodies through reversal the figure of woman as puppet in E.T.A. Hoffmann's famous story 'The Sandman'. Binoculars, a modern device to enhance vision, comically signify the power of the gaze in commercial entertainment. But binoculars are also emblematic of the artist-observer's striving to grasp more of reality than is evident to the naked eye.[23] If Karl is the author's prism through which to reveal a many-facetted New World, then the binoculars signally fail him, for they block rather then enhance his vision of democracy in action. Karl as failed observer and Brunelda, a quondam performer under the audience's gaze who turns the tables, or the binoculars, dimly foreshadow 'Auf der Galerie' (Up in the Gallery), Kafka's much discussed sketch presenting contrasting views of a circus performance: in the first paragraph the young man in the gallery rushes down to rescue an equestrienne from a cruel public and a relentless ringmaster; in the second he weeps without knowing it as the radiant performer and a now grandfatherly ringmaster bow to ecstatic applause. The young man weeps not over the victim to be rescued, but over the triumphant performer who leaves him no role. Comic deflation of the heroic role in oedipal melodrama goes along with sceptical reflection upon the struggle between artist and public in the determination of meaning. Like a Hegelian protagonist, the artist exposes himself to wrest recognition from the public of his vision, but in so doing risks subjection to the status of feminized object of the public gaze. The girl-performer, driven on by the ringmaster and the spectators' sadistic applause, embodies the vulnerable, expressive core of the art-work in a triangle comparable to female singer, but male composer and male audience engaged in the struggle for mastery. At the same time the spectator in the gallery, a male persona, conveys failure to realize in aesthetic form a vision which probes beneath the surface. 'Auf der Galerie' destabilizes masculinity much more radically than *Der Verschollene*. But Brunelda anticipates the equestrienne's double weak yet powerful aspect: she is a vessel of those emotions which are forbidden to proper men, but which she performs for men, thus wielding power over the young men whom she faces down through an expressive excess writ large in her body. She embodies what men must repress if they are to stop being babies and grow up to proper manhood, but what an artist must perhaps acknowledge in order to break through conventional ways of feeling and seeing.

Karl too is a proto-performer, an amateur pianist. But like the young man in the gallery, Karl fails to give his dream aesthetic form, when he cannot find the notes for a new melody he fleetingly hears in his inner ear when performing for Klara. Denying music and desire alike, Karl flees the woman whose name echoes his own. In 'Die Verwandlung' the amateur is Gregor's sister Grete, whose name echoes his own and whom he dreams of sending to the conservatory. Her playing fleetingly evokes a mythical realm of erotic bliss, where human and animal meet, where beauty recognizes the beast, where the self finds completion in the mirror of a sister other-self, a dream brutally dispelled when all the family sees is a creeping insect. Of course, had Grete Samsa gone professional, she might have lost her gift and turned into a shrill, neurotic nag, earth-bound by the weight of flesh. But she might have gone the opposite way to soar like the trapeze artiste in 'Erstes Leid' (First Sorrow), who stays up aloft in the luggage rack even when travelling. Or driven by artistic aspiration, she might have mortified the flesh like the ultra-skinny hero of 'Ein Hungerkünstler' (A Hunger Artist), or sacrificed her body to her art like the singing mouse in 'Josefina, die Sängerin oder Das Volk der Mäuse' (Josephine, the Singer or the Mouse Folk), who throws her head back, throat stretched and diaphragm vibrating in the effort of whistling. Josefina's mouth does not ingest but expresses as she purses her lips to press the air out between delicate front teeth. Yet the thin bodies and Brunelda's fatness are alike in differing from the norm. The thin man, immobilized in his cage and weak with hunger, has handmaidens who help him out; the fat woman, obesely immobilized in her flat, has male servitors who wheel her out, and the limping mouse has her male claque. Like the mouse, Brunelda once performed her coleraturas, but now decently hides her fatness under a blanket when out and about, just as Gregor Samsa hides his awfulness under the sofa. The hunger-artist and the mouse, by contrast, shamelessly exhibit their skinny bodies. But all three performers avoid respectable hard work, claiming as artistes special privileges and services from others. The metamorphosis frees the travelling salesman from his horrible job and instigates special services from Grete. Menninghaus suggests that disgust masks desire. But perhaps it also masks a shadowy, not quite realized authorial identification with Brunelda as a more dangerous, indecently female alter ego than decent, hard-working Karl, who even in the Theatre chooses to continue dutifully as lift boy rather than embrace the risky profession of artiste, as Brunelda once did. Brunelda may be Kafka's most misogynistic creation, yet the echoes and cross-connections with later work suggest unfinished business, even secret empathy with the horrible otherness of this fearful creature trapped in her monstrous body. Kafka returned only intermittently to *Der Verschollene* and finally put it aside once respectable Karl and repulsive Brunelda had merged in the composite figure of decent Gregor Samsa and his indecent body. But this first novel remains a fascinating text in itself and in myriad anticipations of later moments which allow us to glimpse an endlessly transformative imagination at work.

12

André Gide and the Making of the Perfect Child

Naomi Segal

In December 1916 André Gide, then aged just forty-seven, passed a note across a railway carriage to the twenty-six-year-old daughter of his friend and future memoirist Maria Van Rysselberghe. The note said: 'I will only ever love one woman and I can only feel true desires for young boys. But I cannot easily resign myself to seeing you without a child, nor to not having one myself.'[1]

Élisabeth Van Rysselberghe had had an occasional affair with Rupert Brooke between 1910 and 1915, and had been broken-hearted at his death not to have had a child by him. Gide's offer apparently 'dazzled her' (CPD 1, 151), but over the next few years he did little to put it into action; instead he nursed a hope that she would get pregnant 'for him' by his nephew Dominique Drouin or by Marc Allégret, the fourth son of an old family friend. Neither of those plans came to anything and Catherine, Gide's daughter by Élisabeth Van Rysselberghe, was born in 1923.

The true love Gide referred to in the note was for his cousin Madeleine, whom he had known since childhood, had vowed when barely adolescent to protect for ever from the consequences of her mother's adultery, and had married in 1895 after two journeys to North Africa in which he had found 'his normality' in some joyous sexual encounters with young Arab boys.[2] The marriage, he later insisted, had been undertaken in good faith, and there is evidence to suggest that he intended to have children with her; but by a series of failures of desire and communication, the marriage remained unconsummated. What Madeleine knew of Gide's sexual life is impossible to say, but a warm equilibrium reigned between them until, six months after the episode of the note, he fell in love with Marc Allégret. For the first time desire and deep feeling were brought together and dangerously near to the family space.

In June 1918, after much planning and plotting, Gide was about to take Marc to England for the summer months. Madeleine, with whom he had stopped off at their house in Cuverville, a Normandy village, revealed that she knew what was happening. Gide paced up and down all night and then departed in the morning, leaving her a note saying 'that I could no longer stay in Normandy with her, that *I was mouldering there*'.[3] He returned in October, was greeted by her normal smile, and everything seemed as usual until, a month later, while researching his autobiography, he asked to look through her collection of letters from him. She told him that, after contemplating suicide, she had burned them one by one.

What Gide felt he lost in those letters was not simply the gauge of his wife's patient acceptance that he loved her totally in his way. It was something of himself that he had given, and continued to give, into her safe keeping:

> Oh, I know she suffered terribly when I went away with Marc, but why did she have to take it out on the past? [. . .] The best of me is gone now, and there is nothing left to counter-balance the worst. For more than thirty years, whenever I was away for even the shortest time, I had given her—was still giving her—the best of myself, day by day; now suddenly I feel utterly destroyed [. . .] I am suffering as if she had killed our child. (J 3, 1145–46)

Two perfect children emerge then: one the gift he offers to the young feminist in the railway carriage; the other destroyed by his infidelity and his wife's grief. They do not form a parallel, of course, because after all Madeleine's act of destruction was not directed at anything she might deem an offspring: rather that child was Gide himself as unspoilt youth, as perfect author, as potentially a whole made of what was really a part-self. It was years later—when Madeleine's virtuality had resolved itself by death into the newly present shadow of a shadow—that Gide began to understand that the marriage was centred on a more significant non-existent child, the one he had refused to give to her.

During Élisabeth's pregnancy, Gide never doubted for a second that, 'strong personality' as she was,[4] she would bring forth a male child. The very thought of a daughter in that context was impossible; as Maria Van Rysselberghe notes: 'Gide passionately wants Élisabeth to have a boy. He wouldn't know how to bring up a daughter or even be interested in her' (CPD 1, 163). Indeed, when pressed, 'he realizes he has not thought about this [. . .] "I think I would give her a traditional education"' is all he has to suggest.

Gide's daughter Catherine was born on 18 April 1923, while he was away in Morocco. Maria summarizes what he told her friend Loup Mayrisch on his return:

> First of all, a great disappointment that it was a girl: he is totally shocked by this unexpected fact. With a boy, he knows he would have been a good educator; he is certain of it. He would have made him a bold, daring creature—one can never be daring enough. With a girl, he will not know what to do, how to begin. Loup said: 'I know what you're thinking: you'd like her to be brought up as she would have been brought up at Cuverville'. He concedes. With a boy he would never have been in disagreement with Beth or the 'Petite Dame'; with a girl, he might be. The virtues of the Petite Dame are not those he prizes most highly in a woman. (CPD 1, 178–79)

For Gide, the birth of a girl seems to present, as well as an unconscious shock to his desire, a serious logical conundrum: the female child could and even should have belonged to 'Cuverville', as did the now-destroyed effigy of himself as a virtuous child. It was in order to find the good bad boy that he went among independent women.[5]

Here are two versions of Gide's fantasy of the perfect male child.

Les Nourritures terrestres (Fruits of the Earth, 1897) is addressed to, even precipitated by, one might say, the ideal virtual reader, Nathanaël. To him Gide declares that the things in the text 'are no more lies, Nathanaël who will read me, than the name I give you, not knowing yours which belongs to the future'.[6] At both the start and the end of the text, Nathanaël is exhorted to read and then stop reading, desire this address and then discard it, and forget the author: 'Nathanaël, throw away my book, do not be satisfied by it [. . .] It is only *one* of the thousand possible attitudes towards life. Find your own' (GR 248). Thus Gide's desire is inseparable from pedagogy, and the perfect *destinataire* is the youth whom one loves in order to emancipate him from oneself.

The hero of *Les Caves du Vatican* (The Vatican Cellars, 1914), the good bad boy Lafcadio, styles himself 'a creature of inconsequence' (GR 744), so determinedly do he and his acts evade the cause-and-effect of family relations—he is illegitimate—and the motivational reasoning that would encourage detection—he commits a gratuitous murder. He does not fall out of the sculptural hands of the author, of course, nor that of his first seducer, the cleverer Protos. But he carries the glow of a creature new-born, open to formation. In a note for the book, Gide wrote: 'On his arms and thighs and all down his back from the nape of his neck [. . .] he had kept a silky golden-blond down which his mother, laughing, called his milk hair, as the first teeth are called the milk teeth' (GR 1573).

Both Nathanaël and Lafcadio, in different ways, play central roles in a structure that is typical of Gide's fictions: a male chain running both within and beyond the text. In *Les Nourritures terrestres*, we find both a series of mentor/pupil couples that pass from God at one end to the things of the earth at the other, and structures of address explicitly following the full narratological ladder, from real reader, implied reader, narratee, protagonist, narrator, implied author to real author. To summarize the figure of parenthood here that is central to this essay, these chains function on the model of the Platonic pedagogic/pederastic fantasy of a totally male genealogical line in which reproduction is by education rather than bodily generation, and is based on a desire radically excluding the female body.

This idea of a genealogical chain running down a line of one sex only is nothing new, even though it is, in our currently speeding age of reproductive technology, becoming freshly imaginable. Consider the startling but oddly satisfying effect of Samuel Butler's aphorism 'It has, I believe, been often remarked that a hen is only an egg's way of making another egg.'[7] In nature, species that reproduce asexually consist entirely of mothers and daughters; in sexual reproduction, too, it is clear that a male is a female's way of making another female. But the most fundamental fantasy in patriarchal culture has consisted in reversing this so that a woman is understood and disciplined to be a man's way of making another man—the consequences are too familiar and numerous to be detailed here.

In this essay I am looking at how the fantasy of genealogy without heterosexuality haunts both Gide's life and his fiction. He wants to make the perfect male child. He has made many in fiction whose virtual bodies can glow with the sheen of purely textual reproduction; such youths evade ordinary fathers or educators by the further fantasy of their bastardy or their ability to grow beyond the teacher. But what happens when the fantasy demands a real-life satisfaction, the making of the perfect child in the flesh? What a feminist reading may do is explore the effects of this desire when it confronts—either in the pot-luck of life or the exigencies of writing—the need to take account of women in general and sexual dimorphism in particular.

When Gide fell in love with Marc Allégret in 1917, the boy was seventeen; the terms in which he is described in the *Journal* show analogies not only with the glow of Lafcadio, but also the teachability of Nathanaël. In Switzerland in August, Gide declared himself (in a rather mannered third person) to feel 'at forty-eight infinitely younger than he did at twenty' (J 1, 1035),[8] the only cloud on the horizon being 'the fear of seeing the youth grow up too fast'. Marc was the ideal physical object: 'from his face and his skin there radiated a sort of blond glow. The skin of his neck, chest, face and hands, his whole body, was equally warm and golden [. . .] No words can describe the languor, the grace, the voluptuousness of his gaze' (J 1, 1037). Pederasty and pedagogy thus united in one motive, Gide adds: 'I even wonder sometimes if what I love here is not so much the music as the study of the piano, and whether perhaps what drives me is above all the wish to bring one thing to perfection.'[9] When, ten years later, Gide described the pain of rivalry in relation to Marc's closeness to Cocteau, he said: 'My hatred for C[octeau], my greatest suffering, my need to hit out, my life turned upside down, that was Pygmalion finding his statue spoiled, his work of art destroyed; all my work, the trouble I'd taken as an educator, my ideas completely ruined by another person—that "nice" C. That wasn't jealousy, it was something different.'[10]

What all this shows us is that the 'making of the perfect child' is, for Gide, a combination of desire, reproduction, education and production of an aesthetic kind. In Lafcadio Gide made the irresistible hero: in Nathanaël, more daringly, the ideal reader. The text he wrote at around the time of the development of the idea of having an illegitimate child with Élisabeth, the passion for Marc and the crisis in his marriage was one in which the main motif is the 'formation' of a love-object out of an unsexed, unsighted, unknowing 'thing' of clay.

Although completed after Gide's return from England in October 1918, the idea for *La Symphonie pastorale* (The Pastoral Symphony) went back to 1893. As its intensely ironic tone suggests, it was intended to be the 'critique of a form of lying to oneself' (GR 1583).[11] The original title was *L'Aveugle* (The Blind One) which, in its gender ambiguity, both allows the epithet of blindness to be applied as much to its narrator, the pasteur, as to Gertrude, and points to the gender ambiguity which attaches to the latter as a 'found child', who gains her sex as well as her 'soul' through the process of education.

In the analysis which follows, I am going to look particularly at the gender significance of the education of this child. What she represents in terms of the pasteur's desire is in itself complex. He invests in her not only the wish to make something/someone perfect but also to repudiate simultaneously his wife (as joint 'maker'), his children (as those given rather than made, who belong as much, perhaps more, to the unloved wife) and God (who has failed to create a world as perfect for the new child to live in as the pasteur offers her, in what he believes to be a justified fiction). He desires also to assert a Romantic religion of sincerity and impulse—here he contrasts himself with his son Jacques who eventually converts to Catholicism—over a religion of constraint and discipline. In all these impulses he is deplorable and yet he is allowed to arouse our sympathy against everyone and everything else except the acute insight of Gertrude, as she grows into and beyond the education he thinks he can give her. As she begins to understand—what he refuses to admit—that one person's happiness is bought at the expense of others'—she insists: 'I don't want to be happy; I would rather know' (GR 921; p. 61). And this is the real tragedy in this sad story: not so much the impossibility of love without honesty, but the conflict between a child's need for knowledge and an education that restricts it.

This conflict takes in, I believe, the restrictions Gide laid upon himself in translating his male beloved into a female character. This was a move that, in May 1921, he criticized in Proust;[12] yet his *La Symphonie pastorale* appeared in 1919, the same year as *À L'Ombre des jeunes filles en fleurs*, and effectively Gide did the same thing. I want to look not so much at the reasons for the transposition as at its consequences. How does Gertrude follow the trajectory by which, as Freud put it, 'a woman develops out of a child with a bisexual disposition'?[13]

The unconsciously directed nature of the pasteur's search for his object is stressed in the opening pages of his diary, where he describes a journey in the dark, along a 'road I had never ventured down before' (GR 877; p. 9) but from which he glimpses, two kilometres away, a 'mysterious lake' on which he used to skate as a boy. In the obscure corner of a cottage where a dead woman lies, he finds her niece, a huddled heap without sight or language. Just before stumbling on the child, he has said: 'it scarcely seemed likely that in the depths of this wretched dwelling there would be any hidden treasure' (GR 878; p. 11); but of course there is, and he picks it up and takes it home with him.

All the first descriptions of what will become Gertrude stress her indeterminacy: far from being female, she is not yet even human. If Amélie's horrified neuter in reaction to the child her husband brings home—'"What exactly are you intending to do with *that*?"' (GR 881, and see also GR 382)—shocks both him and us, it is not entirely different from his own. The girl is first identified as 'an indeterminate creature'; in the cabriolet she sits slumped on the floor like 'a parcel of flesh without a soul' (GR 880; p. 12) or perhaps, a little more charitably, 'this opaque body [inside which] a soul no doubt waits immured' (p. 13). Surfaces, then, are dark and unreal: depths contain something precious, perhaps inaccessible and probably dangerous. The 'real other' is a remote possibility within a remote possibility.

The girl has no age and no name; both must be given her by the pasteur's family. She has her hair shorn, her clothes burned. The first sounds she makes 'are cries with nothing human in them, like the plaintive yapping of a puppy' (GR 881; p. 14). She gobbles her food down 'with bestial greed' (GR 885, p. 19), more like a carnivore than the pastoral '"lost sheep"' (GR 881, p. 14) the father sententiously announces to his family. She is of course crawling with vermin. It is only when Amélie, whom he accuses of believing charity to be 'an exhaustible treasure' (GR 880; p. 13), gets the task of washing the inert body that Gertrude first acquires a rudimentary gender. Her name—no one seems able or willing to discover her real one—is given to her by Charlotte, the only one of his own children for whom the pasteur has some affection.

When he tries to begin the work of education, the girl's animal status and 'absolute inexpressiveness' (GR 885; p. 19) begin to signify something slightly different: 'as soon as one approached her, her features seemed to harden; they only stopped being inexpressive in order to show hostility; [. . .] I was assailed by a feeling of aversion at the obstinate refusal of this soul.' The being within, then, has to be trained or forced to emerge. It is left to the pasteur's neighbour Dr Martins to suggest both a method and an ideology: Gertrude is not so much 'immured' as herself a thing of mineral. '"You cannot begin to build"', he first advises, '"until you have made sure of solid terrain"' (GR 886;

p. 20). He then compares her to Condillac's 'animated statue', a Galatea brought to life sense by sense, and lastly to 'a deep dark well' (GR 887; p. 21) at the depths of which a hand will finally, suddenly grasp his rope, and then 'tears of gratitude and love will gush forth' from the relieved teacher.

The pedagogic impulse is thus represented as that of an archaeologist, a trainer, a Pygmalion, or a hydraulics engineer. For this is not, as the trilogy will much more boldly be, an examination of what it might mean to educate a young woman. If Gertrude is a female character, it is not because of certain futures made available to her, but because she exists to retrace the feminine teleology from an originary Freudian polymorphism to the destiny of renunciation in a return to the earth; dust to dust, mere body to mere body.

In Gide, as we have seen, good women are meant to be traditional, devoted and essentially resigned. Élisabeth may have been the chosen vessel of his son, but it was Madeleine who should have raised for him a conventional and modest daughter. And despite his resentment following the burning of the letters and the caricature embodied in Amélie, *La Symphonie pastorale* is also a homage to her version of femininity.

The education given to Gertrude marks the mediate position, then, between two states of inanimacy. Like Laura Bridgman, Gertrude is first brought 'out of her darkness' by the sense of touch: it is on her skin, that seemingly impenetrable wall, that words are lined up with things—sense on the outside, enlightenment within. The pasteur will follow this method throughout, filling Gertrude with the image of an arbitrary world he wants to make natural. The parallelism which this text so insistently marks—he as blind or blinder, she teaching as much as taught—opens with a metaphor of touch: 'as I began to guide Gertrude on this twilit road, I myself was only groping my way' (GR 888; p. 22).

When enlightenment is switched on inside, what appears on Gertrude's surface is a series of smiles that flood *his* soul with such 'seraphic joy' (GR 889; p. 24) as he has never experienced with any of his own children; as the smile 'dawns on this statue-like face', it is both an *animation* [the italics are the pasteur's] and a 'birth'. The significance of this parthenogenetic family romance has already been noted: here is the fosterer as male mother, but also as divine Pygmalion, bringing life to a thing of clay. His desire is immediately highlighted by his translation of what he sees as 'not so much intelligence as love'. As we have noted, it is when the pupil refuses that bargain that their world is set for destruction.

Once the first step has been taken, Gertrude advances 'by leaps and bounds as if in mockery of the system' (GR 890; p. 25). Nonetheless, the pasteur never forgets that she 'lived in a state of profound torpor until the day I started looking after her' (GR 891; p. 26). She is a real intellectual—'she would never pretend to understand something, as people so often do [. . .]: until she had got a clear idea of it in her mind, every notion remained a puzzle and an anxiety to her' (GR 894; p. 29)—and her questions, far from responding to a provocation on his part, not only surprise him but force him 'to think again about things I had always taken for granted' (GR 891–92; p. 26). This is not simply '"God revealing to the humble what he hides from the intelligent"' (GR 910; p. 47), as he puts it in order to enjoy the reversal of roles as brief, inconsequential carnival; it is much more dangerously the occasion for the pasteur to create his own universe in supposed response. By reifying the synaesthetic metaphors her disability seems to require, he defines the colour spectrum by the sounds of an orchestra and birdsong as God's plan made audible. He thus 'fills her' with falsehoods that he justifies in terms of her particular bodiedness.

Why does Gertrude have to be a female child taught by a male adult? So that desire can arise without disturbing the *bienséances* of fictional adultery, obviously, but also because the transaction of their pedagogical relation must be a form of transubstantiation. When Amélie teaches her daughter Sarah she reproduces her worse qualities; when Mlle de la M** teaches Gertrude or Gertrude teaches the blind girls, like flows into like in the same way they share poetry or dancing; when the pasteur grapples with his son, similarity breeds rivalry and opposition both sexual and theological. But when the pasteur teaches or loves Gertrude, her 'other' body becomes the site of significant fluids.[14]

Tears are the emanation of the face, its expression in liquid form. Anticipated as the corollary for light dawning in and therefore on that statue-like countenance, they later appear as the medium of affective communication between the couple. Gertrude can hear lies on the man's voice which she then verifies, feeling his tears by 'touching [his] cheeks' (GR 895; p. 31). When she hears Amélie accusing him, he places her hand on his cheek again to prove he has not wept, and she in turn, 'trying to smile [. . .], raised her lovely face to me, and I suddenly saw it was bathed in tears' (GR 898; p. 33).

The image of tears on the face also reappears in the concluding section, after the girl's sight has been restored. Now, back in a state of 'stupor' (GR 926; p. 66), her smile is 'strange, [. . .] strained' and unfamiliar: it 'seemed to stream from her eyes onto her face like tears'.

It seems inevitable then that Gertrude is led to a death by water. Finding on Jacques the face she thought was his, she offers the pasteur the suicide of Narcissus, bending over a stream no longer covered by the minimal skin of ice that tempted both father and son. But when she drowns it is instead as the flower-tressed Ophelia 'with hair of seaweed'. Thus the fluid economy of the girl's education returns the man's mastery to him feminized and undone. His last words, while trying and failing to pray together with his wife, are: 'I felt my heart was more arid than the desert' (GR 930; p. 71).

How, then, does the pederasty/pedagogy plot work when it is transposed into the female? The making of the perfect child here is the premise of both desire and failure. To punish his own failure to hold and shape Marc Allégret (his success, if you like, in finally letting him be Nathanaël rather than Galatea), Gide had to recreate him as fictionally female and then let the resulting mutant die. Yet the real challenge of textual production and eventually fleshly reproduction was to treat the girl as much as a whole, 'bold' human being, and this Gide had to try to do in the years that followed with his daughter Catherine.

Descriptions of Gide contemplating the baby Catherine resemble nothing so much as his interest in botany or entomology: 'he watches her, without letting her see him, as one might watch a plant' (CPD 1, 193); or, in a highly abstracted sense, his capacity for scientific curiosity. When she is just under two, 'he is pitiless in making her try the same thing twenty times over [. . .] The number of times you hear him say: "Leave her! Just leave her!" (CPD 1, 217–18). It is this experiment that he chooses to take further in the trilogy *L'École des femmes* (The School for Wives/Women, 1929), *Robert* (1930) and *Geneviève* (1936). In this text, the desired boy transposed into a girl appears no longer as love-object, but as the subject of a text which is not essentially a love story at all—or if it is a love story, it is a very different one from the surrogate heterosexuality of *La Symphonie pastorale.*

When Gide published *L'École des femmes* Catherine was six, and post-war France was preoccupied by the sudden changes in the situation of women, who had begun to cut their hair, wear short skirts and have raised expectations of careers, sexual equality and new modes of maternity. Victor Margueritte's novel *La Garçonne* (1922) had caused fascinated scandal for its portrayal of lesbianism, free thinking and the claim to unmarried motherhood—the latter tied, in a rarely consistent way, to a long-standing national anxiety about the falling birth-rate.[15]

Gide continued to hold essentially conservative views about women, but to Maria Van Rysselberghe he voiced an interest in the new ideas shared by Élisabeth and her friend Ethel Whitehorn, whom she had met during two years' study at Swanley Horticultural College in Kent in 1912–14. In 1918, for instance, he remarked: 'if Élisabeth and Whity don't succeed in finding a new way of living, outside the conventions, which women will?'(CPD 1, 8–9). But in 1923, three months before the birth of Catherine, he quoted the Margueritte novel—this sentence following his thoughts about a traditional education (cited here on p. 186)—to argue that 'for women, once the age of love is over, it is enough to feel their time is employed in being useful to others' (CPD 1, 163) and Maria recalls how, in his ideas about a utopian future, he had no thoughts about the role of women.

As its title implies, *L'École des femmes* is all about the education of women/wives—and it explores this question in three stages. In the first volume, Éveline writes a two-part diary, one just before and one towards the end of what turns out to be an unhappy marriage. Twenty years and two children after she married the man she naively adored and admired, she has discovered that Robert is fatuous and hollow. Éveline remains what her daughter Geneviève contemptuously calls 'a good woman' [*une honnête femme*] (GR 1298), does not leave her husband because he has convinced her he cannot live without her, and she eventually dies doing war work in a hospital for contagious diseases.

In the second volume, the straw man Robert makes a not always unconvincing attempt to put his side of the story. He believed in Éveline's love, he claims, more than he believed in himself—and here we find echoes of the Gide who never got over the discovery of his wife's anger and could not tolerate or even quite contemplate her existence as a separate person. Robert indicts himself most visibly when he discusses the education of women:

> I could measure the decline of her love by the increasing independence of her mind [for] insubordination is always blameworthy but especially blameworthy in a woman. In the early years of our marriage, and even more during our engagement, Éveline espoused all my opinions and ideas, without criticism [. . .] Our understanding was therefore perfect. (GR 1322)

But, as Éveline starts to assert her own opinions, 'most of our discussions were about the education of our children' (GR 1323). Robert, who believes, like Gide, that 'woman' s role is eminently conservative', finds his daughter Geneviève 'more eager to learn than Gustave and more curious than befits a woman' (GR 1323).

Éveline's virtue keeps her essentially obedient to men; despite what she knows, she still seeks endorsement from her priest, father or doctor. She can slough off Robert along with God, and she can even despise her son, but she cannot slough off duty—this despite knowing that her judgment is entirely rational. This is what makes her, like Madeleine, the heroine of a Corneillien dilemma not exactly between love and duty but between what is true and what is right. She earns a tragic *dénouement*, but it remains a devout one. Gide chooses not to let her husband be a Racinian hero. Éveline's Racinian antagonist is her daughter:

> I have just had a terrible conversation with her, which made me realize that she is the one person I could really have an understanding with but at the same time that I don't want her understanding. For I am afraid that I will find my own thoughts in her, only bolder—so much bolder that they horrify me. All the anxieties and doubts that touched me occasionally have become so many shameless negations in her. No, no, I will not consent to recognize them. (GR 1295)

The history of Gide's production of *Geneviève* is a long tale of struggles with an intractable subject, an uncomfortable voice and an unappealing protagonist; nothing seemed to fit, or to fit properly. Yet the text as it stands would strike most readers as rather well-rounded, finishing as it does on the death of Éveline, the framing motive of Geneviève's narrative, and pointing forward to a conception the protagonist has planned and seems well capable of bringing about; not to let us know which man helps her do so is quite consonant with her intention. Yet Gide sub-titled it '*La Confidence inachevée*' (The Unfinished Confidence) and only a casual line tells us that later she has a son whom she disciplines with occasional corporal punishment. That Gide felt his text was incomplete suggests an obsession rather similar to Freud's in the 'Dora' case history.[16] I would go a little further and argue that by insisting that part of Geneviève is cut off, her creator finds the only way to stop her spontaneously generating, for that is her *raison d'être*.

Gide had set himself the task of 'giving a voice (*prêter la parole*) to the new generation',[17] but their ideas were, he realized already in mid-1933, not really his own. Like alien creatures, those ideas had settled inside him without the 'rootedness' necessary for his usual ironic method whereby an 'offshoot' of his own character was 'transplanted' and allowed to grow to a self-destructive extreme.[18] Whereas it took the shock of the visit to the USSR to excise his desire for the communist romance, his real difficulty with the ideas of the 1930s generation appears more gradually and insidiously through the character of the young feminist. This may have much to do with the absence of libido and the necessity for respect—'can't I fall in love with my fiction any more?' (J 2, 365); 'I know that only the strange and bizarre can delight or induce a state of trance. But [. . .] I owe it to my heroine to remain reasonable, since I have to express myself through her' (J 2, 450)—combined with an instinctive lack of sympathy for feminism.[19] More to the point, the new generation does not wish to borrow his voice.

So he decides eventually to 'cut off' the book at the end of chapter 2, where it would have 'a sort of tolerable conclusion [. . .] though just the opposite of what I had in mind' (J 2 522). In 1933, lamenting the ideas 'which I had found myself forced to take on' (J 2 401), he notes that 'I could no longer push them to the extreme, to the absurd, as I would have been able to do in a novel which could have simultaneously exposed them, gone over them critically and finally rid me of them.' He is unable to empty his system of Geneviève because she is not susceptible to his usual ways of driving inner problems out by 'purgation' or transplantation. At once too alien and too well implanted, like a foetus, she cannot be uprooted without tearing him apart. For a woman could not simply take the man's place in Gide's new genealogy without upturning the whole argument. Instead of entering a triangular bind like his other women,[20] this heroine proposes the nearest possible thing to an exclusively female chain. No wonder he needs to believe he has left the text castrated.

With this in mind, let us enter Geneviève's narrative. As narrator she retraces the steps by which she came, via the desire of an exotic Jewish schoolfriend named Sara and admiration of another, Gisèle, brought up almost without prejudice by an enlightened English mother, to the feminism which Gide had taken it as his task to represent in this fiction.

What does this young woman want? Three things: Sara, to have a baby without marriage, and her mother. All these are ways of engaging in a female-female chain. The first attachment ends in tears: in the face of Jewish over-sophistication, Geneviève becomes excessively naive, tongue-tied with her school-fellows, so shocked at Sara's having posed 'without any clothes on, and in front of her artist father' (GR 1378) that she is forced to agree with her own hated father and falls ill of a hysterical scarlet-fever.

She then perforce transfers her female-female desire to the whole unit of Gisèle and Mme Parmentier, the model daughter-mother couple, in whom emancipation as an idea combines reassuringly with respect for men, uncritical piety, love of flowers and poetry—Geneviève can rail against these quite gently while Gide uses them to anchor his moral decor. Éveline her mother is similar. Supposedly ready to answer all Geneviève's questions with reason and frankness, she tells her nothing about sexual practice and very little about reproduction. Thus both mothers leave the protagonist unsatisfied and focused on the one thing which comes to take up all her conscious thoughts in the final section: the wish to have a child without a husband. This motive is all that is left of the coincidence of feminism with desire, the one trace of Sara that is allowed to remain after her foreign body has been excised, her obsession with '*les filles mères*' (GR 1370). I have left the phrase in French because it carries a number of specific connotations absent in the English equivalent 'unmarried mothers'. *Fille* can mean girl, daughter or prostitute; here it stands awkwardly for unmarried woman. The phrase brings the daughter-mother relation into direct adjectival apposition, and Geneviève immediately lights on it: 'the expression [. . .] had no precise meaning for me and it shocked me a little, though I could not have said why'.[21]

Her motives are initially difficult to work out because her obsession seems so little charged with ordinary desire. When she asks her 'uncle', Dr Marchant, to give her a child, it is clear that she has no wish for the sensualities of pregnancy, birth, lactation or childcare; she has thought no more about these than about the sexual act that she knows must accompany impregnation. So far is this wish dissociated from the only kind of desire she has experienced that when asked whether she would have accepted a male Sara or Gisèle as the father of her child, she demurs at the one and laughs comfortably with the other. His final argument, that he loves his wife,[22] seals both the discussion and, later, the text, when Geneviève understands the greater depth of the attachment between Marchant and Éveline.

What is Geneviève's motive then? Surely it is a realization that the only way to have the mother is to become her. Geneviève's whole text with its liminal presentations (that is, the first and last volumes of Gide's trilogy) is, after all, generated by the death of Éveline. Direct satisfaction is impossible now: her mother is gone, and she cannot have the lesbian love-object, outlawed both by an agreed anti-semitism and by the object's own failure to desire. The self-sufficient unit of Gisèle and Mme Parmentier, so enviably cemented by a dead father rather than like hers riven by a living one, is a pointer to Geneviève's true object. If there could be a female-female couple with no trace of the masculine, that is clearly what she wishes for. But, as we have seen, there cannot. Her mother has stayed *une honnête femme* to the last, loving without consummation, and martyred in uniform still in the service of men. The nearest Geneviève can get to her is by seeking to remake herself as mother and that is why the details do not matter. If there must be a man between them, let him carry the brief afterglow of being the one her mother should have loved.

Why, then, I want finally to ask, having created this 1930s young woman capable of an impressive mixture of intelligence, lesbianism, maternal attachment and feminist social conscience, does Gide end up by 'rewarding' her with a son?

Because after all, as we have seen, he did not take to the trilogy, arguing that the characters never succeeded in interesting him, and so a desultory and conventional closure suited his dissatisfaction. But there is another, more interesting reason: it is also because, actually perhaps, he had gone much further than he wished to go. By the time Gide returned to France after spending the Second World War in North Africa, the real-life Van Rysselberghe family had continued in its genealogy of women-identified-women when Catherine herself had an illegitimate daughter named Isabelle in 1945, who, by a nice coincidence, was born 79 years to the day after her great-grandmother.[23] This female chain, now circle, had both crossed and supported Gide's wish for illegitimacy and for something—to return to that note passed in 1916—that neither the love of a 'good woman' nor 'true desire' for young boys had brought him: the exclusive challenge of women's intelligence and the genealogical chain that runs by both education and reproduction at once. That the fantasy child in this fiction is a boy is a small revenge against a creative identification that shocked even him.

Postscript

Mary Orr

In the round-table discussions that concluded the conference connected to this project, initial response to the individual contributions pursued two more general lines of investigation. The first concerned the nature and direction of current feminist research. Was there a danger, for example, that by not including feminist criticism and rereading of women writer contemporaries to the men singled out for attention by this project, that the category 'women's writing' and its aesthetic impetus would ever be positioned second to the male canon? And did the term 'feminist criticism', in spite of the clearly plural form in which all contributors applied it, fail to differentiate the distinctions between feminisms within the US, UK, or European academies, and thus occlude difference of sex and race in the manner of critics in the school of the Great Tradition? The second point of major interest emerged from others working with feminist critical tools on canonical male writers within European traditions outside those of France and Germany. While some of the detailed debate on certain issues raised by specific contributions appeared marginal to the authors they were studying, the absence of certain specific concerns, as well as the relevance of common themes, similar aesthetic problems and sociological frameworks raised by the contributors, provided a welcome challenge and encouragement to press such feminist critical strategies further with regard to other European literary and aesthetic traditions. If there was one open conclusion to this discussion, it was the real shock expressed concerning the dearth of feminist criticism and scholarship *tout court*, not merely on specific canonical male writers of the period

1770–1936 in a broader European context, but in the light of the unprecedented number of established feminist and gender studies courses in a range of disciplines. In theory, the training is in place to encourage scholars to pursue such interdisciplinary and gender-sensitive research. In practice, such research is much slower to emerge.

The essays which make up this project provide some responses to this astonishment, as well as to anxieties about using the seemingly blanket term, 'feminist criticism'. This volume at the very least offers a clear first step in extending the visibility of feminist research on the twelve authors it highlights. Beyond mere listing or appraisal of often a scant trawl of previous feminist work on a given writer, contributors here provide a set of feminist approaches which not only help to explain these lacunæ, they also unlock much more nuanced readings of well-known texts, and directly challenge some of the received ideas about form, genre or aesthetic priorities attached to particular writers or literary movements such as Realism.

The collection also offers a variety of takes on the same problems, but from two specific cultural angles in the same time-frame. If an agreed misogyny informs the socio-cultural contexts of all the authors examined here, it is explained variously as a form of self-disgust in the case of Baudelaire, catalyst in the case of Stendhal, reagent for Flaubert and Fontane, or direct counterpoint to the strongly pro-women representations of Schiller or Rousseau which destabilize aesthetic conventions and show them often as gendered. Moreover, in the case of the essays on Zola and Gide, there is searching exploration of a deeper misogyny, whether the assumptions underlying Naturalism and its scientific method and male observer, or the desire in the homosexual writer to adopt male reproductive chains alone. Another feature uncovered across various contributions here is enormous sensitivity on the part of writers such as Goethe, Gide and Stendhal to representing, as well as pre-supposing, sophisticated women readers as part of a more complex aesthetic debate on epistemology, its transfer and creative forms. Indeed, redoubtable women are essential to the establishment of the male artist such as Rousseau just as they challenge male notions of womanliness in Fontane.

A further thread running across the collection is the unreliability of the male narrator as explored for example in the works of Hoffmann, Kafka, or Flaubert thanks to the complexities of identity, the irony of omniscient stances, or the play with generic parameters. Indeed, all the contributions in this volume demonstrate that genre and gender are never neat categories. Whether one is an initiator like Rousseau of a form which can more readily adapt to include women's writing (as is certainly the case with autobiography), or a writer re-forging and extending the paradigms of the sonnet (Baudelaire), tragedy (Schiller), the tale (Flaubert and Hoffmann), and the pedagogical impetus of the 'récit' (Gide), feminist scholarship in this volume makes visible and re-evaluates the aesthetic paradigms and assumptions behind each form, and from historically rooted and multiple angles. More alert to the experimentation within canonical forms, this feminist critical approach further challenges the notion of the literary canon itself as some fixed and rigid hierarchy of writing.

Should the hybridity of feminist critical approach represented in this volume still fail to allay anxiety about the cultural differences informing the term 'feminist criticism', the work of the contributors remains cognizant of distinctively US, UK, or European critical heritages and feminist contributions (as the bibliography richly demonstrates), but is work which collectively creates the very dialogue and counterpoint that their studies on individual writers in France and German from the Enlightenment to Modernism convey. In the earliest conception of the project, Heine and Kafka were seen as essential to this cross-border exchange and investigation of the outsider within, concepts amply enlarged by inclusion of Rousseau to frame this debate, just as the invitations to contribute extended any insularity of feminist focus. If one message emerges the more clearly, it is that any single notion of 'feminist criticism' is richly unsettled by the practice(s) employed in the twelve chapters.

With regard to the wider project for feminist scholarship on canonical male European authors beyond this volume on French and German writers from 1770–1936, strategic priorities developed here suggest why informed feminist criticism of the 'male' canon matters. Authorities are as much a certain canon of feminist critics as the phallogocentric bastions of aesthetics and art to be pulled down. There has been no glib reiteration of such feminist frameworks, or use of such jargon in this volume, since these limit and fail to encapsulate the much richer socio-historical contexts brought to bear on the authors treated here. If third-wave feminisms have already pinpointed the blind spots and assumptions of second-wave feminists, especially by focusing on subaltern and postcolonial women and their various politics of writing and art, this volume suggests a different but no less transnational approach, the re-examination of some of the very foundations, socio-critical contexts, generic and aesthetic norms out of and against which twenty-first-century writing springs, and by which the latest forms of cultural representation are still judged. By returning to the heated cross-border exchanges between post-Enlightenment French and German theories of aesthetics from feminist critical standpoints, the developments of two national literatures, the fashioning of their avant-garde movements, and the extension of particular literary genres in the hands of the male writers who informed and developed them, are demonstrably more complex. Furthermore, the seamless, positivistic evolution from pre-Romanticism, Romanticism, Realism to Naturalism and Modernism that is still taught as the model of European aesthetics can no longer be served up. Instead, as demonstrated in this volume, we see the much more problematic questioning of neat 'movements', the grafts of older and innovative forms, the doubling or splitting of roles, the inversion of plot conventions—in short the problematization of a single narrative.

Throughout this volume, the canon in France and Germany of 1770–1936 has been taken as read, but it is the feminist reappraisal of its complexities, as too the understanding of much of feminisms' inheritance from the same base, superstructure and interstices, that emerges as the more interesting with regard to the creative writing of the period. The book-ends of this project question presuppositions about the weight and influence of classical Greek and Latin models on canonical writers in France and Germany concerning rhetoric, art and the role of the artist, just as any putative nostalgia in Gide for example for the Hellenized values of the homoerotic and the male mentor-pupil dyad are decentred by the repercussions of the so-called 'fin-de-siècle' exemplification of decadence and degeneration, but which has been seen in Zola as pathologies of the criminal and her censors. If the great imaginative works have always spilled beyond the neat classifications of reading and criticism imposed upon them, this volume suggests the ways in which twelve representative *œuvres* find renewed interest and relevance when re-appraised by feminist scholarship, but how they in turn continue to hone feminist scholarly method into a more sophisticated instrument.

By also taking on the weight of secondary critical tablets of stone on all of the authors treated in this volume, we suggest a further impact of feminist criticism on canonical writers and their work. This is less a highlighting of the feminist gaps in bibliographies than the refusal to be cowed by received critical wisdom, or to reopen discussion on seemingly well-worked material. As the essays on Heine and Stendhal overtly demonstrate here, there is also the surprising reluctance of feminist critics to engage in depth with canonical male authors whose credentials as proto-feminists make them automatically of prime interest to the multifarious aspects of 'the woman question' in writing. Stendhal's appeal to Beauvoir, as the writings of Baudelaire, Flaubert, Kleist and Kafka among others to Cixous, should have signalled a much more important precedent to contemporary feminist critics than has been the case. As the volume has tacitly indicated, it can be the dangerously similar, rather than the radically other which is the more threatening to neat definition or acceptability of endeavour. The many contradictions and hierarchies established by the critical canon were as constricting to the male writers studied here, as they were exclusionary to women writers. Feminist critical perspectives are well placed to investigate the extent of these constrictions and exclusions, and to contribute further to masculinities theory and approaches to male-authored texts.

Feminist *scholarship* on canonical male writers also presses out a reappraisal of the ingrained notions of scholar as gentleman and critic as male authority, two concepts grounded and developed in the period this book covers. As the work of feminist critics all versed in these sociocritical, historical and aesthetic fields, yet working in academic and educational worlds which are the results of the development of the long nineteenth-century version of the University, feminist scholarship of the rich and nuanced kind that this collection indicates allows scholarship itself, especially its criteria of objective excellence, to be extended and overturned. Again, if there is one point of real leverage feminist critical scholarship in this volume demonstrates, it is the ability to pinpoint contradictions, inconsistencies and double standards, evolutions and volte-faces in writers' works and aesthetic opinions, or mis-matches between theory and practice. The divergence in creative outworking in Schiller's plays of his aesthetic writings, Rousseau's writing as against his political works, Zola's Naturalist novels as compared to his journalism and the *Roman expérimental* or Flaubert's fictions as opposed to his views on art vehemently expressed in his *Correspondance*, provide examples here of the fields for further study but, more importantly, ways to tackle them. Such identification of the unresolved tensions in creative canonical works, together with the purchase on the shifts and variations of knotty problems are strengths of the openly plural feminist approaches developed in each of the contributions here. These offer an exciting point of departure for feminist scholarship on other canonical French and German male writers of the period and beyond in time and space and, by dint of less categorical understanding of the aesthetic values upheld by these, their women counterparts.

What all the contributors in this volume have avoided is hackneyed examination of representations of women, anachronistic application of late-twentieth-century feminist theory or tactics which would exclude all but aesthetic deliberation of forms of *écriture féminine*. However, where earlier debates on aesthetics and the literary canon left woman as muse, model (whether of Madonna or whore) or impossible blue-print in the artist's mind, blue-stocking, hysteric, dark continent or (phallic and castrating) Mother, the essays here negotiate strong female presences and flag up the agency of the intelligent female/feminist reader, thus disrupting preconceived figurative or historical bounds for women in society and in writing. The crimes of such exclusions and false configurations, as pinpointed in this volume especially in the works of Zola, continue to reverberate in all manner of censorship, from codices of banned books, to critical fashion or academic institutional embargo on certain courses and approaches. It is for feminist criticism to continue to uncover and negotiate in canonical works the empowering innovation and challenge, both critical and creative, of past models for the future. Our invitation to students new to the works and authors discussed here, and to researchers alike, is to reread these so-called 'classics' of the French and German canon with a fresh eye sharpened in vision by feminist critical lenses.

Notes

Chapter 1

1. See Thomas P. Saine, 'The World Goethe Lived In: Germany and Europe, 1750–1830' in Lesley Sharpe (ed.) *The Cambridge Companion to Goethe* (Cambridge: Cambridge University Press, 2002) pp. 6–22, for a succinct but thorough account of Goethe's world.
2. See David Hill, 'Introduction' in D. Hill (ed.) *Literature of the Sturm und Drang* (Rochester, NY: Camden House, 2003) pp. 1–44.
3. From the unfinished 'Über den Dilettantismus' in *Johann Wolfgang Goethe: Sämtliche Werke*, ed. by Hendrik Birus and others, 40 vols (Deutscher Klassiker Verlag: Frankfurt/Main, 1987–99) vol. 18, p. 747. Further references to this edition (DK) will be cited by volume and page numbers.
4. Some excellent examples of this work include the titles by Brinker-Gabler, Kord, Möhrmann, and Wurst in the bibliography.
5. Strong challenges to Goethe's position, such as the recent trio of polemical studies by W. Daniel Wilson (*Geheimräte gegen Geheimbünde* (Stuttgart: Metzler, 1991); *Unterirdische Gänge* (Göttingen: Wallstein, 1999); *Das Goethe-Tabu* (Göttingen: Wallstein, 1999)) confirm by their very existence the awesome stature of this poet.
6. See, for example, Deirdre Vincent's 'Mädchen, Frau, Ehefrau . . . Zur Muttergestalt bei Goethe' in Renate Möhrmann (ed.) *Verkitscht, verklärt, vergessen: Die Mutter als ästhetische Figur* (Stuttgart: Metzler, 1996) pp. 92–107. Vincent reviews female roles in various works and concludes that Goethe's preference for young girls accounts for the dearth of mother figures.
7. Katharina Mommsen, 'Goethe as a Precursor of Women's Emancipation' in Clifford Bernd (ed.) *Goethe Proceedings: Essays Commemorating the Goethe Sesquicentennial at the University of California, Davis* (Columbia, South Carolina: Camden House, 1984) pp. 51–65 (p. 63).
8. See Helmut Fuhrmann's criticism ('tollkühne These') in 'Der

schwankende Paris: Bild und Gestalt der Frau im Werke Goethes', *Jahrbuch des Freien Deutschen Hochstifts* (1989) pp. 37–127 (p. 87).

9. See, for example, Ulrike Prokop, *Die Illusion vom grossen Paar: Weibliche Lebensentwürfe im deutschen Bildungsbürgertum 1750–1770* (Frankfurt/Main: S. Fischer, 1991).
10. 'Goethe als Muse: Der Autor und die Schriftstellerinnen seiner Zeit', *Goethe-Jahrbuch* 112 (1995) pp. 183–95.
11. See Becker-Cantarino, 'The Discourse of Patriarchy in Goethe's *Wilhelm Meister*', *Neohelicon* 20 (1993) pp. 137–53. Also, for a recent review of analytical work, see Petra Willim, *So frei geboren wie ein Mann? Frauengestalten im Werk Goethes* (Königstein/Taunus: Helmer, 1997) pp. 7–42.
12. Julie Prandi and others have detailed the varieties of gender transcendence represented by these imposing women. See Prandi, *Spirited Woman Heroes: Major Female Characters in the Dramas of Goethe, Schiller, and Kleist* (Bern, New York: Peter Lang, 1983). See also the items by Wagner and W. Daniel Wilson, 'Amazon, Agitator, Allegory', in the bibliography.
13. *Conversations of Goethe with Johann Peter Eckermann*, trans. by John Oxenford; ed. by J.K. Moorhead (New York: Da Capo Press, 1998) p. 273 (22 October 1828). Passage quoted by Martha Helfer, 'Wilhelm Meister's Women', *Goethe Yearbook* 11 (2002) pp. 229–54 (p. 229).
14. See my 'Star-Gazing: Authority, Instinct, and the Women's World of Goethe's *Stella*', in *Tragedy in Paradise: Family and Gender Politics in German Bourgeois Tragedy 1750–1850* (Columbia, SC: Camden House, 1996) pp. 41–54.
15. 'Goethe as a Critic of Literary Women', in Karl Fink (ed.) *Goethe as a Critic of Literature*, (New York: University Press of America, 1984) p. 177.
16. See Sigrid Damm, *Christiane und Goethe: Eine Recherche* (Frankfurt/Main: Insel, 1998) who lists epithets including 'un bel pezzo di carne, gründlich ungebildet' (Thomas Mann); 'ein rundes nichts' (Charlotte Schiller); and 'eine Blutwurst, die toll geworden sei' (Bettina von Arnim), 9.
17. See 'Der schwankende Paris', p. 51, for a list of examples that includes Adelheid and Maria of *Götz von Berlichingen* and Charlotte and Ottilie of *Die Wahlverwandtschaften*.
18. Lines 6838–39, 6845–47. English translation: Goethe, *Faust I and II*, ed. and trans. by Stuart Atkins (Cambridge, MA: Suhrkamp/Insel, 1984) pp. 175–76. I will use Atkins' translation throughout with two small changes. In one case, I have substituted 'lead' for 'guide' to support my reading of the German and in all cases I have substituted 'Gretchen' for 'Margarete' to avoid confusion. The figure is universally referred to as Gretchen, but her lines are preceded with the full name.
19. See Andre Banuls, 'Familienverhältnisse in Goethes Faust', *Orbis Litterarum* 42 (1987) pp. 332–37.

20. 'Seducing Helena: The Court Fantasy of *Faust II*, Act III', *Goethe Yearbook* 10 (2001) pp. 99–114 (p. 111).
21. Peter Heller comments on the elaborate methods employed in Gretchen's seduction by citing Nietzsche's aphorism 124 from *Menschliches Allzumenschliches II: Der Wanderer und sein Schatten*:
    DIE FAUST IDEE: Eine kleine Nähterin wird verführt und unglücklich gemacht; ein grosser Gelehrter aller vier Fakultäten ist der Übeltäter. Das kann doch nicht mit rechten Dingen zugegangen sein. Nein gewiss nicht! ohne die Beihilfe des leibhaftigen Teufels hätte es der grosse Gelehrte nicht zustande gebracht.—Sollte dies wirklich der grösste deutsche tragische Gedanke sein, wie man unter Deutschen sagen hört?
    Quoted in 'Gretchen: Figur, Klischee, Symbol' in Wolfgang Paulsen (ed.) *Die Frau als Heldin und Autorin* (Bern: Francke, 1979) p. 182.
22. Margaret P. Guenther, '*Faust*: The Tragedy Reexamined' in Susan Cocalis and Kay Goodman (eds) *Beyond the Eternal Feminine: Critical Essays on Women in German Literature* (Stuttgart: Hans Dieter Heinz, 1982) pp. 75–98 (p. 87).
23. To Friedrich Wilhelm Riemer, *Mitteilungen über Goethe. Auf Grund der Ausgabe von 1841 und des handschriftlichen Nachlasses,* ed. by Arthur Pollmer (Leipzig, 1921); quoted in Fuhrmann p. 105 (my translation).
24. The attribution of a lack of humour to feminists is so much a commonplace that it has even entered the discourse of simple witticisms: Question: How many feminists does it take to change a light bulb? Answer: One. And that's not funny.
25. *Mein Genie: Hassliebe zu Goethe & Co.* (Frankfurt/Main: S. Fischer, 1993) pp. 62–69.
26. Lessing's *Miss Sara Sampson* (1755) is generally considered the first German specimen of the genre; Heinrich Leopold Wagner's *Die Kindsmörderin* (1776) is a standard example. Its slight similarities to Goethe's plan for the Gretchen tragedy caused Goethe to accuse Wagner of plagiarism.
27. I have made a similar argument in an essay on the presence of Goethe's *Faust* in Sacher-Masoch's *Venus im Pelz.* In this case there is always a question of who leads/dominates and who follows/submits since the dominatrix is at all times obeying the dominated man, because the terms of her contract to him specify that she is to exact obedience. See 'Das Ewig-Weibliche nasführet dich: Feminine Leadership in Goethe's *Faust* and Sacher-Masoch's *Venus*' in Jane K. Brown and others (eds), *Interpreting Goethe's Faust Today* (Columbia, SC: Camden House, 1994) pp. 112–22.
28. LORD: Though now [Faust] only serves me blindly and ineptly,
    I shall soon lead him into clarity—
    [. . .]
    MEPHISTOPHELES: What'll you bet? You'll lose him yet

If you grant me permission
To lead him gently along my road (l. 309–10, 12–14/p. 10).
Atkins translated 'ihn meine Strasse sacht zu führen' as to *guide* him gently, an alternative translation of 'führen', which Goethe uses in both cases. I have substituted 'lead' and I suspect that Atkins may have used 'guide' to avoid repetition.

Chapter 2

1. See J.-J. Rousseau, *Les Confessions* in *Œuvres complètes*, ed. by Bernard Gagnebin and Marcel Raymond (Paris: Pléiade, 1959) pp. 402–03 (hereafter *OC* I, trans. by J.M. Cohen as *The Confessions* (Harmondsworth: Penguin, 1953) p. 375.
2. *The Odyssey* is a fascinating and complex model in this respect, and one that was important for eighteenth-century understanding of hospitality. See Steve Reece, *The Stranger's Welcome: Oral Theory and the Aesthetics of the Homeric Hospitality Scene* (Ann Arbor: The University of Michigan Press, 1993) for detailed analysis of the key hospitality scenes in Homer. Importantly the *xenia* relationship between peers is one that is inherited. A good man (a good host) will treat beggars well, and the Suitors are shown to be men deserving of punishment by *inter alia* the way they mistreat Odysseus disguised as a beggar. All the same, a beggar would not be treated with the honour that is appropriate for a *xenia*. Importantly, however, a noble guest (or a god) may appear as a beggar (for example, Odysseus appears naked and dirty before Nausicaa) and only emerge in their true light after they have been fed.
3. Of course it is always difficult to mark an origin: some critics would return to Montaigne's *Essays* and others back to St Augustine's *Confessions*. However, it is common for Rousseau's *Confessions* to be picked as the beginning of a peculiarly modern mode of introspective autobiography; see, for example, Michael Sprinker, 'Fictions of the Self: The End of Autobiography' in James Olney (ed.) *Autobiography: Essays Theoretical and Critical* (Princeton: Princeton University Press, 1980).
4. There is considerable material on Rousseau's readership throughout the centuries—some of his readers were and are themselves well-known, and also historians have searched various archives for evidence of the responses of ordinary readers contemporary to Rousseau. See Robert Darnton, 'Readers Respond to Rousseau' in *The Great Cat Massacre And Other Episodes in French Cultural History* (Harmondsworth: Penguin, 1985 [1984]), pp. 209–49, which investigates the archive of the Swiss publishers and book-sellers, Société Typographique de Neuchâtel. See also Claude Labrosse, *Lire au XVIII*[e] *siècle:* La Nouvelle Héloïse *et ses lecteurs* (Lyons: Presses Universitaires de Lyon, 1985). Mary Seidman Trouille, *Sexual Politics in the Enlightenment. Women Writers Read Rousseau* (New York:

State University of New York Press, 1997) analyses Félicité de Genlis, Louise d'Epinay, Manon Roland, Germaine de Staël and Mary Wollstonecraft. I have analysed women writers' readings of Rousseau in 'Rousseau in Daniel Deronda', *Revue de littérature comparée* 56 (1982) pp. 62–77; 'From Eliot's "raw bone" to Gyges' Ring: Two Studies in Intertextuality', *Paragraph* 1 (1983) pp. 44–59; 'Genlis's *Mademoiselle de Clermont:* A Textual and Intertextual Reading', *Australian Journal of French Studies* 37:3 (2000) pp. 331–47; 'The Reworking of *La Nouvelle Héloïse* in Genlis's *Mademoiselle de Clermont*', *French Studies Bulletin* 77 (2000) pp. 7–11.

5. The reasons for this include psychoanalytical, political and stylistic questions. One example of psychobiography is Pierre-Paul Clément, *Jean-Jacques Rousseau de l'éros coupable à l'éros glorieux* (Neuchâtel: La Baconnière, 1976). Felicity Baker uses psychoanalytic structures rather differently; see, for example, her analysis of Book II of the *Confessions*, 'Perverse Scenes of Writing', *Society for Critical Exchange Reports* 10 (1980) pp. 57–71, which draws not only on Freud, but also on Wilfred Bion, André Green and Joyce McDougall as well as the analyses of Rousseau by Paul de Man. The question of transference and counter-transference in readers' response to Rousseau is critical.
6. See Raymond Trousson, *Jean-Jacques Rousseau* (Paris: Tallandier, 1988–89) and Maurice Cranston, *The Noble Savage: Jean-Jacques Rousseau 1754–1762* (Harmondsworth: Allen Lane, 1991) for examples of reactions to Rousseau from Voltaire and others; for O' Brien, see *The Independent Magazine* 12 December 1992, p. 62.
7. See, for one example, Annie Leclerc, *Origines* (Paris: Grasset, 1988).
8. *A Vindication of the Rights of Woman*, ed. by Miriam Brody Kramnick (Harmondsworth: Penguin, 1975), see pp. 173–91.
9. See for example Eva Figes, *Patriarchal Attitudes* (London: Faber, 1970) or Susan M. Okin, *Women in Western Political Thought* (Princeton: Princeton University Press, 1979).
10. Some important work has been influenced by Jacques Derrrida and Paul de Man; for example Peggy Kamuf, *Signature Pieces: On the Institution of Authorship* (Ithaca, NY: Cornell University Press, 1988); Sarah Kofman, *Le Respect des femmes* (Paris: Galilée, 1982). Derrida's main analysis of Rousseau is in *De la grammatologie* (Paris: Les Éditions de Minuit, 1967); for de Man see *Allegories of Reading: Figural Language in Rousseau, Nietzsche, Rilke and Proust* (New Haven: Yale University Press, 1979).
11. See my *Justice and Difference in the Works of Rousseau* (Cambridge: Cambridge University Press, 1993) and *Feminine Economies. Thinking Against the Market in the Enlightenment and the Late Twentieth Century* (Manchester: Manchester University Press, 1997).
12. There is now considerable interest in Rousseau's 'minor' works and even fragments. With respect to autobiography, see, for example, Susan K.

Jackson, *Rousseau's Occasional Autobiographies* (Columbus: Ohio State University Press, 1992).

13. See my 'Language as hospitality: revisiting intertextuality', *Paragraph* 27:1 (2004) pp. 113–27.
14. See Paul Gilroy, *Between Camps: Race, Identity and Nationalism at the End of The Colour Line* (Harmondsworth: Allen Lane, 2000) chapter 2 'Modernity and Infrahumanity' for Kant on the black 'race' and its inferiority. Gilroy takes off from Ronald A.T. Judy, *(Dis)forming the American Canon: African-Arabic Slave Narratives and the Vernacular* (Minnesota: University of Minnesota Press, 1993), chapter 4, section 3 'Kant and the Critique of Pure Negro'. The Kant text which most notoriously uses a raciological model is 'Of National Characteristics, so far as They Depend upon the Distinct Feeling of the Beautiful and Sublime', section 4 of *Observations on the Feeling of the Beautiful and the Sublime* (trans. by John T. Goldthwait, Berkeley and Los Angeles: University of California Press, 1960). Interestingly Kant quotes the 'Swiss' Rousseau on French women as part of his consideration of national characteristics and of feminine hospitality in France (p. 102). Section 3, 'Of the Distinction of the Beautiful and Sublime in the Interrelations of the Two Sexes', would also be relevant to our concerns here. *Perpetual Peace* is in *Perpetual Peace and Other Essays*, trans. by Ted Humphrey (Indianapolis: Hackett Publishing Company, 1983), pp. 107–43. For the rhetoric of hospitality in the Revolution, see Sophie Wahnich, *L'Impossible Citoyen: L'étranger dans le discours de la Révolution française* (Paris: Albin Michel, 1997).
15. Derrida writes: 'Hospitality is culture itself and not simply one ethic amongst others. Insofar as it has to do with the *ethos*, that is, the residence, one's home, the familiar place of dwelling, inasmuch as it is a manner of being there, the manner in which we relate to ourselves and to others, to others as our own or as foreigners, *ethics is hospitality*; ethics is so thoroughly coextensive with the experience of hospitality. But for this very reason, and because being at home with oneself (*l'être-soi chez soi—l'ipséité même*—the other within oneself) supposes a reception or inclusion of the other which one seeks to appropriate, control, and master according to different modalities of violence, there is a history of hospitality, an always possible perversion of *the* law of hospitality (which can appear unconditional), and of the laws which come to limit and condition it in its inscription as a law.' *Cosmopolites de tous les pays, encore un effort!* (Paris: Galilée, 1997) pp. 42–43 (*On Cosmopolitanism and Forgiveness*, trans. by Mark Dooley and Michael Hughes (London: Routledge, 2001) pp. 16–17).
16. Felicity Baker, 'L'esprit de l'hospitalité chez Emile', *Romantisme* 4 (1972) pp. 90–99 analyses hospitality in *Émile* V where it comes closest to the idealized model. Baker argues for its importance in Rousseau's ethics and politics as follows: 'The host who receives strangers generously without

making a material profit from them becomes aware of himself as donor: as he protects others, he recognizes his own strength; as he spends time with other beings, he enriches his mind [*esprit*]; as he lets the stranger depart laden with gifts, his own individual self [*individualité*] is extended. This psychic expansion and reinforcement of the hospitable being, of the *dépositaire* [the one who keeps something safe on behalf of another] are not only a more profoundly interesting gain than any "real" profit: it is even the sole means that Rousseau suggests for preserving individual integrity in the bosom of social belonging' (p. 96, my translation).

17. Hospitality in Homer is, however, by no means straightforward. If we take just the first book of the *Odyssey*, for example, we have three representations of hospitality. While Telemachus's welcome of Mentes (Athene in disguise) seems to fit the paradigm, the focus throughout this first book is more on the abuse of hospitality. The background is Odysseus's fate as the unwilling guest of the nymph Calypso, and the foreground is the situation of Penelope and Telemachus as unwilling hosts to the suitors, who are the epitome of badly-behaved guests. While the virgin and motherless goddess *disguised as a man* (and chieftain, therefore peer) receives appropriate treatment from her male host, in both of the other cases we have open sexual difference and desire—and abuse.
18. *De l'hospitalité: Anne Dufourmantelle invite Jacques Derrida à répondre* (Paris: Calmann-Lévy, 1997), pp. 131–33 (trans. by Rachel Bowlby as *Of Hospitality: Anne Dufourmantelle Invites Jacques Derrida to Respond* (Stanford: Stanford University Press, 2000) pp. 149, 151).
19. See my 'Acceptable hospitality: from Rousseau's Levite to the strangers in our midst today', *Journal of Romance Studies* 3:2 (2003) pp. 1–14.
20. One key issue is the telling of the tale of the rape by the victim, by the 'head of household' and/or by the author. This telling is typically not only a grammatical narrative which may be judged true or false (a series of statements), but also a rhetorical construction which should have a certain effect. The tale may be a spoken or written performance narrowly understood, or may include silent rhetoric, which often has a more powerful effect, such as Lucretia's public suicide or the Levite's dismembering the body of his beloved. The appropriate response of the eighteenth-century recipient of the message may be one of liquefaction—dissolving into tears—although the more virile antique response to the two examples above (and to Helen's rapt) is military action. I have analysed these four examples of episodes of sexual violence in *Justice and Difference*, Chapter Six.
21. Rousseau describes his conversation with Mme de Warens when they are alone as: 'un babil intarissable' (*OC* I, 107), unfortunately translated as 'one interminable gossip' (*The Confessions*, p. 107). The translation takes us in the direction of *society* while I think Rousseau's choice of vocabulary deliberately points to the natural world: *babil,* which is often seen as

childish or feminine babbling (and the *Petit Robert* quotation to support this point is from Rousseau), is also used for brooks, springs or birds. *Intarissable* means something which never stops flowing and is frequently used for water (springs but also tears).

22. Of course his hopes are often dashed. The distinction is not clear cut, as we see with the 'retreat' to the Hermitage which Mme d'Epinay has refurbished for him.
23. Henry Louis Gates Jr. makes the point with respect to early life writings by African Americans who, coming out of slavery, have a desire to have a voice, to be heard, to tell their tale aloud. See *Bearing Witness: Selections from African American Autobiography in the Twentieth Century* (New York: Pantheon Books, 1991).
24. (Paris: Seuil, 1975). Michael Sheringham's *French Autobiography Devices and Desires* (Oxford, Clarendon Press, 1993) does make reference and devotes some analysis to some of the many French women autobiographers (notably Beauvoir, Leduc and Sarraute) but the only authors named in chapter titles are Rousseau, Stendhal, and Leiris. He does not mention, say, Marie Cardinal or Maryse Condé who are the subjects of chapters for Françoise Lionnet below. The recurrent pattern for Sheringham would be as follows: 'Rousseau finds Montaigne evasive; Chateaubriand finds Rousseau unseemly; Stendhal finds Chateaubriand egotistical. There is Rousseau (and Proust) in Gide; Gide in Green; Leiris in Perec. Leiris designates Nerval and Breton as precursors; Genet and Gorz write with and against Sartre; Leduc [finally!] with and against Beauvoir; Sartre and Beauvoir write with and against each other and their acolytes' (pp. 15–16). To those of us cocooned in feminism it is instructive to study books on autobiography and see how Sartre is generally regarded as so much more important for the genre than Beauvoir. Sheringham does focus on women writers in 'Changing the script: women writers and the rise of autobiography' in Sonya Stevens (ed.) *A History of Women's Writing in France* (Cambridge: Cambridge University Press, 2000) pp. 185–203. He is not unreservedly enthusiastic about the phenomenon, characterizing Hélène Cixous's writings, for example, as 'strangely flaccid and verbose', 'indulgent towards themselves' and 'limp' (p. 173). It is tempting to comment on this choice of vocabulary.
25. See, for example, Françoise Lionnet's *Autobiographical Voices: Race, Gender, Self-Portraiture* (Ithaca and London: Cornell University Press, 1989) in the series *Reading Women Writing.*
26. In 'Women's Autobiographical Selves: Theory and Practice' in Shari Benstock (ed.) *The Private Self Theory and Practice of Women's Autobiographical Writings* (Chapel Hill: University of North Carolina Press, 1988), pp. 34–62.
27. To us it may seem that Rousseau was an exceptionally important figure by the time he came to write his autobiography. However, in his view (and

that is the mood of *The Confessions*) he is chiefly a despised outcast who runs the risk of either not being remembered or being portrayed by history as a villain.

28. See Estelle C. Jelinek, 'Introduction' in her *Women's Autobiography: Essays in Criticism* (Bloomington, Indiana University Press, 1980).

Chapter 3

1. See, for example, Ute Gerhard, *Schiller als Religion. Literarische Signaturen des XIX. Jahrhunderts* (Munich: Fink, 1994).
2. On the poem see Ursula Naumann, '"Für einer Zeitung Gnadenlohn"? Schillers Gedicht "Die berühmte Frau" und Sophie Ludwigs Buch *Juda oder der erschlagene Redliche*', *Zeitschrift für deutsche Philologie* 109 (1990), Sonderheft: Schiller. Aspekte neuerer Forschung, pp. 16–26.
3. See *Friedrich Schiller. On the Aesthetic Education of Man in a Series of Letters*, ed. and trans. by Elizabeth M. Wilkinson and L.A. Willoughby (Oxford: Oxford University Press, 1967) p. 57.
4. For a general discussion see Christine Battersby, *Gender and Genius: Towards a Feminist Aesthetics* (London: The Women's Press, 1989).
5. See his letter to Goethe of 6 February 1798.
6. See, for example, the important study by Silvia Bovenschen, *Die imaginierte Weiblichkeit. Exemplarische Untersuchungen zu kulturgeschichtlichen und literarischen Präsentationsformen des Weiblichen* (Frankfurt/Main: Suhrkamp, 1979). More recently Constantin Behler in his study *Nostalgic Teleology: Friedrich Schiller and the Schemata of Aesthetic Humanism*, Stanford German Studies (Berne, Berlin, Frankfurt/Main: Lang, 1995) offers a Foucauldian analysis of enlightenment paradigms as instruments of control and accuses Schiller of being the cultural force behind the rigidity of gender stereotypes that dominated the nineteenth and first half of the twentieth century.
7. This view was reiterated by Susanne Kord in 'Performing Genders: Three Plays on the Power of Women', *Monatshefte* 86 (1994) pp. 95–115.
8. In an early contribution to essays recognizing the gender dimension of the play Volker Klotz asserts that the private issues usurp the public theme in a mixture of classical drama and domestic tragedy. See 'Kronen und lange Haare. Schillers *Maria Stuart*' in Volker Klotz, *Kurze Kommentare zu Stücken und Gedichten*, Hessische Beiträge zur deutschen Literatur (Darmstadt: Roether, 1962) pp. 7–14. An extension of this view is put forward by Sigrid Lange in *Die Utopie des Weiblichen im Drama Goethes, Schillers und Kleists* (Europäische Hochschulschriften 1382, Frankfurt Main, Berlin, Bern: 1993), who sees the fact that Maria exhibits womanly weakness and Elisabeth vanity as the product of Schiller's bourgeois conception of femininity (pp. 110–16).
9. See *Schillers Dramen. Neue Interpretationen*, ed. by Walter Hinderer

(Stuttgart: Reclam, 1979) pp. 174–216. This essay was reprinted in slightly revised form in Hinderer (ed.) *Interpretationen. Schillers Dramen* (Stuttgart: Reclam, 1992) pp. 280–336.

10. See Helmut Fuhrmann, 'Revision des Parisurteils. "Bild" und "Gestalt" der Frau im Werk Friedrich Schillers', *Jahrbuch der Deutschen Schillergesellschaft* 25 (1981) pp. 316–66. The essay is later revised and extended to form part of Fuhrmann's volume *Zur poetischen und philosophischen Anthropologie Schillers. Vier Versuche* (Würzburg: Königshausen und Neumann, 2001) pp. 9–79. Also Hans Peter Herrmann and Martina Herrmann, *Friedrich Schiller. 'Maria Stuart'. Grundlagen und Gedanken zum Verständnis des Dramas* (Frankfurt/Main: Diesterweg, revised edition 1989) esp. pp. 107–12.
11. The tradition–experiment contrast was first suggested by W.F. Mainland in *Schiller and the Changing Past* (London: Heinemann, 1957) pp. 57–86.
12. Immanuel Kant, *Zum ewigen Frieden. Ein philosophischer Entwurf*, ed. by Theodor Valentiner (Stuttgart: Reclam, 1953) p. 53. The translation is my own.
13. 'Politics as a Vocation' in *From Max Weber. Essays in Sociology*, trans., ed. and with an introduction by H.H. Gerth and C. Wright Mills (London: Routledge and Kegan Paul, 6th edn. 1967) p. 123.
14. See Peter Schäublin, 'Der moralphilosophische Diskurs in Schillers *Maria Stuart*', *Sprachkunst* 17 (1986) pp. 141–87.
15. F.J. Lamport puts the contrary argument in 'Krise und Legitimitätsanspruch: *Maria Stuart* als Geschichtstragödie', *Zeitschrift für deutsche Philologie* 109 (1990), Sonderheft: Schiller. Aspekte neuerer Forschung, pp. 134–44.
16. Friedrich Schiller, *Mary Stuart*, trans. and with an introduction and notes by F.J. Lamport (Harmondsworth: Penguin, 2nd edn. 1998), here p. 44. Further references are inserted in the text.
17. For a more negative view of Elisabeth and the claim that Schiller fails to offer a way forward to women as agents of history see Kari Lokke, 'Schiller's *Maria Stuart*: The Historical Sublime and the Aesthetics of Gender', *Monatshefte* 82 (1990) pp. 123–41.
18. For the German original see *Schillers Werke. Nationalausgabe*, ed. by Julius Petersen and others, 42 vols (Weimar: Böhlau, 1943), vol. 20, p. 414 (henceforth NA followed by volume and page number in the text). Translations are from 'On Naïve and Sentimental Poetry', trans. by Julius A. Elias, in H.B. Nisbet (ed.) *German Aesthetic and Literary Criticism: Winckelmann, Lessing, Hamann, Herder, Schiller and Goethe* (Cambridge: Cambridge University Press, 1985) p. 181. Further references will be by page number in the text, following the NA reference.
19. On *Über naive und sentimentalische Dichtung* see Bovenschen pp. 244–56.
20. For a full discussion of this thesis in relation to Schiller's aesthetic thought and to the Platonic tradition see David V. Pugh, *Dialectic of Love: Platonism*

in Schiller's Aesthetics (Montreal and Kingston, London, Buffalo: McGill-Queen's University Press, 1996).

21. For an overview of women's writing and attitudes to it in this period see Jo Catling (ed.) *A History of Women's Writing in Germany, Austria and Switzerland* (Cambridge: Cambridge University Press, 2000) pp. 47–87.
22. See *Schillers Gespräche*, NA 42, 289.
23. For a Marxist interpretation of Schiller's theory of modern literature, see Georg Lukács, 'Schiller's Theory of Modern Literature' in *Goethe and his Age*, trans. by Robert Anchor (London: Merlin Press 1968) pp. 101–35.

Chapter 4

1. On Hoffmann's relationship to Rousseau see my 'Biographie, Autobiographie, Fiktion', full details in the bibliography.
2. See the different interpretations of Nathanael by E. Annuß, 'Maske und Maschine. Künstliche Frauen in Texten von Hoffmann, Villiers und Lem', *Literatur für Leser* 20 (1997) pp. 95–107; S. Asche, *Die Liebe, der Tod und das Ich im Spiegel der Kunst. Die Funktion des Weiblichen in Schriften der Frühromantik und im erzählerischen Werk E.T.A. Hoffmanns*, Hochschulschriften Literaturwissenschaft 69 (Königstein/Ts.: Anton Hain, 1985); H. Cixous, *Prénoms de personne* (Paris: Éditions du Seuil, 1974); M. Kohlenbach, 'Women and Artists: E.T.A. Hoffmann's Implicit Critique of Early Romanticism', *Modern Language Review* 89 (1994) pp. 659–73.
3. See a predominantly negative interpretation of Clara in Annuß, 'Maske und Maschine'; R. Belgardt, 'Der Künstler und die Puppe. Zur Interpretation von Hoffmanns "Der Sandmann"', *German Quarterly* 42 (1969) pp. 686–700; Cixous, *Prénoms de personne*; J.M. Ellis, 'Clara, Nathanael and the Narrator: Interpreting Hoffmann's "Der Sandmann"', *German Quarterly* 54 (1981) pp. 1–18; U. Stadler, 'Der Sandmann' in Brigitte Feldges and Ulrich Stadler (eds) *E.T.A. Hoffmann. Epoche—Werk—Wirkung* (Munich: C.H. Beck, 1986) pp. 135–52.
4. See Asche and P. von Matt, *Die Augen der Automaten. E.T.A. Hoffmanns Imaginationslehre als Prinzip seiner Erzählkunst* (Tübingen: Niemeyer, 1971).
5. See the items in the bibliography by K.-D. Dobat, D. Kremer and M. Momberger. For a critique of deconstructive readings of Hoffmann see my articles 'Karnevaleske Mesalliancen' and 'Narrative Strukturen', also listed in the bibliography.
6. My thanks to Dee Reynolds for help with this translation.
7. See my 'E.T.A. Hoffmann's "Der Sandmann": An Early Example of *Écriture Féminine*? A Critique of Trends in Feminist Literary Criticism', *Women in German Yearbook* 4 (1988) pp. 21–45 (p. 41).
8. L. Irigaray, *Speculum of the Other Woman*, trans. by Gillian C. Gill (Ithaca, NY: Cornell University Press, 1985).

9. For a critique of this tendency see my 'Ahnung des Göttlichen und affizierte Ganglien. Die kontrapunktische Erzähltechnik des *Kater Murr* auf der Schwelle von Romantik zu Moderne' in Nicholas Saul and others (eds) *Schwellen. Germanistische Erkundungen einer Metapher* (Würzburg: Königshausen and Neumann, 1999) pp. 138–51.
10. See the tendency to read Hoffmann as a parodist of Romanticism in the items by J. Schmidt and S. Vietta in the bibliography. W. Nehring, C. Sommerhage, and M. Tatar (also in the bibliography) see Hoffmann as part of the development of Romanticism.
11. See among the many psychoanalytical interpretations the bibliography items by I. Aichinger, S. Freud, and B. Neymeyr; see also the historical psychological analysis by G. Reuchlein.
12. See the bibliography for items by U. Hohoff, G. Saße, and C. Sommerhage.
13. See recently I. Schroeder, 'Das innere Bild und seine Gestaltung. Die Erzählung *Der Sandmann* als Theorie und Praxis des Erzählens', *E.T.A. Hoffmann-Jahrbuch* 9 (2001) pp. 22–33.
14. See P. von Matt and K. Deterding, *Magie des poetischen Raums. E.T.A. Hoffmanns Dichtung und Weltbild*, Beiträge zur neueren Literaturgeschichte, Folge 3, 152 (Heidelberg: Winter, 1999).
15. C. Liebrand, *Aporie des Kunstmythos. Die Texte E.T.A. Hoffmanns*, Rombach Wissenschaften: Reihe Litterae, 42 (Freiburg i. Br.: Rombach, 1996) p. 7.
16. See my critique of Liebrand's first category in 'Heroes and Villains in E.T.A. Hoffmann's "Ritter Gluck"', *Bulletin of the John Rylands University Library of Manchester* 84.3 (2002) pp. 49–66 (p. 59).
17. See J. Butler, *The Psychic Life of Power: Theories in Subjection* (Stanford: Stanford University Press, 1997) p. 11.
18. On the carnival theme, see bibliography for G.R. Kaiser, D. Kremer, 'Literarischer Karneval' and G. Saße; on acting see H. Eilert.
19. That this shared motif is not merely a coincidence is shown by Hoffmann's reference to Goethe's play in *Seltsame Leiden*, H3, 463. J. Simpson, in his essay 'Canny Allusions: *Der Sandmann* as *Kontrafaktur*', *Publications of the English Goethe Society* 71 (2001) pp. 37–49, argues for traces of a *Werther* parody in 'Der Sandmann', but overlooks the fact that Hoffmann's relation to *Werther* is mediated by Goethe's own satire of it.
20. All references to Hoffmann are from *Sämtliche Werke in sechs Bänden*, ed. by Hartmut Steinecke and others (Frankfurt/Main: Deutscher Klassiker Verlag, 1985–2004) and are given as H, followed by volume and page number. All translations are my own. I would like to thank Chris Lyons for checking them.
21. See my 'Der Dichter als Fledermaus bei der Schau des Wunderbaren. Die Poetologie des rechten dichterischen Sehens in Hoffmanns "Der Sandmann" und "Das öde Haus"' in R.J. Kavanagh (ed.) *Mutual*

Exchanges. Sheffield-Münster Colloquium I (Frankfurt/Main: Peter Lang, 1999) pp. 180–92.

22. See B. Dieterle, *Erzählte Bilder. Zum narrativen Umgang mit Gemälden*, Schriften zur Soziosemiotik und Komparatistik: Artefakt, 3 (Marburg: Hitzeroth, 1988); K. Bomhoff, *Bildende Kunst und Dichtung. Die Selbstinterpretation E.T.A. Hoffmanns in der Kunst Jacques Callots und Salvator Rosas* (Freiburg i. Br.: Rombach, 1999). Neither mentions this important difference between Callot and Hoffmann; see on the other hand Kaiser (p. 235), Kremer, 'Literarischer Karneval' and O. Schmidt, '"Die Wundernadel des Meisters"—Zum Bild-Text-Verhältnis in E.T.A. Hoffmanns Capriccio *Prinzessin Brambilla*', *E.T.A. Hoffmann-Jahrbuch* 7 (1999) pp. 50–62 (p. 51).

Chapter 5

1. Margaret Anne Doody, *The True Story of the Novel* (London: Fontana, 1998) p. 440.
2. For comprehensive discussion of this issue see Schor and Cohen in the bibliography.
3. Balzac, pp. 5 and 4 respectively. On Balzac's portrayal of gender differences see Diana Knight, 'Reading as an Old Maid: *La Cousine Bette* and Compulsory Heterosexuality', *Quinquereme* 12:1 (1989) pp. 67–79.
4. This is a recurrent theme of *De la Littérature* (1800) and *De l'Allemagne* (1814). It should, however, be said, that Stendhal does not acknowledge the origin of this idea in Mme de Staël's work.
5. Stendhal, *De l'Amour,* ed. by Henri Martineau (Paris: Classiques Garnier, 1959) p. 200. English translation by Brian Rhys, Stendhal, *Love* (London: Bestseller Library, 1959) p. 148.
6. 'Walter Scott et *la Princesse de Clèves*', *Mélanges de littérature*, vol. 3, *Mélanges critiques*, ed. by Henri Martineau (Paris: Le Divan, 1933) pp. 305–11.
7. *Vie de Henry Brulard*, in Stendhal, *Œuvres intimes*, vol. 2, ed. by V. del Litto, Bibliothèque de la Pléiade (Paris: Gallimard, 1982) [henceforth VHB] p. 536. Translation by John Sturrock, *The Life of Henry Brulard* (London: Penguin, 1995) p. 7.
8. For an account of Stendhal's relations with Mélanie Guilbert, see Jonathan Keates, *Stendhal* (London: Sinclair-Stevenson, 1994) chapter 3.
9. *La Chartreuse de Parme*, in Stendhal, *Romans et nouvelles*, vol. 2, ed. by Henri Martineau, Bibliothèque de la Pléiade (Paris: Gallimard, 1948) Notes, p. 1368.
10. Clara Malraux, 'Les grandes sœurs de Mathilde de la Môle' [sic], *Confluences* no. 4 (1944) pp. 262–64 (p. 263). The remark is cited by Richard Bolster in his *Stendhal, Balzac, et le féminisme romantique*, Lettres

Modernes (Paris: Minard, 1970), one of the earliest and most comprehensive accounts of the presence of women in Stendhal's fiction.

11. Simone de Beauvoir, *Le Deuxième Sexe* (Paris: Gallimard, 1949) (subsequently DS) p. 376; trans. by H.M. Parshley, *The Second Sex* (London: Jonathan Cape, 1953) p. 255 (slightly adapted).
12. See Philippe Berthier, Lamiel, *ou, la boîte de Pandore* (Paris: Presses universitaires de France, 1994) and Clive W. Thompson, Lamiel, *fille du feu: Essai sur Stendhal et l'énergie* (Paris: L'Harmattan, 1997).
13. Naomi Schor, *Breaking the Chain: Women, Theory, and French Realist Fiction, Gender and Culture* (New York: Columbia University Press, 1985) p. 135.
14. Kristeva, *Histoires d'amour* (Paris: Denoël, 1983) pp. 450–52; trans. by Leon S. Roudiez, *Tales of Love* (New York: Columbia University Press, 1987) pp. 363–64.
15. This line of argument is developed at greater length with reference to the novel as a genre from its origins in the ancient world to the present day in the work by Doody cited in note 1.
16. Margaret Cohen, *The Sentimental Education of the Novel* (Princeton, NJ: Princeton University Press, 1999) and Margaret Waller, *The Male Malady: Fictions of Impotence in the French Romantic Novel* (New Brunswick, NJ: Rutgers University Press, 1993).
17. For an account of Duras's work, see Alison Finch, *Women's Writing in Nineteenth-Century France* (Cambridge: Cambridge University Press, 2000) chapter 7, and Rosemary Lloyd, 'The Nineteenth Century: Shaping Women', in Sonya Stephens (ed.) *A History of Women's Writing in France* (Cambridge: Cambridge University Press, 2000) pp. 130–31.
18. For a survey of the social and cultural conditions of women in this period, see Lloyd, ibid. For an account of the downgrading of the legal status of women in the Code Napoléon, see Tetu in the bibliography.
19. Stendhal, *Lettres de Paris par le petit-fils de Grimm, 1825*, ed. by Henri Martineau (Paris: Le Sycomore, 1983) pp. 79, 80. Retranslation into French of Stendhal's 'Letters from Paris, by Grimm's Grandson. No. I', dated 'Paris, December 18, 1824', *The London Magazine* vol. 1 (January 1825) pp. 49–60 (p. 54). These 'letters' were translated into English by one Mrs Sarah Austin, whom Stendhal describes in letters dated 9 January and 6 September 1826 as being too much of a prude to be aware of most of their content. Quoted by José-Luiz Diaz in his 'Présentation' to Stendhal, *Chroniques 1825–1829* ed. by José-Luis Diaz and Henri Martineau (Paris: Sycomore, 1983) pp. 7–44 (pp. 12–13).
20. *Lettres de Paris*, pp. 259–60. Translation, 'Letter no. XII', *London Magazine* vol. 3 (December 1825) pp. 541–50 (p. 544).
21. 'Projet d'article sur *Le Rouge et le Noir*', in Stendhal, *Romans et nouvelles*, vol. 1, ed. by Henri Martineau, Bibliothèque de la Pléiade (Paris: Gallimard, 1952) pp. 700–14 (p. 705). References to *Le Rouge et le Noir* in

this edition are henceforth 'RN' and precede page references to translations of the novel which are taken from Stendhal, *The Red and the Black: A Chronicle of the Nineteenth Century*, trans. by C.K. Scott-Moncrieff, ed. by Ann Jefferson (London: Everyman, 1997). Translations from the 'Projet' are my own.

22. Arnould Frémy in *La Revue de Paris* (August 1838). Quoted in Bolster cited in note 11, p. 44 (my translation).
23. *Lettres de Paris*, pp. 161–62. ['Letter from Paris, no. VI, *London Magazine* vol. 2 (June 1825) pp. 276–90 (p. 284).] For an assessment of Delphine Gay's work as a journalist see Finch cited in note 16, chapter 14.
24. My translation of 'Résponse à un acte d'accusation', ll. 212, 217. On the issue of women as readers of nineteenth-century fiction see Queffélec in the bibliography.
25. On this interesting topic, see Margherita Leoni, *Stendhal: la peinture à l'œuvre* (Paris: L'Harmattan, 1996).
26. *Journal*, 27 September 1811. Extract in *Le Musée idéal de Stendhal*, preface by Dominique Fernandez, ed. by Ferrante Ferranti (Paris: Stock, 1995) p. 86. Unless otherwise stated, all references to Stendhal's writings on art will be to this edition (henceforth *Musée*), since illustrations are provided for all the references. Translations are mine.
27. On Clélia in this context, see my *Stendhal La Chartreuse de Parme* (London: Grant and Cutler, 2003) pp. 65–69.

Chapter 6

1. George F. Peters, *The Poet as Provocateur: Heinrich Heine and His Critics* (Rochester: Camden House, 2000) p. 156.
2. Rudolf Walter Leonhardt, *Das Weib, das ich geliebet hab: Heines Mädchen und Frauen* (Hamburg: Hoffmann und Campe, 1975); and Dolf Sternberger, *Heinrich Heine und die Abschaffung der Sünde* (Frankfurt/Main: Suhrkamp, 1976). Sternberger's work does not really focus on women in Heine. Peters does not mention a more important book on the topic: Diana Lynn Justis's *The Feminine in Heine's Life and Œuvre* (New York: Peter Lang, 1997). In the works by men on Heine's women, he could also have included Adolph Kohut's *Heinrich Heine und die Frauen* (Berlin: Alfred H. Fried, 1888).
3. Ingrid Straube, *Heinrich Heines Frauen: Ein Gespräch* (Aachen: Rimbaud Presse, 1986).
4. Indeed, Justis suggests that Heine learned a great deal about women's subjugation from Rahel, and that he shared Sand's views on marriage and other topics related to women (pp. 123–69).
5. John Fuegi, *Brecht and Company: Sex, Politics, and the Making of Modern Drama* (New York: Grove Press, 1994).
6. References to the original German are based on *Heinrich Heine. Historisch-*

kritische Gesamtausgabe der Werke, ed. by Manfred Windfuhr and others, 16 vols (Hamburg: Hoffmann und Campe, 1973–97). This is abbreviated to DHA, followed by volume and page number. Translations are taken from Hal Draper's renditions in *The Complete Poems of Heinrich Heine: A Modern English Version* (Boston: Suhrkamp/Insel, 1982); page numbers follow the reference to the German original.

7. These remarks appeared in the *Blätter für literarische Unterhaltung* in a review of *Gedichte* by Gustav Pfizer (Nr. 181, 30 June 1835, p. 346).
8. See Jost Hermand, 'Erotik im Juste milieu: Heines "Verschiedene"', in *Mehr als ein Liberaler: Über Heinrich Heine* (Frankfurt/Main: Peter Lang, 1991) pp. 111–25.
9. See my 'Heine and Utopia', *Heine-Jahrbuch* 27 (1988) pp. 86–112.
10. *The Doctrine of Saint-Simon: An Exposition*, First Year, 1828–29, trans. by Georg G. Iggers (New York: Schocken, 1972) p. 85.

Chapter 7

1. In this essay, I quote from Baudelaire's *Œuvres complètes,* ed. by Claude Pichois, 2 vols (Paris: Gallimard, 1975–76) (henceforth OC followed by the volume and page number), and from *Correspondance*, ed. by Claude Pichois, 2 vols (Paris: Gallimard, 1973) (henceforth C followed by volume and page number). Translations of the poems are by James McGowan (Oxford: Oxford University Press, 1993); page references follow the reference from the original. All other translations are my own.
2. This poem was excised from the volume as a result of the 1857 trial in which the poet and his publisher were found guilty of offences to public morality.
3. For more subtle and nuanced readings of this poem see Ainslee Armstrong McLees, 'Baudelaire's "Une Charogne": Caricature and the Birth of Modern Art', *Mosaic* 21.4 (1988) pp. 111–22; Patrick Labarthe, 'La "mise en crise" de la relation amoureuse dans *Les Fleurs du mal*' in Steve Murphy (ed.) *Lectures des* Fleurs du mal (Rennes: Presses Universitaires de Rennes, 2002) pp. 115–26. Susan Wolf's 'Baudelaire's Sepulchres' in L. Porter (ed.) *Approaches to Teaching Baudelaire's* Flowers of Evil (New York: Modern Language Association, 2000) pp. 123–29 offers a sophisticated psychoanalytical framework for responding to Baudelaire's depictions of dead and mutilated women.
4. As expressed in Baudelaire's letter to Nadar of 14 May 1859 (C 1, 573).
5. See his letter to Sainte-Beuve dated January 1862 (C 2, 219).
6. As Jérôme Thélot argues in his standard, although contested, study *Baudelaire: violence et poésie* (Paris: Gallimard, 1993).
7. For further discussion of this see Peter Dayan, 'Baudelaire at his Latrine: Motions in the Petits poèmes en prose and in George Sand's novels', *French Studies* 48.4 (1994) pp. 416–24.

8. Ross Chambers, *Mélancolie et Opposition* (Paris: Corti, 1987).
9. Rosemary Lloyd, 'Dwelling in Possibility: Encounters with the Other in Baudelaire's Spleen de Paris', *Australian Journal of French Studies* 29.1 (1992) pp. 68–77.
10. Mary Ann Caws, 'What can a woman do for the late Henry James?', *Raritan* 14.1 (1994) pp. 1–17.
11. Particularly illuminating on this is Roger Williams, *The Horror of Life* (Chicago: University of Chicago Press, 1980).
12. Gustave Flaubert, *Correspondance*, ed. by Jean Bruneau. 5 vols (Paris: Gallimard, 1973–) vol. 2 p. 304.
13. On this see Michael Danahy, 'Marceline Desbordes-Valmore et la fraternité des poètes', *Nineteenth-Century French Studies* 19.3 (1991), pp. 386–93; Rosemary Lloyd, 'Baudelaire, Marceline Desbordes-Valmore et la fraternité des poètes', *Bulletin baudelairien* 26.2 (1991) pp. 65–77 and Wendy Greenberg, *Uncanonical Women: Feminine Voice in French Poetry 1830–1871* (Amsterdam: Rodopi, 1999) chapter 4.
14. Tamara Bassim, *La Femme dans l'œuvre de Baudelaire* (Neuchâtel: La Baconnière, 1974).
15. Edward Ahearn, 'Black Woman, White Poet: Exile and Exploitation in Baudelaire's Jeanne Duval', *French Review* 51 (1977) pp. 212–20 and Griselda Pollock, *Differencing the Canon: Feminist Desire and the Writing of Art's Histories* (London: Routledge, 1999).
16. Kerry Weinberg, 'Women of Eliot and Baudelaire: The Boredom, the Horror and the Glory', *Modern Language Studies* 14.3 (1984) pp. 31–42; Jean Anderson, 'Baudelaire misogyne: vers une lecture féministe des *Fleurs du mal*', *New Zealand Journal of French Studies* 8.1 (1987) pp. 16–28; Ross Chambers, 'Irony and Misogyny: Authority and the Homosocial in Baudelaire and Flaubert', *Australian Journal of French Studies* 26.3 (1989) pp. 272–88; and Peggy Kamuf, 'Baudelaire's modern woman', *Qui parle* 4.2 (1991) pp. 1–7.
17. Elaine DalMolin, *Cutting the Body: Representing Woman in Baudelaire's Poetry, Truffaut's Cinema, and Freud's Psychoanalysis* (Ann Arbor: University of Michigan Press, 2000).
18. Marie Maclean, *Narrative as performance: the Baudelairean experiment* (London: Routledge, 1988); Sima Godfrey, '"Mère des souvenirs": Baudelaire, Memory and Mother', *L'Esprit créateur* 25.2 (1985) pp. 32–44 and Margaret Miner, '(S)(m)othering Baudelaire' in Patricia Ward (ed.) *Baudelaire and the Poetics of Modernity* (Nashville: Vanderbilt University Press, 2001) pp. 157–71.
19. Amy Ransom, '"Mon semblable, ma mère": Woman, Subjectivity and Escape in *Les Fleurs du Mal*', *Paroles Gelées: UCLA French Studies* 11 (1993) pp. 31–55.
20. As is Elissa Marder's optic in *Temporal Disorders in the Wake of Modernity*

(*Baudelaire and Flaubert*) (Palo Alto, CA: Stanford University Press, 2001).

21. Rosemary Lloyd, 'Hypocrite brother, Hypocrite sister: changing genders in *Les Fleurs du mal*', *French Studies* (1999) pp. 167–75 and *Baudelaire's World* (Ithaca, NY: Cornell University Press, 2002). The question of cross-gendered reading is the focus of more general studies such as those by Fetterley, Peterson and Showalter in the bibliography.
22. Gretchen Schultz, 'Baudelaire's Lesbian Connections' in L. Porter (ed.) *Approaches to Teaching Baudelaire's* Flowers of Evil (New York: Modern Language Association, 2000).
23. See Judith Butler, *Gender Trouble* (New York: Routledge, 1990).
24. Peter Gay, *Schnitzler's Century: The Making of Middle-Class 1815–1914* (New York: Norton, 2002).
25. For the question of education for women of the period see Anderson, Heywood, Knottnerus and Mayeur in the bibliography.
26. Tony Hunt defines this rhetorical term as 'paradoxical notions involving natural impossibilities, especially through inversion of the natural order of things' in *Villon's Last Will: Language and Authority in the* Testament (Oxford: Clarendon Press, 1996) p. 146.
27. For an exploration of this concept see for instance Julia Kristeva, *Pouvoirs de l'horreur* (Paris: Seuil, 1980) especially pp. 21–29.
28. For an attempt to write the biography of Jeanne Duval through a reading of *Les Fleurs du Mal*, above all as a person of colour, see Emmanuel Richon, *Jeanne Duval et Charles Baudelaire: Belle d'abandon* (Paris: L'Harmattan, 1998).
29. Jean-Paul Sartre, *Baudelaire* (Paris: Gallimard, 1946) passim. For a more standard biographical analysis, see Claude Pichois, *Baudelaire* trans. by Graham Robb (London: Hamish Hamilton, 1987). For more recent work on the mother, see Irigaray in the bibliography.
30. See also Baudelaire's review of Léon Cladel's *Les Martyrs ridicules* (OC 2, 187). For further exploration of this topic, see Micale and Goldstein in the bibliography.
31. Following the work of Jennifer Radden (ed.) *The Nature of Melancholy: From Aristotle to Kristeva* (Oxford: Oxford University Press, 2000).

Chapter 8

1. One of Flaubert's earliest references to muscular as opposed to feminine forms comes before he corresponds with Louise Colet, and is in his letter of 7 June 1844 to Louis de Cormenin in the context of a desire to belong to an *all-male* enclave of writers: 'I'm flattered to see that you are at one with me in your hatred of Saint-Beuve and his crowd. Above all, I like the sentence which is nervy, substantial, clear, with rippling muscles and swarthy skin: I like male and not female sentences such as those of

Lamartine so often and to a lesser extent, those of Villemain.' *Gustave Flaubert: Correspondance I, 1830–1851*, ed. by Jean Bruneau (Paris: NRF Gallimard, 1973), p. 210 (my translation and henceforth C).

2. For differing approaches to the study of Flaubert's female correspondents, see James Smith Allen, *Poignant Relations: Three Modern French Women* (Baltimore and London: The Johns Hopkins University Press, 2000); Janet Beizer, *Ventriloquized Bodies: Narratives of Hysteria in Nineteenth-Century France* (Ithaca and London: Cornell University Press, 1993) and Martine Reid, *Flaubert correspondant* (Paris: SEDES, 1995).
3. Among Flaubert's 'feminist' critics of a number of hues are Luzette Czyba, *Mythes et Idéologie de la Femme dans les Romans de Flaubert* (Lyon: Presses Universitaires de Lyon, 1983) Naomi Schor, *Breaking the Chain: Women, Theory and French Realist Fiction* (New York: Columbia University Press, 1985), and Mary Orr, *Flaubert: Writing the Masculine* (Oxford: Oxford University Press, 2000).
4. Jonathan Culler's *Flaubert: the Uses of Uncertainty* (London: Elek, 1974), the work of Eugene Donato, *The Script of Decadence: Essays on the Fictions of Flaubert and the Poetics of Romanticism* (Oxford: OUP, 1993) and Naomi Schor and H.F. Majewski (eds) *Flaubert and Postmodernism* (Lincoln Nebraska: University of Nebraska Press, 1984) offer rather different spins on a deconstructed Flaubert, and deconstruction as a critical tool which denies or facilitates a gender agenda.
5. Subsequent references to these works by Flaubert are from the two-volume *Œuvres complètes*, ed. by Bernard Masson (Paris: Seuil, 1964), vol. 2, henceforth OC. Translations are my own.
6. On the wider subject of the history of French Feminism, see Albistur and Rendall in the bibliography.
7. For an elucidation of Flaubert's unsettling, violent, sadean, macabre writing, see for example Yvonne Bargues Rollins, *Le Pas de Flaubert: une danse macabre* (Paris: Champion, 1998).
8. Gender criticism of Flaubert's last works is perhaps represented less from feminist than from homosexual-homosocial angles. See for example Lawrence Schehr, *Rendering French Realism* (Stanford: Stanford University Press, 1997).
9. Flaubert's famous remark about the stupidity [bêtise] of conclusions, 'Ineptitude consists in desiring to conclude', is advanced on his first major trip to the Middle East in the context of the preposterousness of Auguste Comte's *Essai de Philosophie positive* in a letter to his friend Louis Bouilhet of 4 September 1850 written from Damascus (C 679).
10. For a feminist reading of Flaubert's *Trois Contes* including their endings see Aimée Israel Pelletier, *Flaubert's Straight and Suspect Saints* (Amsterdam & Philadelphia: The John Benjamins Publishing Company, 1991).
11. *Bouvard et Pécuchet* has been classified generically in a range of different

ways. See for example Donato, *The Script of Decadence* and Orr, *Writing the masculine*, chapter 6.

12. Such as Louise Colet? It lies outside this paper to examine this crucial yet problematic relationship. See Francine du Plessix Gray, *Rage and Fire: A life of Louise Colet, Pioneer Feminist, Literary Star, Flaubert's Muse* (New York: Simon and Schuster, 1994).
13. See Mary Orr, *Madame Bovary: representations of the masculine* (Bern: Peter Lang, 1999) pp. 169–210 for a discussion of Flaubert's representations of marriage and the 'happy ever after' through the prism of Charles' two unions and marriage to Emma by the end of the first third of the novel.
14. The shock is also that such a scene has not one but two Biblical precedents, the raising of the Widow's son by Elijah and a similar resurrection miracle by Elisha.
15. For a study of the Trial of Flaubert's *Madame Bovary*, see Dominic LaCapra, Madame Bovary *on Trial* (Ithaca and London: Cornell University Press, 1982).
16. See my essay 'Death and the *Post Mortem* in Flaubert's Works' in Tim Unwin (ed.) *The Cambridge Companion to Flaubert* (Cambridge; Cambridge University Press, 2004) chapter 7 for a fuller discussion of the problematic nature of these *dénouements*.
17. My reading is in direct counterpoint to Elizabeth Bronfen's in *Over her dead body: Death, Femininity and the Aesthetic* (Manchester: Manchester University Press, 1992).
18. That this second attempt may also have been a near miss for such an adept executioner is suggested in the gruesome close-up detail of John's head at the end of the tale where there is evidence that the cut to the lower jaw was not clean.
19. Critics usually read this scene is evidence of Félicité's potential sainthood, not for its literal meaning of narrow escape.
20. *Writing the Masculine*, chapter 6.
21. Key critics of this novel always interpret the failures as humorous bungling, or hypothesize categories of discipline which are seen to determine which field of research the two protagonists take next.
22. See Jacques Neefs, 'La Nuit de Noël: *Bouvard et Pécuchet*', in *Gustave Flaubert 3: Mythes et religions 2* (Paris: Lettres Modernes, Minard, 1988) pp. 35–61 and more recently Andrew Cuthbert, *Les Champs des Connaissances: Myth and Metaphysics in the Late Works of Flaubert* (unpublished PhD thesis, University of Exeter, 2003), pp. 94–108 for analyses of this scene.
23. While these two preliminary viewpoints seem to follow gender stereotypes, the unreliable female servant voice and the voice of 'male' medical science as authority, gendering of the voice of the final statement is extremely problematic.

Chapter 9

1. German references are to Theodor Fontane, *Sämtliche Werke*, ed. by Edgar Gross and Kurt Schreinert, 24 vols (Munich: Nymphenburger Verlag, 1959–75), abbreviated as NFA, followed by the number of the volume and page. Translated quotations from *Effi Briest* are taken from, Theodor Fontane, *Effi Briest*. Translated by Hugh Rorrison and Helen Chambers (London: Angel Books, 1995). The page number follows the NFA reference in brackets in the text.
2. Helen E. Chambers, *The Changing Image of Theodor Fontane* (Columbia: Camden House, 1999) pp. 91–96, surveys feminist criticism, including the first extended academic study of his work by Helene Herrmann, 'Theodor Fontanes *Effi Briest*. Die Geschichte eines Romans', *Die Frau* 19 (1912) pp. 543–54, 610–25, 677–94.
3. Alistair Fowler, *Kinds of Literature* (Oxford: Clarendon Press, 1982) p. 215; quoted in Harold Bloom, *The Western Canon. The Books and School of the Age* (London: Papermac 1994) p. 21.
4. My discussion of Spielhagen's theories is based on Friedrich Spielhagen, *Beiträge zur Theorie und Technik des Romans* (Leipzig: Verlag von L. Staackmann, 1883).
5. See John R. Reed, *Victorian Conventions* (Ohio: Ohio University Press, 1975).
6. Bodo Rollka, *Die Belletristik in der Berliner Presse des 19. Jahrhunderts* (Berlin: Colloquium Verlag, 1985) p. 396.
7. For individual objections to Zola among Fontane's contemporaries see *Romantheorie Dokumente ihrer Geschichte in Deutschland seit 1880*, ed. by Eberhard Lämmert (Athenäum Taschenbücher, 1984) pp. 1–11; Fontane's views are quoted on pp. 16–17.
8. See Michael Glowinski, 'Der Dialog im Roman', *Poetica* 6, 1974, pp. 1–16.
9. 'Der Held im Roman. Mit besonderer Beziehung auf George Eliot's *Middlemarch*' (1874) *Beiträge* p. 99.
10. David Blackbourn, *The Fontana History of Germany 1780–1918: The Long Nineteenth Century* (London: Fontana Press, 1997) p. 377. The phrases 'manly cause', 'manly project' are taken from Blackbourn (passim).
11. This description is applied to the legendary Queen Luise, wife of Frederick William III of Prussia, by Heinrich von Treitschke, *Ausgewählte Schriften*, vol. 1 (Leipzig: Hirzel, 1917) pp. 276–77.
12. See Nancy Birch Wagner, *Goethe as Cultural Icon: Intertextual Encounters with Stifter and Fontane*, North American Studies in Nineteenth-Century German Literature, vol. 17 (New York: Peter Lang, 1994), to which I am indebted for much of my understanding of Fontane's reading of Goethe.
13. See Fontane's letter to his sister, Elise, 5 August 1859 in *Theodor Fontane. Briefe an seine Familie*. Erster Band (Berlin: Friedrich Fontane and Co., 1905) p. 109.

14. This phrase and the reference to 'the great precursors' belong to the terminology of Harold Bloom, *The Anxiety of Influence: A Theory of Poetry* (London and Oxford: Oxford University Press, 1973).
15. Birgit Panke-Kochinke, *Die anständige Frau* (Pfaffenweiler: Centaurus-Verlagsgesellschaft, 1991) p. 1.
16. See Marianne Kesting, 'Frau Penelope Swinegel' in *Literaturen. Das Journal für Bücher und Themen* 04/02 (Schwerpunkt: Fontane und die Frauen) pp. 12–17 (p. 19) on Fontane's wife Emilie.
17. See *Theodor Fontane und Martha Fontane. Ein Familienbriefnetz,* ed. by Regina Dieterle (Berlin, New York: Walter de Gruyter, 2002). *Meine liebe Mete. Ein Briefgespräch zwischen Eltern und Tochter*, ed. by Gotthart Erler (Berlin: Aufbau Taschenbuch, 2001). Emilie und Theodor Fontane, *Der Ehebriefwechsel in 3 Bänden*, ed. by Gotthart Erler, Große Brandenburger Ausgabe (Berlin: Aufbau Verlag, 1998).
18. Regina Dieterle, *Vater und Tochter. Erkundung einer erotisierten Beziehung in Leben und Werk Theodor Fontanes* (Bern, Berlin, Frankfurt/Main: Peter Lang, 1996).
19. Fontane to Marie Uhse, 13 November 1895, in *Briefe Theodor Fontanes. Zweite Sammlung*, ed. by Otto Pniower and Paul Schlenther, vol. 2 (Berlin: F. Fontane and Co., 1910), p. 366.
20. Klaus Peter Schuster, *Effi Briest. Ein Leben nach christlichen Bildern.* Studien zur deutschen Literatur, vol. 55 (Tübingen: Niemeyer, 1978).
21. World's Classics (London and Oxford: Oxford University Press, 1998) p. 1.
22. World's Classics (London and Oxford: Oxford University Press, 1960) p. 176.
23. Sibylle Wirsing, 'Der Fürst und das Mädchen' in *Literaturen* (note 16) pp. 30–33, discusses the connections between Effi's family and the rise of Prussia.
24. Rudolf Helmstetter, *Die Geburt des Realismus aus dem Dunst des Familienblatts. Fontane und die öffentlichkeitsgeschichtlichen Rahmenbedingungen des Poetischen Realismus* (München: Fink, 1998) p. 192.
25. Jeffrey Schneider, 'Masculinity, Male Friendship, and the Paranoid Logic of Honor in Theodor Fontane's *Effi Briest*', in *German Quarterly* 75 (2002) pp. 265–81; Schneider finally cautions against such a reading.
26. Manfred Allenhöfer, *Vierter Stand und alte Ordnung bei Fontane. Zur Realistik des bürgerlichen Realismus*, Stuttgarter Arbeiten zur Germanistik (Stuttgart: Hans-Dieter Heinz Akademischer Verlag, 1986) p. 78, argues that in later novels central figures are shadowed by members of the fourth estate whom they recognize as superior.
27. See my '"A visibly-appointed stopping-place": Narrative Endings at the End of the Century', in Patricia Howe and Helen Chambers (eds) *Theodor Fontane and the European Context. Literature, Culture and Society in*

Prussia and Europe (Amsterdam and Atlanta GA: Rodopi, 2001) pp. 137–51.

28. Translations from *Der Stechlin* are my own.
29. Monika Wienfort, 'Fontane und der Adel. Beobachtungen zum *Stechlin*', *Fontane Blätter*, 76/2003, pp. 126–33 sees Dubslav's decision not to remarry as a motif contradicting bourgeois criticism of the aristocracy's marriages for profit, disguised as idiosyncratic theology.
30. On Fontane's Melusine figures see the entries for Renate Schäfer and Hubert Ohl in the bibliography.
31. Edda Ziegler, 'Die Zukunft der Melusinen. Weiblichkeitskonstruktion in Fontanes Spätwerk', in *Theodor Fontane: Am Ende des Jahrhunderts*, vol. 2: Sprache. Ich. Roman. Frau p. 175.
32. Harold Bloom, *The Western Canon*, p. 30. There have been four films, fifty translations in twenty-nine languages and a parodic sequel of *Effi Briest*. I am indebted to my late colleague Derek Glass for information about translations.
33. F. Th. Vischer, 'Der Heerd der Familie ist der wahre Mittelpunct des Weldbildes im Roman', in *Aesthetik oder Wissenschaft des Schönen 1857* § 881, quoted in Hartmut Steinecke, *Romantheorie und Romankritik in Deutschland*, vol. 2 (Stuttgart: Metzler, 1976) p. 266.
34. Sigmund Freud, 'The Uncanny', in *Collected Papers*, vol. 4, trans. by Joan Riviere (New York: Basic Books, Inc, 1959) pp. 368–407.

Chapter 10

1. Moloch, 'Prédictions pour 1890', *La Silhouette*, 29 December (1889) p. 1.
2. Maurice Talmeyr, 'L'Élection Zola', *Gil Blas*, 6 May (1890) p. 1.
3. In addition to Brunetière, elected over Zola in June 1893, others who drew votes in this election included the royalist historian Paul Thureau-Dangin and Ernest Lavisse. On the candidates, see 'Sous le Coupole', *Le Matin*, 27 April (1890) pp. 1–2. On the Zola elections, see Francis Lacoste, 'L'Académie contre Zola: Autour de la Reception de Pierre Loti', *Excavatio*, 2 (Fall 1993), 142–55; and Lacoste, 'Zola et L'Académie', *Excavatio*, 6–7 (1995), pp. 210–29. A list of the 700 Academicians elected since the Institute's 1635 origins appears on its website www.academie-francaise.fr/immortels. On the Academy's history, see Marc Fumaroli, 'La Coupole' in *Les Lieux de Mémoire*, ed. Pierre Nora (1984–92; rpt. Paris: Gallimard Quarto, 1997) vol. 2, pp. 1923–82.
4. Talmeyr in note 2, p. 1. On national identity and cultural politics, see, in the bibliography, Lebovics and my 'Olympia devient française'.
5. Daniel Milo, 'Les Classiques scolaires' in *Les Lieux de Mémoire* quoted in note 3, vol. 2, p. 2119.
6. As note 5, vol. 2, p. 2087.
7. Michèle Sacquin (ed.) *Zola*, Exhibition catalogue, Paris, Bibliothèque

Nationale de France, 18 October 2002–19 January 2003 (Paris: Fayard, 2002).

8. See David Bagueley and Dorothy Speirs, *Bibliographie de la critique sur Émile Zola: 1864–1970* and *1971–1980* (Toronto: University of Toronto Press, 1976 and 1982), and the online continuation for 1981–2003, at http://www.dur.ac.uk/SMEL/depts/french/Bagueley/Bibliog/.
9. For a perspective on the dominance of textual 'genetics' in French Zola studies, see Jean-Pierre Leduc-Adine (ed.) *Zola, genèse de l'œuvre* (Paris: CNRS, 2002), and Gisèle Séginger (ed.) *Zola à l'œuvre* (Strasbourg: Presses Universitaires de Strasbourg, 2003).
10. Naomi Schor, 'Mother's Day: Zola's Women', *Diacritics* 5, no. 4 (1975) pp. 11–17; *Zola's Crowds* (Baltimore: Johns Hopkins University Press, 1978); *Breaking the Chain: Women, Theory, and French Realist Fiction* (New York: Columbia University Press, 1985), especially pp. 29–47; *Reading in Detail* (New York: Methuen, 1987) pp. 110–30; Charles Bernheimer, *Figures of Ill Repute: Representing Prostitution in Nineteenth-Century France* (Cambridge, MA: Harvard University Press, 1989) pp. 200–233; David F. Bell, *Models of Power: Politics and Economics in Zola's Rougon Macquart* (Lincoln, Nebraska: University of Nebraska Press, 1988); Peter Brooks, *Body Work: Objects of Desire in Modern Narrative* (Cambridge, MA: Harvard University Press, 1993) pp. 123–61; Janet Beizer, *Ventriloquized Bodies: Narratives of Hysteria in Nineteenth-Century France* (Ithaca: Cornell University Press, 1994); Dorothy Kelly, 'Gender, Metaphor, and Machine: *La Bête humaine*', *French Literature Series* 16 (1989) pp. 110–22.
11. As put forward by, among others, Joan Scott, Eve Sedgwick, and Judith Butler in the bibliography.
12. Dorothy Kelly, 'Experimenting on Women: Zola's Theory and Practice of the Experimental Novel' in Margaret Cohen and Christopher Prendergast (eds) *Spectacles of Realism: Gender, Body, Genre* (Minneapolis: University of Minnesota Press, 1995) pp. 231–46; Sharon Marcus, *Apartment Stories* (Berkeley: University of California Press, 1999) pp. 166–98.
13. 'Figures du Féminin', *Cahiers naturalistes* 73 (1999); Sylvie Collot, *Lieux du désir: topologie amoureuse de Zola* (Paris: Hachette, 1992).
14. This essay is based on a study of 45 contemporary newspapers and magazines which I examined from the novel's first appearance in the biweekly *La Vie populaire* to the November 1890 vote.
15. Jules Huret, 'Les Deux Lutteurs', *L'Écho de Paris*, 7 December (1889) p. 2. The word 'curiosity' is from Paul d'Armon, 'La Bête humaine', *Le Voltaire*, 10 mars (1890) p. 1.
16. D'Armon in note 15.
17. D'Armon in note 15.
18. Zola, 'Au rédacteur', *Le Journal des débats*, 18 November (1889) p. 1.
19. Huret in note 15.
20. Huret in note 15. Zola expresses further confusion in an interview with

Philippe Gilla, 'L'Académie française et "La Bête humaine"', *Le Figaro*, 4 March (1890) p. 1.

21. Both posters belong to the Henri Céard Collection of the Paris Musée Carnavalet, respectively Inventaire AFF 2697 and AFF 1367. I am grateful to curator Jocelyne Van Deputte for help with this research.
22. By early December 1889 the press was writing about offensive 'affiches' as though the smaller one had simply added insult to injury (E. Pelca, 'Carnet littéraire', *Le Gaulois*, 4 December [1889] p. 2). E. Lepelletier argued already in late November in the daily paper *Paris* that the poster and what he called 'the prospectus'—therefore both images—contributed to dooming Zola's Academy campaign ('Chronique. Le roman-feuilleton à l'académie', *Paris*, 22 November [1889] p. 1). Two detailed descriptions of the poster, one of which calls it the 'première affiche', enable us to be certain that the colour poster caused the initial scandal: Mario Prax, 'Ce n'est pas de lui', *Le Charivari*, 22 November (1889) p. 1 and Henry Fouquier, 'La Vie de Paris', *Le XIXe Siècle*, 21 November (1889) p. 1. The editorialist 'Scaramouche' complained in *Le Gaulois* about 'a large image representing a man who wants to violate a woman'—a description that could well apply to either image ('L'art et la morale', *Le Gaulois*, 22 November [1889] p. 1). The novel's first instalment, with the illustration that appeared on the smaller poster, was published in *La Vie populaire* on 14 November 1889.
23. Prax in note 22. Rape within marriage was not considered a crime in France until the late twentieth century.
24. Émile Zola, *La Bête humaine* (1890; rpt. Paris: Garnier-Flammarion, 1972), 68–69, hereafter *BH*. Translations are mine.
25. See Émile Zola, 'Documents préparatoires', *Les Rougon-Macquart*, ed. by Armand Lanoux and Henri Mitterand (Paris: Gallimard Pléiade, 1966), vol. 5, pp. 1729–81, esp. 1735; and *Carnets d'enquêtes*, ed. by Henri Mitterand (Paris: Plon, 1986), pp. 499–554.
26. See, in the bibliography, my 'Censoring the Realist Gaze' and *Scenes of Seduction*, pp. 162–96.
27. Zola's *Le Roman expérimental* (Paris: Charpentier, 1880) p. 8 (hereafter *RE*) discusses Balzac's *La Cousine Bette* which, as I have shown in *Scenes of Seduction* (pp. 162–96), is one of the novels through which the pejorative discourse of 'realism' was elaborated in the 1840s.
28. See Kelly in note 12, pp. 231–46.
29. The critics of Realism, as I have shown in 'Censoring the Realist Gaze' pp. 28–67, quoted in note 26, obsessively compared the novels they loathed to the morgue and pathological wax museums.
30. Examples include Felicien Champsaur, 'La Queue du romantisme', *L'Événement*, 12 March (1890) p. 1 and Alfred Barbou, 'Chronique de la semaine', *Le Journal illustré*, 11 May (1890) p. 146.

31. Alain Pagès, *La Bataille littéraire: Essai sur la réception du naturalisme à l'époque de Germinal* (Paris: Séguier, 1989).
32. Jonathan Crary, *Techniques of the Observer* (Cambridge, MA: MIT Press, 1990), 9, 16, 6.
33. On nineteenth-century literary censorship, see my *Scenes of Seduction*, pp. 199–248; 'Censoring the Realist Gaze'; and 'The Limits of Reformism: The Novel, Censorship, and the Politics of Adultery in Nineteenth-Century France' in Deirdre Lynch and William B. Warner (eds) *Cultural Institutions of the Novel* (Chapel Hill: Duke University Press, 1996), pp. 335–68.
34. Louis Legrand, 'Le Naturalisme', *Le Courrier français*, 30 March (1890) p. 5. On the censorship of this image, see 'Poursuites contre le Courrier Français', *Le Courrier français*, 4 May 1890, pp. 2–5. I discuss the censorship battles of this journal in the book I am completing, *Desires to Censor*.
35. Legrand's tamer 'Le Romantisme', *Courrier français*, 30 March (1890) p. 4, showed a man holding a peacock quill gazing up at a nude woman in front of a gothic stained glass window.
36. I have discussed these battles in 'Dressed Down: Lingerie, Popular Prints, and the Voyeur's Censored Look in Third Republic France' (College Art Association Conference, Los Angeles, 1998).
37. For more on Zola and Manet see Clayson in the bibliography.
38. Jean-Louis Forain, 'Les Deux Zola', *Le Courrier français*, 16 November (1890) p. 1.
39. See John Grand-Carteret, *Zola en images* (Paris: Juven, 1907).
40. 'La Bête Humaine', *L'Art Moderne*, 27 April (1890), p. 1.
41. Jules Lemaître, 'La Bete humaine', *Le Figaro*, 8 March (1890) p. 1.
42. Armand de Pontmartin, 'La Bête humaine par Émile Zola', *Gazette de France*, 23 March (1890) p. 1.
43. 'La Folie du crime', *Le Matin*, 20 February (1890) p. 1.
44. Caliban, 'L'Atavisme', *Le Figaro*, 16 March (1890) p. 1.
45. D'Armon in note 15, p. 1.
46. E. Lepelletier, 'Chronique des livres, La Bête humaine', *L'Écho de Paris*, 11 March (1890) p. 2. Zola's notes for the novel explicitly evoke these crimes (Zola, *Ébauche*, f° 348–49, 357, cited by Gisèle Séginger, 'Commentaires: la Genèse' in *La Bête humaine* (Paris: Livre de poche, 1997) p. 445.
47. 'Zola sur une locomotive', *L'Illustration*, 8 March (1890) p. 1.
48. Georges Laroche, 'La Bête humaine de Saint Louis', *Le Siècle*, 29 March (1890) p. 2.
49. L. Serizier, 'Chronique parisien: La Tête coupée', *Le Siècle*, 1 April (1890) p. 2.
50. See Ruth Harris, 'Murder under Hypnosis in the Case of Gabrielle Bompard: Psychiatry in the Courtroom in Belle Époque Paris' in W.F. Bynum and others (eds) *Anatomy of Madness* (London: Tavistock, 1986)

vol. 2, pp. 197–241; Pierre Darmon, *La Malle à Gouffé* (Paris: Denoël, 1988) and *Procès Eyraud-Bompard, procès-verbaux d'audiences tirés de la Gazette des tribunaux* (Paris: n.p., 1891).

51. Henri Meyer, 'L'Affaire Gouffé: L'Accomplissement du crime', *Le Journal illustré*, 2 February (1890) pp. 36–37; 'L'Affaire Gouffé', *Le Petit Journal. Supplément illustré*, 20 December (1890) p. 8.
52. F. de Haenen, 'L'Affaire Gouffé. Le service anthropométrique du Palais de Justice prenant le signalement de Gabrielle Bompard', *L'Illustration*, 1 February (1890) p. 91. *L'Illustration* proclaimed her 'une déséquilibrée, une névrosée, une hystérique au premier chef' (cited in Darmon in note 50, p. 137).
53. 'Le Crime. L'opinion de Zola', *La Lanterne*, 28 January (1890) p. 1.
54. Had *La Bête humaine* been published a year earlier, Zola noted (Laroche in note 48, p. 2) that critics would have accused it of influencing Bompard.
55. Edmond Le Roy, 'Gabrielle Bompard d'après Zola', *Le Figaro*, 29 January (1890) p. 2.
56. See note 53.
57. See note 55.
58. 'Autour de l'Affaire Gouffé', *L'Estafette*, 23 December (1890) p. 1.
59. See note 55.
60. See note 58.
61. The conservative *Figaro* was the fifth largest newspaper in 1880 with a circulation of 104,924, numbers close to those of 1890. On the French Press of the period see Bellanger in the bibliography.
62. *Le Journal des débats*, 16 November 1889, p. 1; Zola, 'Au rédacteur', in note 18, p. 1. Zola accused the editor of opposing his Academy candidacy.
63. Charles Bigot suggested in an otherwise positive review, 'Chronique littéraire: La Bête humaine', *Le Siècle*, 10 March (1890) p. 2, that if the novel fell into the hands of 'some deranged man' that it might push him over the edge into a bloody obsession.
64. Zola, 'Lettre à la Jeunesse' in *RE* 60, cited by Kelly in note 12, p. 232.
65. See Kelly in note 12 for Zola's anxieties about female sentimentality.
66. Cesare Lombroso, 'La "Bête humaine" et l'anthropologie criminelle', *La Revue des revues* 4 (1892) pp. 260–64.
67. Guglielmo Ferrero, 'Le Mensonge et la Véracité chez la Femme criminelle', *Archives d'anthropologie criminelle* 8 (1893) pp. 138–49, especially p. 138; Raymond Ryckère, *La Femme en prison et devant la mort* (Lyon: Storck, 1898) pp. 70–71.
68. Michelle Perrot, 'Délinquance et système pénitentiaire en France au XIXe siècle', *Annales, ESC* 30, no. 1, Jan.-Feb. (1975) p. 72.
69. See D.A. Miller, *The Novel and the Police* (Berkeley: University of California Press, 1987); and my *Scenes of Seduction*, pp. 1–59.
70. Judith Walkowitz, *City of Dreadful Delight: Narratives of Sexual Danger in Late-Victorian London* (Chicago: University of Chicago Press, 1992). For

perceptive analyses of French nineteenth-century crime discourses, see Kalifa and Shapiro in the bibliography.

71. D'Armon in note 15, p. 2.
72. 'La Bête humaine' in note 40, p. 2; and Caliban in note 44, p. 1.
73. During the criminal investigation, Misard claims he has seen Cabuche peeping (*BH*, 360).
74. A. Robida, 'Pot Bouille', *La Caricature*, 13 May (1882), p. 3.
75. This is the complaint of Pontmartin, note 42.
76. Many thanks to the three readers whose queries sharpened this text: Mary Orr, Emily Apter, and Maurice Samuels.

Chapter 11

1. Max Brod, *Über Franz Kafka* (Frankfurt/Main: Fischer Taschenbuch, 1974) p. 120.
2. Walter H. Sokel, *Franz Kafka. Tragik und Ironie* (Frankfurt/Main: Fischer Taschenbuch, 1976).
3. Larysa Mykyta, 'Woman as the Obstacle and the Way', *MLN* 95 (1980) pp. 627–40.
4. Gilles Deleuze and Féliz Guattari, *Kafka: Toward a Minor Literature*, trans. by Dana Polan (Minneapolis: University of Minnesota Press, 1975) p. 68.
5. Elias Canetti, *Der andere Prozeß. Kafkas Briefe an Felice* (Munich: Hanser, 1984); Detlev Kremer, *Kafka. Die Erotik des Schreibens* (Frankfurt/Main: Athenäum, 1989).
6. Ritchie Robertson, *Kafka: Judaism, Politics, and Literature* (Oxford: Clarendon, 1985); Otto Weininger, *Geschlecht und Charakter* (Munich: Matthes and Seitz, 1980; orig 1903).
7. Sander Gilman, *Franz Kafka: The Jewish Patient* (New York, London: Routledge, 1995); Rainer Stach, *Kafkas erotscher Mythos. Eine ästhetische Konstruktion des Weiblichen* (Frankfurt/Main: Fischer Taschenbuch, 1987); Mark Anderson, *Kafka's Clothes: Ornament and Aestheticism in the Habsburg 'Fin de Siècle'* (Oxford: Clarendon, 1992); Dagmar Lorenz, 'Kafka and gender' in Julian Preece (ed.) *The Cambridge Companion to Kafka* (Cambridge University Press, 2002) pp. 169–88.
8. Frank Möbus, *Sünden-Fälle. Geschlechtlichkeit in Erzählungen Franz Kafkas* (Göttingen: Wallstein, 1994).
9. Julia Kristeva, *Powers of Horror: An Essay on Abjection*, trans. by Leon S. Roudiez (New York: Columbia University Pres, 1982); Anne Fuchs, *A Space of Anxiety: Dislocation and Abjection in Modern German-Jewish Literature* (Amsterdam: Rodopi, 1999).
10. Winifried Menninghaus, *Ekel. Theorie und Geschichte einer starken Empfindung* (Frankfurt/Main: Suhrkamp Taschenbuch, 1999).
11. Elizabeth Boa, *Kafka: Gender, Class and Race in the Letters and Fictions* (Oxford: Clarendon, 1996).

12. G.W.F. Hegel, *Phenomenology of Spirit* (Oxford: Oxford University Press, 1977; orig. 1806) pp. 111–19.
13. Leopold von Sacher-Masoch, *Venus im Pelz. Mit einer Studie über den Masochismus von Gilles Delueze* (Frankfurt/Main: Insel, 1980; orig. 1869).
14. The short stories and sketches referred to can all be found in *The Collected Short Stories of Franz Kafka*, ed. by N.N. Glatzer (Harmondsworth: Penguin, 1988) and Franz Kafka, *Die Erzählungen. Originalfassung* (Frankfurt/Main: Fischer Taschenbuch, 1996).
15. Page numbers for the text in translation refer to Franz Kafka, *The Man Who Disappeared (Amerika)*, trans. by M. Hofmann (Harmondsworth: Penguin, 1996). Page numbers for the German original refer to Franz Kafka, *Der Verschollene (Amerika)*. Roman Originalfassung (Frankfurt/Main: Fischer Taschenbuch, 1994).
16. J.M. Barrie's *Peter Pan, or the Boy who wouldn't grow up* (1904), and the story version 'Peter and Wendy' (1911) are symptomatic of a flight from masculinity in the Age of Empire.
17. On body culture, the striving to harden and cleanse the body through exercise, modern hygiene, and healthy diet, see Anderson, *Kafka's Clothes*, pp. 74–97.
18. M.M. Bakhtin, *Rabelais and his World*, trans. by Hélène Iswolsky (Bloomington: Indiana University Press, 1984) pp. 368–81.
19. See Möbus, *Sünden-Fälle*, p. 122; on homosexuality and youth culture see Ulfried Geuter, *Homosexualität in der deutschen Jugendbewegung. Jungenfreundschaft und Sexualität im Diskurs von Jugendbewegung, Psychoanalyse und Jugendpsychologie am Beginn des 20. Jahrhunderts* (Frankfurt/Main: Suhrkamp, 1994).
20. Gail H. Hart, 'Das Ewig-Weibliche nasführet dich: Feminine Leadership in Goethe's *Faust* and Sacher-Masoch's *Venus*' in Jane Brown and others (eds), *Interpreting Goethe's Faust Today* (Rochester, NY: Camden House, 1994) pp. 112–22.
21. On changing gender discourse see Claudia Honegger, *Die Ordnung der Geschlechter. Die Wissenschaften vom Menschen und das Weib 1750–1850* (Frankfurt/Main: Campus, 1991).
22. See Naomi Ritter, *Art as Spectacle: Images of the Entertainer since Romanticism* (Columbia and London: University of Missouri Press, 1989) pp. 68–90 on Kafka within the tradition of poetological reflection through the metaphor of performance art.
23. On motifs including binoculars in the context of technological developments in visual culture see Carolin Duttlinger, *Kafka, Photography and Visual Culture*, unpublished Ph.D. thesis (University of Cambridge, 2002).

Chapter 12

1. Maria Van Rysselberghe, *Les Cahiers de la Petite Dame*, 2 vols (henceforth CPD): vol. 1 (Paris: Gallimard, 1973); vol. 2 (Paris: Gallimard, 1974); CPD 1, p. 150.
2. André Gide, *Souvenirs et voyages*, ed. by Pierre Masson (Paris: Gallimard, 2001) (henceforth J3); J3, p. 310.
3. Jean Schlumberger, *Madeleine et André Gide* (Paris: Gallimard, 1956) p. 90, italics are Gide's.
4. This term is used, in inverted commas in the original, by Catherine Gide in her introduction to the edition of her mother's letters of 1924–28 to her mother, Élisabeth Van Rysselberghe, *Lettres à la Petite Dame* (Paris: Gallimard, 2000) p. 16.
5. The term 'good bad boy' is one of a series conceived by Leslie Fiedler in his *Love and Death in the American Novel* (London: Jonathan Cape [1960, 1966], 1970).
6. André Gide, *Romans, récits et soties, œuvres lyriques*, ed. by Yvonne Davet and Jean-Jacques Thierry (Paris: Gallimard, 1958) (henceforth GR) p. 153.
7. Samuel Butler, *Life and Habit* (London: Trübner, 1878) p. 134.
8. André Gide, *Journal 1887–1925*, ed. by Éric Marty (Paris: Gallimard, 1996) (henceforth J 1); J 1, p. 1035.
9. The educational motive is, itself, also haunted by a female figure: in April 1918, Gide noted that his obsession with forming or 'retouching' Marc was probably a trait he had inherited from his mother (J 1, p. 1063).
10. Léon Pierre-Quint, *André Gide: L'Homme, sa vie, son œuvre* (Paris: Stock, 1952) p. 391.
11. References to the text of *La Symphonie pastorale* are followed by the corresponding page in the standard translation, André Gide, *The Pastoral Symphony*, trans. by Dorothy Bussy (Harmondsworth: Penguin, 1974 [1919]).
12. See J 1, 1126–27: 'He said he regretted the "indecisiveness" that had made him fill out the heterosexual parts of his book by transposing all his most graceful, tender and charming homosexual memories into the "shade of young girls in flower", with the result that nothing was left for *Sodome et Gomorrhe* but grotesque and abject aspects. But he seemed very upset when I said it seemed as though he was deliberately stigmatizing uranism. He protested; and I came to realize that what we find ignoble, ridiculous or disgusting does not appear so repulsive to him.'
13. Sigmund Freud, 'Femininity', trans. by James Strachey, *The Pelican Freud Library*, 15 vols (Harmondsworth: Penguin, 1979–86) vol. 2, p. 149.
14. On the gender of body fluids, see my *André Gide: Pederasty and Pedagogy* (Oxford: Oxford University Press, 1998) chapter 1, and Naomi Segal, 'The common touch' in Mandy Merck (ed.) *After Diana* (London: Verso, 1998), pp. 131–45. In relation to this text, see Alain Goulet, 'La figuration

du procès littéraire dans l'écriture de *La Symphonie pastorale*' in *La Revue des lettres modernes*, 331–35 (1972), pp. 27–56, reprinted in translation in David Walker (ed.) *André Gide* (London and New York: Longman, 1996) pp. 27–56.

15. It also includes a startling example of a woman initiating coitus interruptus. For a fuller picture of this period, see for example Bard, Gordon and Cross, McMillan, Roberts, and Smith in the bibliography. In a broader European context, the influence of Havelock Ellis, Ellen Key and other new theorists of love and marriage was much debated, as had been the scandalous publication in 1907 by Léon Blum (discussed in a mainly anti-Semitic tone, by Gide in *Corydon* [1911, 1920, 1924]) of *Du mariage*.
16. See Toril Moi, 'Representations of patriarchy: sexuality and epistemology in Freud's "Dora'" in Charles Bernheimer and Claire Kahane (eds) *In Dora's Case* (London: Virago, 1985). Emily Apter in her *André Gide and the Codes of Homotextuality* (Saragota, Calif: ANMA Libri, 1987) pp. 125–26 and 129–30 draws a comparison between this case history and *La Porte étroite*.
17. André Gide, *Journal 1926–1950*, ed. by Martine Sagaert (Paris: Gallimard, 1997), (henceforth J 2) p. 401.
18. See the letter to Scheffer reproduced in vol. IV of the *Œuvres complètes*, ed. by Louis Martin-Chauffier (Paris: Gallimard, 1933), 615–17.
19. See for example J 2 pp. 622, 738 and 842.
20. See my *André Gide*, chapter 3.
21. For a brilliant reading of this motif in another eccentric young woman who reached textual existence in the 1930s, see Jean Allouch, *Marguerite ou l'Aimée de Lacan* (Paris: EPEL, 1994) pp. 420–21 where he observes the closeness between the notion of *being* a 'fille-mère' and the *relation* of daughter to mother.
22. A revealing discussion of this moment appears in CPD 2, pp. 526–27.
23. By another nice coincidence, this is also the year in which the vote was granted to French women.

Bibliography of Secondary Literature

1. General Works

Albistur, Maïte and Daniel Armogathe, *Histoire du féminisme français du moyen âge à nos jours* (Paris: des femmes, 1977).

Anderson, R. D., *Education in France 1848–1870* (Oxford: Clarendon Press, 1975).

Bakhtin, M.M., *Rabelais and his World*, trans. by Hélène Iswolsky (Bloomington: Indiana University Press, 1984).

Bard, Christine, *Les Filles de Marianne* (Paris: Fayard, 1995).

Battersby, Christine, *Gender and Genius: Towards a Feminist Aesthetics* (London: The Women's Press, 1989).

Blackbourn, David, *The Fontana History of Germany 1780–1918: The Long Nineteenth Century* (London: Fontana Press, 1997).

Bloom, Harold, *The Anxiety of Influence: A Theory of Poetry* (London and Oxford: Oxford University Press, 1973).

——*The Western Canon: The Books and School of the Age* (London: Macmillan, 1994).

Bovenschen, Silvia, *Die imaginierte Weiblichkeit. Exemplarische Untersuchungen zu kulturgeschichtlichen und literarischen Präsentationsformen des Weiblichen* (Frankfurt/Main: Suhrkamp, 1979).

Brinker-Gabler, Gisela (ed.) *Deutsche Dichterinnen vom 16. Jahrhundert bis zur Gegenwart* (Frankfurt/Main, 1978).

——(ed.) *Deutsche Literatur von Frauen*. 2 vols (Munich: Beck, 1988).

Brinkmann, Richard (ed.) *Begriffsbestimmung des literarischen Realismus*, Wege der Forschung Bd. CCXII (Darmstadt: Wissenschaftliche Buchgesellschaft, 1974).

Bronfen, Elizabeth, *Over her dead body: Death, Femininity and the Aesthetic* (Manchester: Manchester University Press, 1992).

Brooks, Peter, *Body Work: Objects of Desire in Modern Narrative* (Cambridge: Harvard University Press, 1993).

Butler, Judith, *Gender Trouble* (New York: Routledge, 1990).

—— *Bodies that Matter* (New York: Routledge, 1993).

——*The Psychic Life of Power: Theories in Subjection* (Stanford: Stanford University Press, 1997).

Cixous, Hélène, *Prénoms de personne* (Paris: Éditions du Seuil, 1974).

Cohen, Margaret, *The Sentimental Education of the Novel* (Princeton, NJ: Princeton University Press, 1999).

Crary, Jonathan, *Techniques of the Observer* (Cambridge, MA: MIT Press, 1990).

Darnton, Robert, *The Great Cat Massacre And Other Episodes in French Cultural History* (Harmondsworth: Penguin, 1985 [1984]).

Derrida, Jacques, *De la grammatologie* (Paris: Les Editions de Minuit, 1967) trans. by Gayatri Chakravorty Spivak, *Of Grammatology* (Baltimore: The Johns Hopkins University Press, 1974).

——*Cosmopolites de tous les pays, encore un effort!* (Paris: Galilée, 1997). (*On Cosmopolitanism and Forgiveness*, trans. by Mark Dooley and Michael Hughes (London: Routledge, 2001)).

——*De l'hospitalité: Anne Dufourmantelle invite Jacques Derrida à répondre* (Paris: Calmann-Lévy, 1997). (*Of Hospitality. Anne Dufourmantelle Invites Jacques Derrida to Respond* trans. by Rachel Bowlby (Stanford: Stanford University Press, 2000)).

Doody, Margaret Anne, *The True Story of the Novel* (London: Fontana, 1998).

Ellis, Havelock, *Marriage Today and Tomorrow* (San Francisco: The Westgate Press, 1929).

Fetterley, Judith, *The Resisting Reader* (Bloomington, IN: Indiana University Press, 1978).

Fiedler, Leslie, *Love and Death in the American Novel* (London: Jonathan Cape [1960, 1966], 1970).

Figes, Eva, *Patriarchal Attitudes* (London: Faber, 1970).

Finch, Alison, *Women's Writing in Nineteenth-Century France* (Cambridge: Cambridge University Press, 2000).

Flynn, Elizabeth and Patrocinio Schweikart (eds) *Gender and Reading: Essays on Genders, Texts, and Contexts* (Baltimore: Johns Hopkins University Press, 1986).

Fowler, Alastair, *Kinds of Literature* (Oxford: Clarendon Press, 1982).

Freud, Sigmund, 'The Uncanny' in: *Collected Papers*, vol. 4, trans. by Joan Riviere (New York: Basic Books 1959) pp. 368–407.

Freud, Sigmund, 'Femininity', trans by James Strachey, *The Pelican Freud Library*, 15 vols (Harmondsworth: Penguin, 1979–86) vol. 2.

Geuter, Ulfried, *Homosexualität in der deutschen Jugendbewegung.*

Jungenfreundschaft und Sexualität im Diskurs von Jugendbewegung, Psychoanalyse und Jugendpsychologie am Beginn des 20. Jahrhunderts (Frankfurt/Main: Suhrkamp, 1994).

Goldstein, Jan, 'The Uses of Male Hysteria: Medical and Literary Discourse in Nineteenth-Century France' *Representations* 34 (1991) pp. 134–65.

Gordon, Felicia and Máire Cross, *Early French Feminisms 1830–1940* (Cheltenham and Brookfield: Edward Elgar, 1996).

Hegel, G.W.F., *Phenomenology of Spirit* (Oxford: Oxford University Press, 1977).

Heywood, Colin, *Childhood in Nineteenth-Century France: Work, Health, and Education among the 'classes populaires'* (Cambridge: Cambridge University Press, 1988).

Honegger, Claudia, *Die Ordnung der Geschlechter. Die Wissenschaften vom Menschen und das Weib 1750–1850* (Frankfurt/Main: Campus, 1991).

Irigaray, Luce, *Le Corps-à-corps avec la mère* (Montréal: Pleine Lune, 1981).

——*Speculum of the Other Woman*, trans. by Gillian C. Gill (Ithaca, NY: Cornell University Press, 1985).

Key, Ellen, *Love and Marriage*, trans. by Arthur G. Chater, critical intro. by Havelock Ellis (New York and London: G. P. Putnam's Sons, 1911).

Knottnerus, J. David and Frédérique Van de Poel-Knottnerus, *The Social Worlds of Male and Female Children in the Nineteenth-Century French Educational System: Youth, Rituals, and Elites* (New York: Edwin Mellen Press, 1999).

Kord, Susanne, *Ein Blick hinter die Kulissen: Deutschsprachige Dramatikerinnen im 18. und 19. Jahrhundert* (Stuttgart: Metzler, 1992).

——*Sich einen Namen machen: Anonymität und weibliche Autorschaft 1700–1900* (Stuttgart: Metzler, 1996).

Kristeva, Julia, *Pouvoirs de l'horreur* (Paris: Seuil, 1980). Trans by Leon S. Roudiez, *Powers of Horror: An Essay on Abjection* (New York: Columbia University Press, 1982).

——*Histoires d'amour* (Paris: Denoël, 1983), trans. by Leon S. Roudiez, *Tales of Love* (New York: Columbia University Press, 1987).

Löffler, Sigrid, 'Wer sagt uns, was wir lesen sollen? Die Bücherflut, die Kritik und der literarische Kanon', Bithell Memorial Lecture, 2002 (London: University of London School of Advanced Studies, 2003).

Margueritte, Victor, *La Garçonne* (Paris: Flammarion, 1922).

Matlock, Jann, *Scenes of Seduction: Prostitution, Hysteria, and Reading Difference in Nineteenth-Century France* (New York: Columbia University Press, 1994).

Mayeur, F., *L'Éducation des jeunes filles en France au dix-neuvième siècle* (Paris: Presses Universitaires de France, 1979).

McMillan, James F., *Housewife or Harlot* (New York: St Martin's Press, 1981).

Menninghaus, Winfried, *Ekel. Theorie und Geschichte einer starken Empfindung* (Frankfurt/Main: Suhrkamp, 1999).

Micale, Mark, 'Charcot and the Idea of Hysteria in the Male: Gender, Mental Science, and Medical Diagnosis in Late Nineteenth-Century France' *Medical History* 34 (1990) pp. 363–411.

Möhrmann, Renate (ed.) *Die andere Frau: Emanzipationsansätze deutscher Schriftstellerinnen im Vorfeld der achtundvierziger Revolution.* (Stuttgart: Metzler, 1977).

Nye, Robert A., *Masculinity and Male Codes of Honor in Modern France* (Oxford: Oxford University Press, 1993).

Okin, Susan M., *Women in Western Political Thought* (Princeton: Princeton University Press, 1979).

Olney, James (ed.), *Autobiography: Essays Theoretical and Critical* (Princeton: Princeton University Press, 1980).

Peterson, Carla, *The Determined Reader: Gender and Culture in the Novel from Napoleon to Victoria* (New Brunswick, NJ: Rutgers University Press, 1985).

Queffélec, Lise, 'Le lecteur du roman comme lectrice: stratégies romanesques et stratégies critiques sous la Monarchie de Juillet', *Romantisme* 53 (1986) pp. 9–21.

Radden, Jennifer (ed.) *The Nature of Melancholy: From Aristotle to Kristeva* (Oxford: Oxford University Press, 2000).

Reed, John R., *Victorian Conventions* (Ohio: Ohio University Press, 1975).

Rendall, Jane, *The Origins of Modern Feminism: Women in Britain, France and the US, 1789–1960* (London: MacMillan, 1985).

Reuchlein, Georg, *Bürgerliche Gesellschaft, Psychiatrie und Literatur. Zur Entwicklung der Wahnsinnsthematik in der deutschen Literatur des späten 18. und frühen 19. Jahrhunderts* (Munich: Fink, 1986).

Ritter, Naomi, *Art as Spectacle: Images of the Entertainer since Romanticism* (Columbia and London: University of Missouri Press, 1989).

Roberts, Mary Louise, *Civilization without Sexes* (Chicago and London: University of Chicago Press, 1994).

Sacher-Masoch, Leopold von, *Venus im Pelz. Mit einer Studie über den Masochismus von Gilles Deleuze* (Frankfurt/Main: Insel, 1980; orig. 1869).

Schor, Naomi, *Breaking the Chain: Women, Theory, and French Realist Fiction* (New York: Columbia University Press, 1985).

——*George Sand and Idealism, Gender and Culture* (New York: Columbia University Press, 1993).

Scott, Joan, *Gender and the Politics of History* (New York: Columbia University Press, 1988).

Sedgwick, Eve, *Between Men: English Literature and Male Homosocial Desire* (New York: Columbia University Press, 1985).

Showalter, Elaine (ed.) *Speaking of Gender* (New York: Routledge, 1989).

Singley, Carol J. and Susan Elizabeth Sweeney (eds) *Anxious Power: Reading, Writing and Ambivalence in Narrative by Women* (New York: State University of New York Press, 1993).

Smith, Paul, *Feminism and the Third Republic* (Oxford: Clarendon Press, 1996).

Spielhagen, Friedrich, *Beiträge zur Theorie und Technik des Romans* (Leipzig: Staackmann, 1883).

Steinecke, Harmut, *Romantheorie und Romankritik in Deutschland* vol. 2 (Stuttgart: Metzler, 1976).

Tetu, Jean-François, 'Remarques sur le statut juridique de la femme au xixe siècle' in Roger Bellet (ed.) *La Femme au 19e siècle: Littérature et idéologie* (Lyon: Presses universitaires de Lyon, 1979).

Waller, Margaret, *The Male Malady: Fictions of Impotence in the French Romantic Novel* (New Brunswick, NJ: Rutgers University Press, 1993).

Weinberg, Kerry, 'Women of Eliot and Baudelaire: The Boredom, the Horror and the Glory' *Modern Language Studies* 14.3 (1984) pp. 31–42.

Weininger, Otto, *Geschlecht und Charakter* (Munich: Matthes & Seitz, 1980; orig. 1903).

Williams, Roger, *The Horror of Life* (Chicago: University of Chicago Press, 1980).

Wollstonecraft, Mary, *A Vindication of the Rights of Woman*, ed. by Miriam Brody Kramnick (Harmondsworth: Penguin, 1975).

Wurst, Karin, *Frauen und Drama im achtzehnten Jahrhundert.* (Cologne: Böhlau, 1991).

2. Works on Specific Authors

'L'Affaire Gouffé', *Le Petit Journal. Supplément illustré*, 20 December (1890) p. 8.

Ahearn, Edward, 'Black Woman, White Poet: Exile and Exploitation in Baudelaire's Jeanne Duval' *French Review* 51 (1977) pp. 212–20.

Aichinger, Ingrid, 'E.T.A. Hoffmanns Novelle "Der Sandmann" und die Interpretation Sigmund Freuds', *Zeitschrift für deutsche Philologie* 95 (1976) Sonderheft E.T.A. Hoffmann, pp. 113–32.

Allen, James Smith, *Poignant Relations: Three Modern French Women* (Baltimore and London: The Johns Hopkins University Press, 2000).

Allenhöfer, Manfred, *Vierter Stand und alte Ordnung bei Fontane. Zur Realistik des bürgerlichen Realismus*, Stuttgarter Arbeiten zur Germanistik (Stuttgart: Hans-Dieter Heinz, 1986).

Allouch, Jean, *Marguerite ou l'Aimée de Lacan* (Paris: EPEL, 1994).

Anderson, Jean, 'Baudelaire misogyne: vers une lecture féministe des *Fleurs du mal*' *New Zealand Journal of French Studies* 8.1 (1987) pp. 16–28.

Anderson, Mark, *Kafka's Clothes: Ornament and Aestheticism in the Habsburg 'Fin de Siècle'* (Oxford: Clarendon, 1992).

Annuß, Evelyn, 'Maske und Maschine Künstliche Frauen in Texten von Hoffmann, Villiers und Lem', *Literatur für Leser* 20 (1997) pp. 95–107.

Apter, Emily, *André Gide and the Codes of Homotextuality* (Saragota, Calif: ANMA Libri, 1987).

Armon, Paul d', 'La Bête humaine', *Le Voltaire*, 10 mars (1890) p. 1.

Asche, Susanne, *Die Liebe, der Tod und das Ich im Spiegel der Kunst. Die Funktion des Weiblichen in Schriften der Frühromantik und im erzählerischen Werk E.T.A. Hoffmanns,* Hochschulschriften Literaturwissenschaft, 69 (Königstein/Ts.: Anton Hain, 1985).

'Autour de l'Affaire Gouffé', *L'Estafette*, 23 December 1890, p. 1.

Bagueley, David and Dorothy Speirs, *Bibliographie de la critique sur Émile Zola: 1864–1970* and *1971–1980* (Toronto: University of Toronto Press, 1976 and 1982).

Baker, Felicity, 'L'esprit de l'hospitalité chez Emile', *Romantisme* 4 (1972) pp. 90–99.

——'Perverse Scenes of Writing', *Society for Critical Exchange Reports* 10 (1980) pp. 57–71.

Balzac, Honoré de, 'Avant-propos', *La Comédie humaine*, vol. 1, Bibliothèque de la Pléiade, ed. by Marcel Bouteron and Roger Pierrot (Paris: Gallimard, 1935).

Banuls, Andre, 'Familienverhältnisse in Goethes Faust', *Orbis Litterarum* 42 (1987) pp. 332–37.

Barbou, Alfred, 'Chronique de la semaine', *Le Journal illustré*, 11 May (1890) p. 146.

Bassim, Tamara, *La Femme dans l'œuvre de Baudelaire.* Neuchâtel: La Baconnière, 1974.

Beauvoir, Simone de, *Le Deuxième Sexe* (Paris: Gallimard, 1949), trans. by H. M. Parshley, *The Second Sex* (London: Jonathan Cape, 1953).

Becker-Cantarino, Barbara, 'Goethe as a Critic of Literary Women' in Karl Fink (ed.) *Goethe as a Critic of Literature* (New York: University Press of America, 1984) pp. 160–81.

——'The Discourse of Patriarchy in Goethe's *Wilhelm Meister*', *Neohelicon* 20 (1993) pp. 137–53.

——'Witch and Infanticide: Imaging the Female in *Faust* I', *Goethe Yearbook* 7 (1994) pp. 1–22.

——' "Meine Mutter, die Hur, die mich umgebracht hat." Die Kindsmörderin als literarisches Sujet' in Renate Möhrmann (ed.) *Verklärt, verkitscht, vergessen: Die Mutter als ästhetische Figur*, (Stuttgart: Metzler, 1996) pp. 107–29.

Behler, Constantin, *Nostalgic Teleology. Friedrich Schiller and the Schemata of Aesthetic Humanism* (Bern, Berlin, Frankfurt/Main: Lang, 1995).

Beizer, Janet, *Ventriloquized Bodies: Narratives of Hysteria in Nineteenth-Century France* (Ithaca, NY: Cornell University Press, 1994).

Belgardt, Raimund, 'Der Künstler und die Puppe. Zur Interpretation von Hoffmanns "Der Sandmann"', *The German Quarterly* 42 (1969) pp. 686–700.

Bell, David F., *Models of Power: Politics and Economics in Zola's Rougon Macquart* (Lincoln, Nebraska: University of Nebraska Press, 1988).

Bernheimer, Charles, *Figures of Ill Repute: Representing Prostitution in Nineteenth-Century France* (Cambridge, MA: Harvard University Press, 1989).

Berthier, Philippe, Lamiel, *ou, la boîte de Pandore* (Paris: Presses Universitaires de France, 1994).

'La Bête Humaine', *L'Art Moderne*, 27 Avril 1890, pp. 1–3.

Bigot, Charles, 'Chronique littéraire: La Bête humaine', *Le Siècle*, 10 March (1890) p. 2.

Birch Wagner, Nancy, *Goethe as Cultural Icon: Intertextual Encounters with Stifter and Fontane*, North American Studies in Nineteenth-Century German Literature 17 (New York: Peter Lang, 1994).

Boa, Elizabeth, *Kafka: Gender, Class and Race in the Letters and Fictions* (Oxford: Clarendon, 1996).

Bolster, Richard, *Stendhal, Balzac, et le féminisme romantique*, Lettres Modernes (Paris: Minard, 1970).

Bomhoff, Katrin, Bildende Kunst und Dichtung. Die Selbstinterpretation E.T.A. Hoffmanns in der Kunst Jacques Callots und Salvator Rosas (Freiburg i. Br.: Rombach, 1999).

Brod, Max, *Über Franz Kafka* (Frankfurt/Main: Fischer Taschenbuch, 1974).

Butler, Samuel, *Life and Habit* (London: Trübner, 1878).

Caliban, 'L'Atavisme', *Le Figaro*, 16 March 1890, p. 1.

Canetti, Elias, *Der andere Prozeß. Kafkas Briefe an Felice* (Munich: Hanser, 1984).

Caws, Mary Ann. 'What can a woman do for the late Henry James?', *Raritan* 14.1 (1994) pp. 1–17.

Chambers, Helen E., *The Changing Image of Theodor Fontane* (Columbia, SC: Camden House, 1999).

Chambers, Ross, *Mélancolie et Opposition* (Paris: Corti, 1987).

——'Irony and Misogyny: Authority and the Homosocial in Baudelaire and Flaubert', *Australian Journal of French Studies* 26.3 (1989) pp. 272–88.

Champsaur, Felicien, 'La Queue du romantisme', *L'Événement*, 12 March (1890) p. 1.

Clément, Pierre-Paul, *Jean-Jacques Rousseau de l'éros coupable à l'éros glorieux* (Neuchâtel: La Baconnière, 1976).

Cohen, Margaret, *The Sentimental Education of the Novel* (Princeton, NJ: Princeton University Press, 1999).

Collot, Sylvie, *Lieux du désir: topologie amoureuse de Zola* (Paris: Hachette, 1992).

Cranston, Maurice, *The Noble Savage: Jean-Jacques Rousseau 1754–1762* (Harmondsworth: Allen Lane, 1991).

Culler, Jonathan, *Flaubert: the Uses of Uncertainty* (London: Elek, 1974).

Cuthbert, Andrew, *Les Champs des Connaissances: Myth and Metaphysics in the Late Works of Flaubert* (unpublished PhD thesis, University of Exeter, 2003) 94–108.

Czyba, Luzette, *Mythes et Idéologie de la Femme dans les Romans de Flaubert* (Lyon: Presses Universitaires de Lyon, 1983).

DalMolin, Elaine, *Cutting the Body: Representing Woman in Baudelaire's Poetry, Truffaut's Cinema, and Freud's Psychoanalysis* (Ann Arbor: University of Michigan Press, 2000).

Damm, Sigrid, *Christiane und Goethe: Eine Recherche*. (Frankfurt/Main: Insel, 1998).

Danahy, Michael, 'Marceline Desbordes-Valmore et la fraternité des poètes' *Nineteenth-Century French Studies* 19.3 (1991) pp. 386–93.

Darmon, Pierre, *La Malle à Gouffé* (Paris: Denoël, 1988).

Dayan, Peter, 'Baudelaire at his Latrine: Motions in the Petits poèmes en prose and in George Sand's novels' *French Studies* 48.4 (1994) pp. 416–24.

Deleuze, Gilles and Féliz Guattari, *Kafka: Toward a Minor Literature*, trans. by Dana Polan (Minneapolis: University of Minnesota Press, 1975).

Delf von Wolzogen, Hanna (ed.), *Theodor Fontane: Am Ende des Jahrhunderts. Internationales Symposium des Theodor-Fontane-Archivs zum 100. Todestag Theodor Fontanes, 13–17 September 1998 in Potsdam,* 3 vols (Würzburg: Königshausen and Neumann, 2000).

De Man, Paul, *Allegories of Reading: Figural Language in Rousseau, Nietzsche, Rilke and Proust* (New Haven: Yale University Press, 1979).

Deterding, Klaus, *Magie des poetischen Raums. E.T.A. Hoffmanns Dichtung und Weltbild*, Beiträge zur neueren Literaturgeschichte, Folge 3, 152 (Heidelberg: Winter, 1999).

Dieterle, Bernard, *Erzählte Bilder. Zum narrativen Umgang mit Gemälden*, Schriften zur Soziosemiotik und Komparatistik: Artefakt, 3 (Marburg: Hitzeroth, 1988).

Dieterle, Regina, *Vater und Tochter. Erkundung einer erotisierten Beziehung in Leben und Werk Theodor Fontanes* (Bern, Berlin, Frankfurt/Main: Lang, 1996).

Dobat, Klaus-Dieter, *Musik als romantische Illusion. Eine Untersuchung zur Bedeutung der Musikvorstellung E.T.A. Hoffmanns für sein literarische Werk* (Tübingen: Niemeyer, 1984).

Donato, Eugene *The Script of Decadence: Essays on the Fictions of Flaubert and the Poetics of Romanticism* (Oxford: Oxford University Press, 1993).

Duennebier, Anna, *Mein Genie: Hassliebe zu Goethe & Co.* (Frankfurt/Main: Fischer, 1993).

Duttlinger, Carolin, *Kafka, Photography and Visual Culture*, unpublished PhD thesis (University of Cambridge, 2002).

Eilert, Heide, *Theater in der Erzählkunst. Eine Studie zum Werk E.T.A. Hoffmanns* (Tübingen: Niemeyer, 1977).

Ellis, John M., 'Clara, Nathanael and the Narrator: Interpreting Hoffmann's "Der Sandmann"', *The German Quarterly* 54 (1981) pp. 1–18.

Ferrero, Guglielmo, 'Le Mensonge et la Véracité chez la Femme criminelle', *Archives d'anthropologie criminelle* 8 (1893) pp. 138–49.

'Figures du Féminin', *Cahiers naturalistes* 73 (1999).

'La Folie du crime', *Le Matin*, 20 February 1890, p. 1.

'Fontane und die Frauen' in: *Literaturen. Das Journal für Bücher und Themen*, 04/02, pp. 10–36.

Forain, Jean-Louis, 'Les Deux Zola', *Le Courrier français*, 16 November (1890) p. 1.

Fouquier, Henry, 'La Vie de Paris', *Le XIXe Siècle*, 21 November (1889) p. 1.

Friedman, Susan Stanford, 'Women's Autobiographical Selves: Theory and Practice' in Shari Benstock (ed.) *The Private Self: Theory and Practice of Women's Autobiographical Writings* (Chapel Hill: University of North Carolina Press, 1988) pp. 34–62.

Fuchs, Anne, *A Space of Anxiety: Dislocation and Abjection in Modern German-Jewish Literature* (Amsterdam: Rodopi, 1999).

Fuhrmann, Helmut, 'Der schwankende Paris: Bild und Gestalt der Frau im Werke Goethes', *Jahrbuch des Freien Deutschen Hochstifts* (1989) pp. 37–127.

——'Revision des Parisurteils. "Bild" und "Gestalt" der Frau im Werk Friedrich Schillers', *Jahrbuch der Deutschen Schillergesellschaft* 25 (1981) pp. 316–66.

——*Zur poetischen und philosophischen Anthropologie Schillers. Vier Versuche* (Würzburg: Königshausen und Neumann, 2001).

Fumaroli, Marc, 'La Coupole' in *Les Lieux de Mémoire*, ed. by Pierre Nora (1984–92; rpt. Paris: Gallimard Quarto, 1997) vol. 2, pp. 1923–82.

Gates Jr., Henry Louis, *Bearing Witness: Selections from African American Autobiography in the Twentieth Century* (New York: Pantheon Books, 1991).

Gay, Peter, *Schnitzler's Century: The Making of Middle-Class Culture, 1815–1914* (New York and London: Norton, 2002).

Gerhard, Ute, *Schiller als Religion. Literarische Signaturen des XIX. Jahrhunderts* (Munich: Fink, 1994).

Gilman, Sander, *Franz Kafka: The Jewish Patient* (New York, London: Routledge, 1995).

Gilroy, Paul, *Between Camps: Race, Identity and Nationalism at the End of the Colour Line* (Harmondsworth: Allen Lane The Penguin Press, 2000).

Glowinski, Michael, 'Der Dialog im Roman', *Poetica* 6 (1974) pp. 1–16.

Godfrey, Sima, '"Mère des souvenirs": Baudelaire, Memory and Mother' *L'Esprit créateur* 25.2 (1985) pp. 32–44.

Goulet, Alain, 'La figuration du procès littéraire dans l'écriture de *La Symphonie pastorale*' in *La Revue des lettres modernes*, 331–335 (1972) pp. 27–56, reprinted in translation in David Walker (ed.), *André Gide* (London and New York: Longman, 1996).

Grair, Charles. 'Seducing Helena: The Court Fantasy of *Faust II*, Act III', *Goethe Yearbook* 10 (2001) pp. 99–114.

Grand-Carteret, John, *Zola en images* (Paris: Juven, 1907).

Gray, Francine du Plessix, *Rage and Fire: a Life of Louise Colet, Pioneer Feminist, Literary Star, Flaubert's Muse* (New York: Simon and Schuster, 1994).

Greenberg, Wendy, *Uncanonical Women: Feminine Voice in French Poetry (1830–1871)* (Amsterdam: Rodopi, 1999).

Guenter, Margaret P. '*Faust*: The Tragedy Re-examined' in Susan Cocalis and Kay Goodman (eds) *Beyond the Eternal Feminine: Critical Essays on Women in German Literature* (Stuttgart: Hans Dieter Heinz, 1982) pp. 75–98.

Haenen, F. de, 'L'Affaire Gouffé: Le service anthropométrique du Palais de Justice prenant le signalement de Gabrielle Bompard', *L'Illustration*, 1 February (1890) p. 91.

Harris, Ruth, 'Murder under Hypnosis in the Case of Gabrielle Bompard: Psychiatry in the Courtroom in Belle Époque Paris' in W.F. Bynum and others (eds) *Anatomy of Madness* (London: Tavistock, 1986) vol. 2: Institutions and Society, pp. 197–241.

Hart, Gail K., 'Das Ewig-Weibliche nasführet dich: Feminine Leadership in Goethe's *Faust* and Sacher-Masoch's *Venus*' in Jane K. Brown and others (eds) *Interpreting Goethe's Faust Today* (Columbia, SC: Camden House, 1994) pp. 112–22.

——*Tragedy in Paradise: Family and Gender Politics in German Bourgeois Tragedy 1750–1850* (Columbia, SC: Camden House, 1996).

Helfer, Martha, 'Wilhelm Meister's Women', *Goethe Yearbook* 11 (2002) pp. 229–54.

Heller, Peter, 'Gretchen: Figur, Klischee, Symbol' in Wolfgang Paulsen (ed.) *Die Frau als Heldin und Autorin* (Bern: Francke, 1979) pp. 174–95.

Helmstetter, Rudolf, *Die Geburt des Realismus aus dem Dunst des Familienblatts. Fontane und die öffentlichkeitsgeschichtlichen Rahmenbedingungen des Poetischen Realismus* (Munich: Fink, 1998).

Hermand, Jost. 'Erotik im Juste milieu: Heines "Verschiedene"' in *Mehr als ein Liberaler: Über Heinrich Heine* (Frankfurt/Main: Peter Lang, 1991) pp. 111–25.

Herrmann, Hans Peter, and Martina Herrmann, *Friedrich Schiller. 'Maria Stuart' Grundlagen und Gedanken zum Verständnis des Dramas* (Frankfurt/Main: Diesterweg, revised edition 1989).

Herrmann, Helene, 'Theodor Fontanes *Effi Briest. Die Geschichte eines Romans' in Die Frau* 19 (1912) pp. 543–54, 610–25, 677–94.

Hohoff, Ulrich, *E.T.A. Hoffmann. Der Sandmann Textkritik, Edition, Kommentar* (Berlin, New York: de Gruyter, 1988).

Holub, Robert C., 'Heine and Utopia', *Heine-Jahrbuch* 27 (1988) pp. 86–112.

Howe, Patricia and Helen Chambers (eds), *Theodor Fontane and the European Context. Literature, Culture and Society in Prussia and Europe* (Amsterdam and Atlanta, GA: Rodopi, 2001).

Huret, Jules, 'Les Deux Lutteurs', *L'Écho de Paris*, 7 December (1889) p. 2.

Jackson, Susan K., *Rousseau's Occasional Autobiographies* (Columbus: Ohio State University Press, 1992).

Jefferson, Ann, *Stendhal, La Chartreuse de Parme* (London: Grant and Cutler, 2003).

Jelinek, Estelle C. (ed.), *Women's Autobiography: Essays in Criticism* (Bloomington: Indiana University Press, 1980).

Judy, Ronald A.T., *(Dis)forming the American Canon: African-Arabic Slave Narratives and the Vernacular* (Minnesota: University of Minnesota Press, 1993).

Justis, Diana Lynn, *The Feminine in Heine's Life and Œuvre* (New York: Lang, 1997).

Kaiser, Gerhard R., 'Hoffmanns *Prinzessin Brambilla* als Antwort auf Goethes *Römisches Karneval.* Eine Lektüre im Lichte Baudelaires' in Klaus Manger (ed.) *Italienbeziehungen des klassischen Weimar* (Tübingen: Niemeyer, 1997) pp. 215–42.

Kamuf, Peggy, *Signature Pieces On the Institution of Authorship* (Ithaca, New York: Cornell University Press, 1988).

——'Baudelaire's modern woman', *Qui parle* 4.2 (1991) pp. 1–7.

Kant, Immanuel, *Observations on the Feeling of the Beautiful and the Sublime*, trans. by John T. Goldthwait (Berkeley and Los Angeles: University of California Press, 1960).

——*Perpetual Peace and Other Essays*, trans. by Ted Humphrey (Indianapolis: Hackett Publishing Company, 1983).

Keates, Jonathan, *Stendhal* (London: Sinclair-Stevenson, 1994).

Kelly, Dorothy, 'Gender, Metaphor, and Machine: *La Bête humaine*', *French Literature Series* 16 (1989) pp. 110–22.

——'Experimenting on Women: Zola's Theory and Practice of the Experimental Novel' in Margaret Cohen and Christopher Prendergast (eds) *Spectacles of Realism: Gender, Body, Genre* (Minneapolis: University of Minnesota Press, 1995) pp. 231–46.

Klotz, Volker, 'Kronen und lange Haare. Schillers *Maria Stuart*' in Volker Klotz, *Kurze Kommentare zu Stücken und Gedichten* (Darmstadt: Roether, 1962) pp. 7–14.

Knight, Diana, 'Reading as an Old Maid: *La Cousine Bette* and Compulsory Heterosexuality', *Quinquereme* 12:1 (1989) pp. 67–79.

Kofman, Sarah, *Le Respect des femmes* (Paris: Galilée, 1982).

Kohlenbach, Margarete, 'Women and Artists: E.T.A. Hoffmann's Implicit Critique of Early Romanticism', *Modern Language Review* 89 (1994) pp. 659–673.

Kohut, Adolph, *Heinrich Heine und die Frauen* (Berlin: Alfred H. Frieds Verlag) 1888.

Kord, Susanne, 'Performing Genders: Three Plays on the Power of Women', *Monatshefte* 86 (1994) pp. 95–115.

Kremer, Detlev, *Kafka. Die Erotik des Schreibens* (Frankfurt/Main: Athenäum, 1989).

——*Romantische Metamorphosen. E.T.A. Hoffmanns Erzählungen* (Stuttgart: Metzler, 1993).

——'Literarischer Karneval. Groteske Motive in E.T.A. Hoffmanns *Prinzessin Brambilla*', *E.T.A. Hoffmann-Jahrbuch* 3 (1995) pp. 15–30.

——*E.T.A. Hoffmann. Erzählungen und Romane* (Berlin: Erich Schmidt, 1999).

Labarthe, Patrick. 'La "mise en crise" de la relation amoureuse dans *Les Fleurs du mal*' in Steve Murphy (ed.) *Lectures des* Fleurs du mal (Rennes: Presses universitaires de Rennes, 2002) pp. 115–26.

Labrosse, Claude, *Lire au xviii*[e] *siècle:* La Nouvelle Héloïse *et ses lecteurs* (Lyons: Presses Universitaires de Lyon, 1985).

LaCapra, Dominic, Madame Bovary *on Trial* (Ithaca and London: Cornell University Press, 1982).

Lacoste, Francis, 'L'Académie contre Zola: Autour de la Reception de Pierre Loti', *Excavatio* 2 (1993) pp. 142–55.

——'Zola et L'Académie', *Excavatio* 6–7 (1995) pp. 210–29.

Lämmert, Eberhard (ed.), *Romantheorie. Dokumente ihrer Geschichte in Deutschland seit 1880* (Königstein/Taunus: Athenäum Taschenbücher, 1984).

Lamport, F.J., 'Krise und Legitimitätsanspruch. *Maria Stuart* als Geschichtstragödie', *Zeitschrift für deutsche Philologie* 109 (1990), Sonderheft: Schiller. Aspekte neuerer Forschung pp. 134–44.

Lange, Sigrid, *Die Utopie des Weiblichen im Drama Goethes, Schillers und Kleists* (Frankfurt/Main., Berlin, Bern: Lang, 1993).

Laroche, Georges, 'La Bête humaine de Saint Louis', *Le Siècle*, 29 mars (1890) p. 2

Leclerc, Annie, *Origines* (Paris: Grasset, 1988).

Leduc-Adine, Jean-Pierre (ed.), *Zola, genèse de l'œuvre* (Paris: CNRS, 2002).

Legrand, Louis, 'Le Naturalisme', *Le Courrier français*, 30 March (1890) p. 5.

——'Le Romantisme', *Le Courrier français*, 30 March (1890) p. 4.

Lejeune, Philippe, *Le Pacte autobiographique* (Paris: Seuil, 1975).

Lemaître, Jules, 'La Bête humaine', *Le Figaro*, 8 Mars (1890) p. 1.

Leonhardt, Rudolf Walter, *Das Weib, das ich geliebet hab: Heines Mädchen und Frauen* (Hamburg: Hoffmann und Campe, 1975).

Leoni, Margherita, *Stendhal: la peinture à l'œuvre* (Paris: L'Harmattan, 1996).

Lepelletier, E., 'Chronique des livres, La Bête humaine', *L'Écho de Paris*, 11 March (1890) p. 2.

——'Chronique. Le roman-feuilleton à l'académie', *Paris*, 22 November (1889) p. 1

Le Roy, Edmond, 'Gabrielle Bompard d'après Zola', *Le Figaro*, 29 January (1890) p. 2.

Liebrand, Claudia, *Aporie des Kunstmythos Die Texte E.T.A. Hoffmanns*,

Rombach Wissenschaften: Reihe Litterae, 42 (Freiburg i. Br.: Rombach, 1996).

Lionnet, Françoise, *Autobiographical Voices: Race, Gender, Self-Portraiture* (Ithaca and London: Cornell University Press, 1989).

Lloyd, Rosemary, 'Baudelaire, Marceline Desbordes-Valmore et la fraternité des poètes', *Bulletin baudelairien* 26.2 (1991) pp. 65–74.

——'Hypocrite brother, Hypocrite sister: changing genders in *Les Fleurs du mal*', *French Studies* (1999) pp. 167–75.

——'The Nineteenth Century: Shaping Women' in Sonya Stephens (ed.) *A History of Women's Writing in France* (Cambridge: Cambridge University Press, 2000).

——*Baudelaire's World* (Ithaca, NY: Cornell University Press, 2002).

Lokke, Kari, 'Schiller's *Maria Stuart*: The Historical Sublime and the Aesthetics of Gender', *Monatshefte* 82 (1990) pp. 123–41.

Lombroso, Cesare, 'La "Bête humaine" et l'anthropologie criminelle', *La Revue des revues* 4 (1892) pp. 260–64.

Lorenz, Dagmar, 'Kafka and gender' in Julian Preece (ed.) *The Cambridge Companion to Kafka* (Cambridge University Press, 2002) pp. 169–88.

Lukács, Georg, 'Schiller's Theory of Modern Literature' in *Goethe and his Age*, trans. by Robert Anchor (London: Merlin Press 1968) pp. 101–35.

Maclean, Marie, *Narrative as Performance: the Baudelairean Experiment* (London: Routledge, 1988).

Malraux, Clara, 'Les grandes sœurs de Mathilde de la Môle' [sic], *Confluences* no. 4 (1944) 262–64.

Marcus, Sharon, *Apartment Stories* (Berkeley: University of California Press, 1999) pp. 166–98.

Marder, Elissa. *Temporal Disorders in the Wake of Modernity (Baudelaire and Flaubert)* (Palo Alto, CA: Stanford University Press, 2001).

Matlock, Jann, 'Censoring the Realist Gaze' in Margaret Cohen and Christopher Prendergast (eds) *Spectacles of Realism: Gender, Body, Genre* (Minneapolis: University of Minnesota Press, 1995) pp. 28–67.

——*Scenes of Seduction* (New York: Columbia University Press, 1994).

——'The Limits of Reformism: The Novel, Censorship, and the Politics of Adultery in Nineteenth-Century France' in Deirdre Lynch and William B. Warner (eds) *Cultural Institutions of the Novel* (Chapel Hill: Duke University Press, 1996) pp. 335–68.

——'Dressed Down: Lingerie, Popular Prints, and the Voyeur's Censored Look in Third Republic France' (Los Angeles: College Art Association, 1998).

——'Olympia devient française, ou comment la modernité a perdu la mémoire' in *Ruptures: De la discontinuité dans la vie artistique* (Paris: Louvre and ENSBA, 2002) pp. 165–216.

Matt, Peter von, *Die Augen der Automaten. E.T.A. Hoffmanns Imaginationslehre als Prinzip seiner Erzählkunst* (Tübingen: Niemeyer, 1971).

McLees, Ainslee Armstrong, 'Baudelaire's "Une Charogne": Caricature and the Birth of Modern Art' *Mosaic* 21.4 (1988) pp. 111–22.

Meyer, Henri, 'L'Affaire Gouffé: L'Accomplissement du crime', *Le Journal illustré*, 2 February (1890) pp. 36–37.

Miller, D.A., *The Novel and the Police* (Berkeley: University of California Press, 1987).

Milo, Daniel, 'Les Classiques scolaires' in *Les Lieux de Mémoire*, ed. Pierre Nora 1984–92; rpt. Paris: Gallimard Quarto, 1997) vol. 2: La Nation, p. 2119.

Miner, Margaret. '(S)(m)othering Baudelaire' in Patricia Ward (ed.) *Baudelaire and the Poetics of Modernity* (Nashville: Vanderbilt University Press, 2001) pp. 157–71.

Möbus, Frank, *Sünden-Fälle. Geschlechtlichkeit in Erzählungen Franz Kafkas* (Göttingen: Wallstein, 1994).

Möhrmann, Renate (ed.) *Verkitscht, verklärt, vergessen: Die Mutter als ästhetische Figur* (Stuttgart: Metzler, 1996).

Moi, Toril, 'Representations of patriarchy: sexuality and epistemology in Freud's "Dora"' in Charles Bernheimer and Claire Kahane (eds) *In Dora's Case* (London: Virago, 1985).

Moloch, 'Prédictions pour 1890', *La Silhouette*, 29 December (1889) p. 1.

Momberger, Manfred, *Sonne und Punsch. Die Dissemination des romantischen Kunstbegriffs bei E.T.A. Hoffmann*, Literatur in der Gesellschaft Neue Folge, 9 (Munich: Fink, 1986).

Mommsen, Katharina, 'Goethe as a Precursor of Women's Emancipation' in Clifford Bernd (ed.) *Goethe Proceedings: Essays Commemorating the Goethe Sesquicentennial at the University of California, Davis* (Columbia, SC: Camden House, 1984) pp. 51–65.

Mossman, Carol A., *The Narrative Matrix: Stendhal's* Le Rouge et le Noir (Lexington, KY: French Forum, 1984).

Mykyta, Larysa, 'Woman as the Obstacle and the Way', *MLN* 95 (1980) pp. 627–40.

Naumann, Ursula '"Für einer Zeitung Gnadenlohn"? Schillers Gedicht "Die berühmte Frau" und Sophie Ludwigs Buch *Juda oder der erschlagene Redliche*', *Zeitschrift für deutsche Philologie* 109 (1990) Sonderheft: Schiller. Aspekte neuerer Forschung, pp. 16–26.

Neefs, Jacques, 'La Nuit de Noël: *Bouvard et Pécuchet*' in *Gustave Flaubert 3: Mythes et religions 2* (Paris: Lettres Modernes, Minard, 1988) pp. 35–61.

Nehring, Wolfgang, 'E.T.A. Hoffmanns Erzählwerk: Ein Modell und seine Variationen', *Zeitschrift für deutsche Philologie* 95 (1976) Sonderheft, pp. 3–24.

Neymeyr, Barbara, 'Narzistische Destruktion. Zum Stellenwert von Realitätsverlust und Selbstentfremdung in E.T.A. Hoffmanns Nachtstück *Der Sandmann*', *Poetica* 29 (1997) pp. 499–531.

Ohl, Hubert, 'Melusine als Mythos bei Theodor Fontane' in Helmut

Koopmann (ed.) *Mythos und Mythologie in der Literatur des 19. Jahrhunderts* (Frankfurt/Main: Klostermann, 1979) pp. 289–305.

Orr, Mary, *Madame Bovary: representations of the masculine* (Bern: Peter Lang, 1999).

——*Flaubert: Writing the Masculine* (Oxford: Oxford University Press, 2000).

——'Death and the *Post Mortem* in Flaubert's Works' in Tim Unwin (ed.) *The Cambridge Companion to Flaubert* (Cambridge; Cambridge University Press, 2004) chapter 7.

Pagès, Alain, *La Bataille littéraire: Essai sur la réception du naturalisme à l'époque de Germinal* (Paris: Séguier, 1989).

Panke-Kochinke, Birgit, *Die anständige Frau* (Pfaffenweiler: Centaurus-Verlagsgesellschaft, 1991).

Pelca, E., 'Carnet littéraire', *Le Gaulois*, 4 December (1889) p. 2.

Perrot, Michelle, 'Délinquance et système pénitentiaire en France au xixe siècle', *Annales, ESC* 30, No. 1 Jan.–Feb. (1975) p. 72.

Pelletier, Aimée Israel, *Flaubert's Straight and Suspect Saints* (Amsterdam and Philadelphia: The John Benjamins Publishing Company, 1991).

Peters, George F., *The Poet as Provocateur: Heinrich Heine and His Critics* (Rochester: Camden House, 2000).

Pichois, Claude. *Baudelaire.* Trans. Graham Robb. (London: Hamish Hamilton, 1987).

Pierre-Quint, Léon, *André Gide: L'Homme, sa vie, son œuvre* (Paris: Stock, 1952).

Pollock, Griselda, *Differencing the Canon: Feminist Desire and the Writing of Art's Histories* (London: Routledge, 1999).

Pontmartin, Armand de, 'La Bête humaine par Émile Zola', *Gazette de France*, 23 March (1809) p. 1.

'Poursuites contre le Courrier Français', *Le Courrier français*, 4 May (1890) pp. 2–5.

Procès Eyraud-Bompard, procès-verbaux d'audiences tirés de la Gazette des tribunaux (Paris: n.p., 1891).

Prandi, Julie, *Spirited Woman Heroes: Major Female Characters in the Dramas of Goethe, Schiller, and Kleist.* (Berne, New York: Peter Lang, 1983).

Prax, Mario, 'Ce n'est pas de lui', *Le Charivari*, 22 November (1889) p. 1.

Prokop, Ulrike, *Die Illusion vom großen Paar: Weibliche Lebensentwürfe im deutschen Bildungsbürgertum 1750–1770* (Frankfurt/Main: S. Fischer, 1991).

Pugh, David V., *Dialectic of Love: Platonism in Schiller's Aesthetics* (Montreal and Kingston, London, Buffalo: McGill-Queen's University Press, 1996).

Ransom, Amy, '"Mon semblable, ma mere": Woman, Subjectivity and Escape in *Les Fleurs du Mal*', *Paroles Gelées: UCLA French Studies* 11 (1993) pp. 31–55.

Reece, Steve, *The Stranger's Welcome: Oral Theory and the Aesthetics of the*

Homeric Hospitality Scene (Ann Arbor: The University of Michigan Press, 1993).

Reid, Martine, *Flaubert correspondant* (Paris: SEDES, 1995).

Richon, Emmanuel, *Jeanne Duval et Charles Baudelaire: Belle d'abandon* (Paris: L'Harmattan, 1998).

Robertson, Ritchie, *Kafka: Judaism, Politics, and Literature* (Oxford: Clarendon Press, 1985).

Roland, Mme., *Mémoires de Madame Roland*, ed. by Paul de Roux (Paris: Mercure de France, 1986), trans. by Evelyn Shuckburgh, *The Memoirs of Madame Roland* (London: Barrie and Jenkins, 1989).

Rollins, Yvonne Bargues, *Le Pas de Flaubert: une danse macabre* (Paris: Champion, 1998).

Rollka, Bodo, *Die Belletristik in der Berliner Presse des 19. Jahrhunderts* (Berlin: Colloquium Verlag, 1985).

Ryckère, Raymond, *La Femme en prison et devant la mort* (Lyon: Storck, 1898) pp. 70–71.

Saße, Günter, 'Die Karnevalisierung der Wirklichkeit. Vom "chronischen Dualismus" zur "Duplizität der irdischen Seins" in Hoffmanns *Prinzessin Brambilla*', *E.T.A. Hoffmann-Jahrbuch* 9 (2001) pp. 55–69.

Sacquin, Michèle (ed.) *Zola*, Exhibition catalogue, Paris, Bibliothèque Nationale de France, 18 October 2002–19 January 2003 (Paris: Fayard, 2002).

Sartre, Jean-Paul, *Baudelaire* (Paris: Gallimard, 1946).

Sautermeister, Gert, '*Maria Stuart*' in Walter Hinderer (ed.) *Schillers Dramen. Neue Interpretationen* (Stuttgart: Reclam, 1979) pp. 174–216; reprinted in slightly revised form in Hinderer (ed.) *Interpretationen. Schillers Dramen* (Stuttgart: Reclam, 1992) pp. 280–336.

Scaramouche, 'L'art et la morale', *Le Gaulois*, 22 November (1889) p. 1.

Schäfer, Renate, 'Fontanes Melusine-Motiv', *Euphorion* 56 (1962) pp. 69–104.

Schäublin, Peter, 'Der moralphilosophische Diskurs in Schillers *Maria Stuart*', *Sprachkunst* 17 (1986) pp. 141–87.

Schehr, Lawrence, *Rendering French Realism* (Stanford: Stanford University Press, 1997).

Schlaffer, Hannelore, 'Goethe als Muse: Der Autor und die Schriftstellerinnen seiner Zeit', *Goethe Jahrbuch* 112 (1995) pp. 183–95.

Schlumberger, Jean, *Madeleine et André Gide* (Paris: Gallimard, 1956).

Schmidt, Jochen, 'Die Krise der romantischen Subjektivität: E.Th.A. Hoffmanns Künstlernovelle "Der Sandmann" in historischer Perspektive' in Jürgen Brummack and others (eds) *Literaturwissenschaft und Geistesgeschichte. Festschrift für Richard Brinkmann* (Tübingen: Niemeyer, 1981) pp. 348–70.

Schmidt, Olaf, '"Die Wundernadel des Meisters"—Zum Bild-Text-Verhältnis in E.T.A. Hoffmanns Capriccio *Prinzessin Brambilla*', *E.T.A. Hoffmann-Jahrbuch* 7 (1999) pp. 50–62.

Schmidt, Ricarda, 'E.T.A. Hoffmann's "Der Sandmann": An Early Example of *Écriture Féminine*? A Critique of Trends in Feminist Literary Criticism', *Women in German Yearbook* 4 (1988) pp. 21–45.

——'Karnevaleske Mesalliancen oder der Autor als Bauchredner der Sprache? Eine Analyse Bachtinscher Ansätze für die Interpretation des Traumes in Hoffmanns "Die Abenteuer der Sylvester-Nacht" im Lichte malerischer Intertexte' in Sheila Dickson and Mark G. Ward (eds) *Romantic Dreams. Proceedings of the Glasgow Conference, April 1997* (Glasgow: University of Glasgow French and German Publications, 1998) pp. 77–97 (plus 12 pages of unnumbered illustrations).

——'Ahnung des Göttlichen und affizierte Ganglien. Die kontrapunktische Erzähltechnik des *Kater Murr* auf der Schwelle von Romantik zu Moderne' in Nicholas Saul and others (eds) *Schwellen. Germanistische Erkundungen einer Metapher* (Würzburg: Königshausen and Neumann, 1999) pp. 138–51.

——'Der Dichter als Fledermaus bei der Schau des Wunderbaren. Die Poetologie des rechten dichterischen Sehens in Hoffmanns "Der Sandmann" und "Das öde Haus'" in R.J. Kavanagh (ed.) *Mutual Exchanges. Sheffield-Münster Colloquium I* (Frankfurt/Main: Peter Lang, 1999) pp. 180–92.

——'Narrative Strukturen romantischer Subjektivität in E.T.A. Hoffmanns *Die Elixiere des Teufels* und *Der Sandmann*', *Germanisch-Romanische Monatsschrift* 49.2 (1999) pp. 143–160.

——'Heroes and Villains in E.T.A. Hoffmann's "Ritter Gluck"', *Bulletin of the John Rylands University Library of Manchester* 84.3 (2002) pp. 49–66.

——'Biographie, Autobiographie, Fiktion: Die Funktion von Rousseaus *Confessions* für die Konstruktion von Identität in Hoffmanns *Kater Murr*' in Sheila Dickson and Walter Pape (eds) *Romantische Identitätskonstruktionen: Nation, Geschichte und (Auto-) Biographie. Glasgower Kolloquium der Internationalen Arnim-Gesellschaft. Schriften der Internationalen Arnim-Gesellschaft 4* (Tübingen: Niemeyer, 2003) pp. 193–216.

Schneider, Jeffrey, 'Masculinity, Male Friendship, and the Paranoid Logic of Honor in Theodor Fontane's *Effi Briest*', *German Quarterly* 75 (2002) pp. 265–81.

Schor, Naomi, 'Mother's Day: Zola's Women', *Diacritics* 5, no. 4 (1975) pp. 11–17.

——*Zola's Crowds* (Baltimore: Johns Hopkins University Press, 1978).

——*Breaking the Chain: Women, Theory, and French Realist Fiction* (New York: Columbia University Press, 1985).

——*Reading in Detail* (New York: Methuen, 1987) 110–30.

Schor Naomi and H.F. Majewski (eds) *Flaubert and Postmodernism* (Lincoln, Nebraska: University of Nebraska Press, 1984).

Schroeder, Irene, 'Das innere Bild und seine Gestaltung. Die Erzählung *Der*

Sandmann als Theorie und Praxis des Erzählens', *E.T.A. Hoffmann-Jahrbuch* 9 (2001) pp. 22–33.

Schultz, Gretchen, 'Baudelaire's Lesbian Connections' in L. Porter (ed.) *Approaches to Teaching Baudelaire's* Flowers of Evil (New York: Modern Language Association, 2000).

Schuster, Klaus Peter, *Effi Briest. Ein Leben nach christlichen Bildern*. Studien zur deutschen Literatur 55 (Tübingen: Niemeyer, 1978).

Seele, Astrid, *Frauen um Goethe* (Reinbeck: Rowohlt, 1997).

Segal, Naomi, *André Gide: Pederasty and Pedagogy* (Oxford: Oxford University Press, 1998).

——'The common touch' in Mandy Merck (ed.) *After Diana* (London: Verso, 1998) pp. 131–45.

Séginger, Gisèle, 'Commentaires: la Genèse' in Émile Zola, *La Bête humaine* (Paris: Livre de Poche, 1997).

Serizier, L., 'Chronique parisien: La Tete coupée', *Le Siècle*, 1 April (1890) p. 2.

Shapiro, Ann-Louise, *Breaking the Codes: Female Criminality in Fin-de-Siècle Paris* (Stanford: Stanford University Press, 1996).

Sheringham, Michael, *French Autobiography: Devices and Desires* (Oxford: Clarendon Press, 1993).

——'Changing the script: women writers and the rise of autobiography' in Sonya Stevens (ed.) *A History of Women's Writing in France* (Cambridge: Cambridge University Press, 2000) pp. 185–203.

Simpson, James, 'Canny Allusions: *Der Sandmann* as *Kontrafaktur', Publications of the English Goethe Society* 71 (2001) pp. 37–49.

Sokel, Walter H., *Franz Kafka. Tragik und Ironie* (Frankfurt/Main: Fischer Taschenbuch, 1976).

Sommerhage, Claus, 'Hoffmanns Erzähler. Über Poetik und Pathologie in E.T.A. Hoffmanns Nachtstück "Der Sandmann"', *Zeitschrift für deutsche Philologie* 106 (1987) pp. 512–34.

'Sous le Coupole', *Le Matin*, 27 April 1890, pp. 1–2.

Stach, Reiner, *Kafkas erotscher Mythos. Eine ästhetische Konstruktion des Weiblichen* (Frankfurt/Main: Fischer, 1987).

Stadler, Ulrich, 'Der Sandmann' in Brigitte Feldges and Ulrich Stadler, *E.T.A. Hoffmann. Epoche—Werk—Wirkung*, Beck'sche Elementarbücher (Munich: C.H. Beck, 1986) pp. 135–52.

Sternberger, Dolf, *Heinrich Heine und die Abschaffung der Sünde* (Frankfurt/Main: Suhrkamp, 1976).

Still, Judith, 'Rousseau in Daniel Deronda', *Revue de littérature comparée* 56 (1982) pp. 62–77.

——'From Eliot's "raw bone" to Gyges' Ring: Two Studies in Intertextuality', *Paragraph* 1 (1983) pp. 44–59.

——*Justice and Difference in the Works of Rousseau* (Cambridge: Cambridge University Press, 1993).

——*Feminine Economies. Thinking Against the Market in the Enlightenment and the Late Twentieth Century* (Manchester: Manchester University Press, 1997).

——'Genlis's *Mademoiselle de Clermont*: A Textual and Intertextual Reading', *Australian Journal of French Studies* 37:3 (2000) pp. 331–47.

——'The Reworking of *La Nouvelle Héloïse* in Genlis's *Mademoiselle de Clermont*', *French Studies Bulletin* 77 (2000) pp. 7–11.

——'Acceptable hospitality: from Rousseau's Levite to the strangers in our midst today', *Journal of Romance Studies* 3:2 (2003) pp. 1–14.

——'Language as hospitality: revisiting intertextuality via *Monolingualism of the Other*', *Paragraph* 27:1 (2004) pp. 113–27.

Straube, Ingrid. *Heinrich Heines Frauen: Ein Gespräch* (Aachen: Rimbaud Presse, 1986).

Talmeyr, Maurice, 'L'Élection Zola', *Gil Blas*, 6 May 1890, p. 1.

Tatar, Maria, 'E.T.A. Hoffmann's "Der Sandmann": Reflection and Romantic Irony', *Modern Language Notes* 95 (1980) pp. 585–608.

Thélot, Jérôme, *Baudelaire: violence et poésie* (Paris: Gallimard, 1993).

Thompson, C. W., Lamiel, *fille du feu: Essai sur Stendhal et l'énergie* (Paris: L'Harmattan, 1997).

Trouille, Mary Seidman, *Sexual Politics in the Enlightenment. Women Writers Read Rousseau* (New York: State University of New York Press, 1997).

Trousson, Raymond, *Jean-Jacques Rousseau* 2 vols (Paris: Tallandier, 1988–89).

Van Rysselberghe, Élisabeth, *Lettres à la Petite Dame* (Paris: Gallimard, 2000).

Vietta, Silvio, 'Romantikparodie und Realitätsbegriff im Erzählwerk E.T.A. Hoffmanns', *Zeitschrift für deutsche Philologie* 100 (1981) pp. 575–91.

Vincent, Deirdre, 'Mädchen, Frau, Ehefrau. . . . Zur Muttergestalt bei Goethe' in Möhrmann (ed.) *Verkitscht, verklärt, vergessen* pp. 92–107.

Wagner, Irmgard, 'Vom Mythos zum Fetisch: Die Frau als Erlöserin in Goethes klassischen Dramen', *Goethe Yearbook* 5 (1990) pp. 121–43.

Wahnich, Sophie, *L'Impossible Citoyen: L'étranger dans le discours de la Révolution française* (Paris: Albin Michel, 1997).

Walkowitz, Judith, *City of Dreadful Delight: Narratives of Sexual Danger in Late-Victorian London* (Chicago: University of Chicago Press, 1992).

www.academie-francaise.fr/immortels

www.dur.ac.uk/SMEL/depts/french/Bagueley/Bibliog/

Waller, Margaret, *The Male Malady: Fictions of Impotence in the French Romantic Novel* (New Brunswick, NJ: Rutgers University Press, 1993).

Wienfort, Monika, 'Fontane und der Adel. Beobachtungen zum *Stechlin*', *Fontane Blätter* 76 (2003) pp. 126–33.

Willim, Petra, *So frei geboren wie ein Mann? Frauengestalten im Werk Goethes* (Königstein/Taunus: Helmer, 1997).

Wilson, W. Daniel, 'Amazon, Agitator, Allegory: Political and Gender Cross(-Dress)ing in Goethe's *Egmont*' in Alice Kuzniar (ed.) *Outing*

Goethe and His Age (Stanford: Stanford University Press, 1986) pp. 125–46.

Wolf, Susan, 'Baudelaire's Sepulchres' in L. Porter (ed.) *Approaches to Teaching Baudelaire's* Flowers of Evil (New York: Modern Language Association, 2000) pp. 123–29.

Zola, Émile, 'Le Crime. L'opinion de Zola', *La Lanterne*, 28 January (1890) p. 1.

——'Au rédacteur', *Le Journal des débats*, 18 November (1889) p. 3.

——'L'Académie française et "La Bête humaine"', interview with Philippe Gilla, *Le Figaro*, 4 March (1890) p. 1.

——'Documents préparatoires', *Les Rougon-Macquart*, ed. by Armand Lanoux and Henri Mitterand (Paris: Gallimard Pléiade, 1966) vol. 5, pp. 1729–81.

——*Carnets d'enquêtes*, ed. by Henri Mitterand (Paris: Plon, 1986) pp. 499–554.

'Zola sur une locomotive', *L'Illustration*, 8 March 1890, p. 1.

Index